Negotiating Public Services in the Congo

State, Society and Governance

**Edited by Tom De Herdt
and Kristof Titeca**

ZED

Negotiating Public Services in the Congo: State, Society and Governance was first published in 2019 by Zed Books Ltd, The Foundry, 17 Oval Way, London SE11 5RR, UK.

www.zedbooks.net

Editorial Copyright © Tom De Herdt and Kristof Titeca 2019
Copyright in this Collection © Zed Books 2019

The right of Tom De Herdt and Kristof Titeca to be identified as the editors of this work has been asserted by them in accordance with the Copyright, Designs and Patents Act, 1988.

Typeset in Plantin MT Std by seagulls.net
Index by Ed Emery
Cover design by Keith Dodds
Cover photo © Sven Torfinn/Panos

A catalogue record for this book is available from the British Library

ISBN 978-1-78699-399-1 hb
ISBN 978-1-78699-400-4 pb
ISBN 978-1-78699-401-1 pdf
ISBN 978-1-78699-402-8 epub
ISBN 978-1-78699-403-5 mobi

Contents

List of Figures, Tables and Boxes

Figures

Tables

Boxes

About the Contributors

Klara Claessens is a postdoctoral researcher at the Department of Earth and Environmental Sciences, Division of Geography and Tourism, KU Leuven and at the Institute of Development Policy, University of Antwerp. She works on land governance in the Great Lakes Region.

Camilla Lindström is a PhD candidate at the Institute of Development Studies, Sussex University. She works on governance, state-building and aid negotiations in central Africa, with a particular focus on the Democratic Republic of Congo. She has long-term experience of working in international development

Albert Malukisa Nkuku is Professor at the Catholic University of Congo and Postdoctoral Researcher at the Institute of Development Policy and Management, University of Antwerp. He works on urban governance in Kinshasa and other major cities of the Democratic Republic of Congo.

Jean-Pierre Mpiana Tshitenge is a professor at the Faculty of Social, Administrative and Political Sciences at the University of Kinshasa, where he is also the faculty's academic secretary. He is also affiliated researcher at the Pôle SuD of the University of Liège and member of the Association for the Anthropology of Social Change and Development (APAD). His latest research interests are on university governance and public service delivery.

Stylianos Moshonas is a postdoctoral researcher at the Institute of Development Policy, University of Antwerp. His research focuses on the political economy of development and public sector reforms, mainly in sub-Saharan Africa and especially the Democratic Republic of Congo.

Aymar Nyenyezi Bisoka is a postdoctoral researcher at the Centre for Development Studies, Université Catholique de Louvain, at the Institute of Development Policy, University of Antwerp and the Centre for Reference and Expertise on Central Africa. He works on the post-conflict development and the political ecology of natural resources in the Great Lakes Region.

Stéphanie Perazzone completed her PhD in International Relations/Political Science at the Graduate Institute of International and Development Studies, and holds a post-doctoral research and teaching position at the University of Geneva's Faculty of Social Sciences. She works on the micro-sociology of governance and political violence in the Democratic Republic of Congo, on qualitative methods in international political inquiry and on state formation in sub-saharan Africa..

Randi Solhjell is a postdoctoral fellow associated with the Norwegian Police University College and the Center for Research on Extremism at the University of Oslo. She holds a PhD from the London School of Economics and has worked in particular on statehood, perceptions of public goods and citizenship in the Democratic Republic of Congo.

Michel Thill is a PhD student with the Department of Conflict and Development at Ghent University. His research examines the daily negotiation of public order in the city of Bukavu in the Democratic Republic of the Congo, with a particular focus on the work of the police and police–civil relations. Michel is a Doctoral Research Fellow at Ghent University's Conflict Research Group and a Fellow of the Rift Valley Institute.

Preface

Like states, book projects exist both as an idea and as a set of practices. The idea for this book emerged when both of us saw interesting links between the work we had been doing previously about public services in the Congo, and the work of others. While public services can be seen and analysed as the public face of the state, it is also useful to ask what lies behind this face: what processes have given it the shape it currently has? This question is perhaps more relevant today than previously in the Congo, as on the one hand state infrastructure has been withering away in the midst of the "post-conflict state reconstruction" of recent decades", while on the other hand public services continue to be provided. Taking stock of what functions and why, the book also aims to contribute to the debate on public services in the context of "real" or "hybrid" governance beyond the state. Does the state still play a role, or is it no longer relevant? What does this imply for regulatory coherence and legitimacy of the governance arrangements in place? How are elements of the state administration, general population or other non-state actors benefiting (or not) from the governance arrangements in place? And last but not least, how does international aid help or complicate this picture?

We noticed that other researchers were also working along these lines, sometimes departing from other types of literature or research traditions, but always working on empirical material based on fieldwork in the DRC. Empirically, the different case-study chapters address a wide range of public services (education, justice, waste, public transport, health) in specific areas of the DRC. We also added a number of chapters exploring the links between public services and the state in the DRC from a wider perspective.

The catalyst that put the idea of this book into practice was the "power, policy and politics" project we have been involved in since 2017, part of the Sustainable Livelihoods Research Consortium managed by the Overseas Development Institute for DfID. The project allowed us to invite others to step in, to engage in additional fieldwork and to take the time to spell out the common thread. We also thank the editors of Zed and the two anonymous reviewers for their comments. And finally, we also thank Patrick Edmond for helping us with language and layout issues.

Tom De Herdt and Kristof Titeca,
Antwerp and Kampala

I
Introduction: Negotiating Public Services in the Congo

Tom De Herdt and Kristof Titeca

How are public services governed in the Democratic Republic of Congo (DRC)? The case studies contained herein all explain how, and under what conditions, the state administration of the DRC – in conjunction with a variety of other actors – really works to provide public services. True, sometimes it simply fails to provide such services (as we will detail for a service such as waste collection). But many other public services continue to be provided in the DRC, even outliving the state of the DRC itself at the moment it was described, sometimes (but not always) quite aptly, as a "forsaken black hole characterized by calamity, chaos, confusion" (Trefon, 2009, p. 3).

In the following sections of this introduction, we unpack the various layers which help us understand the ways in which public services are delivered. First, we explain the basic analytical premise of the book: that a "real", or "everyday", governance perspective is needed to understand public service provision in the DRC, which can be characterized as a "weblike society" in which the state is not the only actor organizing governance. We further unpack this by looking at the complex "rentscape" in the DRC – namely, the ways in which public services are being financed. Second, we connect these elements to previous literature on the state in Africa, and the DRC more particularly, analysing what light they might shed on regulatory practices, on the level and agents of change, and on the formal/informal discussion. In doing so, we also present the various chapters of this volume.

Real governance

Olivier de Sardan (2008) coined the term "real governance" to invite researchers to extend their gaze beyond formal state rules, particularly in contexts in which a variety of actors, both state and non-state, contribute to governance and public services. Olivier de Sardan also added the "real" or "everyday" adjective to the object of analysis so as to contrast such an approach from normative approaches that, implicitly or explicitly, analyse actual governance practices against a standard of "good" governance supposedly characterizing Western democracies (2008, p. 1; see also: Blundo & Le Meur, 2008). The argument is not so much about questioning the definition of "good" governance or rethinking the frontier between "good" and "bad". Rather, the point is that the first step in promoting institutional change necessarily needs to be defined in terms of what actually exists, who is involved and for what reasons, and how it has been evolving.

Consequently, we need to focus on how public services and state institutions function on a day-to-day basis, and how they have been doing so almost *despite* the state. Moreover, we need to engage in an empirical analysis of the everyday institutional landscape and how this has been evolving. It is particularly important this is done before we start imagining how it might be affected by reform policies or development interventions, or under which circumstances it might evolve differently.

As we will argue below, the perspective has a general appeal. But we also think it is particularly appropriate for the context of the DRC. This is due to two related reasons: a historically evolved institutional complexity on the one hand, and a complex landscape of rents on the other.

Real governance in space and time: A weblike society

The adjective "real" first of all reflects a decentred state-in-society (Migdal & Schlichte, 2005), or "public authority from below" (Hoffmann & Kirk, 2013), perspective that sees the public sector as an institutional hybrid (Meagher, De Herdt & Titeca, 2014) where different forms of authority and sources of legitimacy may operate in uneasy discordance at the same time (De Herdt, 2015). As one of the first authors to set aside a state-centric perspective, Joel Migdal suggested that states should be regarded as embedded in "weblike societies", which

> ... host a mélange of fairly autonomous social organizations ...
> There may be no one ballgame, no single manager of power ...
> In many Third World countries, many ballgames may be played
> simultaneously. In weblike societies, although social control is
> fragmented and heterogeneous, this does not mean that people
> are not being governed; they most certainly are. The allocation of
> values, however, is not centralized. Numerous systems of justice
> operate simultaneously. (Migdal, 1988, p. 39)

More recently, and among similar lines, Christian Lund proposed that the state should be conceived of as "the amalgamated result of the exercise of power by a variety of local institutions and the imposition of external institutions, conjugated with the image of a state" (2006, p. 86). Likewise, Bierschenk underlines the "cobbled together" (*bricolé*) nature of the state; that is, its "heterogeneity" (Bierschenk, 2010, p. 2). Throughout the years, a variety of terms have been used to refer to these processes: an active work of "bricolage" (Cleaver, 2014), "assemblage" (Li, 2005), "negotiation" (Hagmann & Péclard, 2010; Englebert & Tull, 2013) or "real governance" (De Herdt & Olivier de Sardan, 2015; Olivier de Sardan, 2010; Titeca & De Herdt, 2011), a practice-based governmental rationality that is bound to be imperfect, provisional, emergent (Hoffman & Kirk, 2013), oftentimes suspended (Schlichte, 2008) and, ultimately, elusive (Mitchell, 1991).

How characteristic is the "weblike society" description of states for the African continent? There are different views on this. One position is to conceive the complexity of governance as a fairly universal phenomenon, as testified by scholarship on the United States (Hallet & Ventresca, 2006; Lipsky, 1972; Ostrom, 1972), Germany (Bosetzky, 2019), the United Kingdom (Rose, 1999) or France (Bourdieu, 1990). This position contests the possibility of analysing the state as autonomous from society, and instead seeks to understand public bureaucracy as "a configuration of social processes" (Bierschenk, 2010, p. 13). In recent work, for instance, Migdal and Schlichte propose distinguishing between "the image of the state", in general, as "a coherent, controlling organization in a territory, which is a representation of the people bounded by that territory", on one hand, and, on the other, "state practices", or "the diverse, multiple actions of state actors as well as the myriad responses and interactions between state officials and non-state actors" (2005, p. 15). Their work, and that of others (e.g. Li, 2007, Rose, 1999), is largely inspired by Foucault, who had France in mind when he claimed that "maybe, after all, the state is no more than a composite reality and a mythicized abstraction, whose importance is a lot more limited than many of us think" (Foucault, 1991, p. 103). In the history of academic writing on the state in Africa, this literature provided for a welcome alternative way of thinking about statehood during a period when the dominant writings on the African state were only seeing "collapse" (Milliken & Krause, 2003), "disintegration" (Zartman, 1995) and "failure" (Rotberg, 2004).

At the same time, questions could be asked about the time-specific and space-specific character of these dynamics: to what extent are these dynamics new, or characteristic of a particular place? Many authors do indeed situate a weblike society, or some of its close cousins, in a particular place or time. The problem is that the coordinates of place and time may differ from author to author, and sometimes they do so quite spectacularly. For instance, while Migdal thought his concept to be relevant for the so-called "Third World" in general (Migdal, 1988), Hagmann and Péclard see what they call "negotiated statehood" as a "central process and a recurrent theme of the history of statehood in Africa", and state that negotiability has been "part and parcel of state formation in Africa since the early colonial times" (2010, p. 557). However, their timing is contested, or at least nuanced, by others. Crawford Young would characterize the colonial state and its aftermath rather as an exceptional period of an integral and authoritarian state, lasting well beyond formal independence. Only after the era of the "postcolonial state" came to an end, around the 1990s, were African states pressed to democratize and "opened space for a multitude of actors" (2004, p. 25). For Thomas Callaghy too, the crucial change took place around the 1990s, when Mobutu's Zaire transformed into a "lame Leviathan", "an archipelago state, both functionally and territorially – a group of islands of control and extraction which kept the stumbling system alive by focusing on the most profitable forms and locations of resource pillage" (2001, p. 109). In opposition to this view, Lemarchand (1988) would rather link what he called the privatization of the African state to the *lack* of democratic pressures, and for that reason he discerns a change in the state system's logic in the early 1970s: because of the absence of electoral pressure, the patronage characterizing the young African democracies of the 1960s transmuted into the appropriation of public office not for amassing public support but for personal gain. Later-on, a "governance without government" literature to the contrary attributes the emergence of "parallel or semi-autonomous power systems that govern access to security and resources" (Vlassenroot & Raeymaekers, 2008, p. 50) neither to democratization, nor its disappearance, but to "a context of crisis and violent conflict" which has "apparently given life to a more commodified, indirect form of statehood that drives the middle ground between formal and informal, state and non-state spheres of authority and regulation" (2008, p. 51). Englebert and Tull turn this around, arguing that it is not the context of crisis and violent conflict that impacts on the structure of governance, but rather that violence itself should be seen as part of a political negotiation strategy, "one of the manifestations of its essential characteristics, which is primarily contestation" (2013, p. 6). In other words, different authors situate their own variety of "weblike society" in a different time-period or space because they also vary in attributing a particular cause to the phenomenon they observe.

Still others wouldn't look at political drivers but rather focus on economic ones. The late 1970s and early 1980s were a particularly important moment in this regard. After having accumulated extensive debts in a period of cheap money, sub-Saharan African states in the early 1980s were obliged to implement policies of structural adjustment as a condition of managing this debt. They were no longer able to pay the salaries of civil servants, and public services in general deteriorated (Bates, 2008; Bierschenk, 2010, pp. 7–8; Van de Walle, 2001). A key element of these policies was the strong decline in public resources to pay for civil servants. The state no longer being able to provide these, civil servants have to look out for them themselves. This is a process described by Blundo as the "informal privatization" (2006, p. 805) of the state by civil servants who use their state position, or what Englebert (2009) describes as the capacity of legal command, to look for revenue. In this situation, state administrations profoundly changed, and a struggle for revenue became a central defining characteristic of the functioning of the civil service. Certainly, in the DRC administrations were transformed into "parcels of power", in which "each position in the administration providing not only a wage, but also an opportunity for appropriation" (De Herdt, Marivoet & Muhirigwa, 2015, p. 49).

But do we have to make a choice here, in attributing the ultimate causes of the weblike society either to particular political factors like colonization, democracy or war, or to economic factors like structural adjustment, and hence situating the time and place of weblike societies differently? Perhaps the more appropriate conclusion is that all these elements may have played a role in configuring the particular weblike society we encounter in today's Africa, together with drivers of governance complexity that should be traced back much further in time. In their analysis of village politics in Benin, for instance, Bierschenk and Olivier de Sardan (2003) picture the era of Structural Adjustment as merely one additional layer of institutional development, adding to an already complex landscape fundamentally marked by the as yet incomplete process of state formation in Africa. Over time, a variety of political authorities have been piling up on top of each other: customary institutions of different types, religious authorities, state authorities, etc.:

> When a new form of political authority is set up (either by the
> State or by development agencies) it does not substitute for the
> layers of institutionality already in place but adds to them. This
> is what gives village power its polycephalous character. There
> are layers of power and legitimacy dating from different periods.
> None of them has truly disappeared, but all have been recycled
> and reconstituted, interlinked and interwoven in a coexistence
> which sometimes is only peaceful in appearance. (Olivier de
> Sardan, 2011, p. 8)

More recently, through the development reforms demanded by the
donor organizations, a whole range of new institutions were established,
parallel to existing ones, and often working outside the state apparatus.
In the words of Thomas Bierschenk: "More than 50 years of development policy have not led to the homogenization of these institutional
arrangements, instead they became more and more complex" (2010,
p. 7). In other words, instead of an absence of governance, the state is
only one of the many actors providing governance. Through this institutional layering, various actors with their own form of authority and
legitimacy exist alongside each other in the same socio-political space.
Particularly at the local level, the state is only one among a variety of
actors, in which a variety of relationships exist between a variety of
actors, characterized by "multiplex" ties. As a result:

> Owing to their incapacity to institutionalize and thus limit
> the legitimate use of violence, and their inability to establish
> themselves at local level, contemporary African states have,
> to date, proved extremely fragile, and their processes of state
> formation still appear to be reversible. Phases characterized
> by the firm implantation of state power in "civil society" have
> alternated with periods of recession in a process involving the
> tightening and loosening of state control since the advent of
> colonial rule. (Bierschenk & Olivier de Sardan, 2003, p. 148)

In short, as the institutional shape of the public sector in sub-
Saharan African countries is the product of different historical layers,
adding to rather than replacing the variety in meaning systems, rules
and actors, there is not a shortage of regulation, as suggested by a
"failed state" perspective, but rather an excess of rules (Li, 2007;
Olivier de Sardan, 2015).

This has an important consequence for understanding how social
change can work, and also not work. What is introduced at the national

level is neither directly applied at the local level, nor simply rejected. Put another way, changes at the national level are not necessarily implemented at the local level in the ways intended. In the words of Bierschenk and Olivier de Sardan: "The superimposition of centres of power and instances of regulation – each with its own rules, legitimacy and political personnel – in the absence of any real hierarchy is the major defining principle of the local political arenas" (2003, p. 154). Put differently: if national changes are implemented at the local level, they do so through processes of translation, interconnecting a diversity of only partly compatible logics. Indeed, administrative action is not monopolized by the state alone, but results from the interaction between a broad range of actors (civil servants, intermediaries, users), making use of rules and logics which are not limited to the public sphere, and which are therefore almost continuously re-negotiated by local public servants (Blundo, 2006, Brandt, 2017).

Real governance in a complex rentscape

In order to further unpack the plural context in which governance takes place in the DRC, and the processes of negotiation it entails, it is worthwhile zooming in on the flows of economic rents controlled or influenced by governance processes. Importantly, while the State in the DRC functions on the basis of revenues and a budget voted in parliament, this is only one side to the story.

The DRC is commonly depicted as "surviving to a great extent thanks to the assistance of the international financial institutions and the influx of resources for mining rights from nontraditional partners such as China" (Kaiser & Wolters, 2012, p. 71). Other authors too are focusing on the interface between the national and the international level to explain crucial political dynamics in the DRC (Autesserre, 2009; Koddenbrock, 2012; Stearns, 2013; Trefon, 2011; Veit, 2008). However, it is our contention that the importance of the international sphere needs to be put into the perspective of a much wider landscape of rents, in which international rents play an important, but not a predominant, role.

This "rentscape" is composed, first of all, by the state budget managed by the Central Bank. Then come equally official budgets managed by either lower tiers of government (provinces and lower-level decentralized entities) or international organizations. Whereas the public revenue wielded by the lower tiers can be estimated at 5% of the central-level budget, the international aid budget hovers around a third of this budget. Even if this international aid flow is far from negligible, its importance must be situated in a wider rentscape where the "public budget" is composed not just of the official financial flows. Another important category of rents is represented by what Williams and Ghonda call "parafiscal" revenue, that is revenues collected by "many government services ... to be used for their own purposes rather than being transferred to the Treasury" (2012, p. 12). Parafiscal revenue can be earned by both state and non-state service providers. Prud'homme coined the concept of "informal tax", defining it as the "nonformal means utilized to finance the provision of public goods and services" (Prud'homme, 1992). However, the formal/informal duality would suggest that "formal" is unambiguous. In many cases, this is not so. As we documented in the case of school costs (Titeca & De Herdt, 2011), the legal framework around the fees paid by parents to schools is so self-contradictory that it is as easy to find an official document justifying these fees as to find one declaring them illegal. Williams and Ghonda's concept of parafiscal revenue rather refers to the non-centralized form of management of these revenues than to the informal origins of them, which seems descriptively more accurate.

Taking a closer look at this parafiscal revenue allows us a better understanding of the negotiated nature of public services. First, the importance of parafiscal revenue in the DRC highlights the de facto blurring of boundaries between "state" and "society", and between "public" and "private". This is related to the historic importance of non-state service providers: the (colonial) state subcontracted much of its service delivery and taxation work to non-state actors (Hoffmann, Vlassenroot & Marchais, 2016; Poncelet, André & De Herdt, 2010), such as churches. This is particularly clear in the education sector: the way in which the system of school fees is currently set up is reminiscent of the well-known logic of indirect rule in a concessionary state (Naseemullah & Staniland, 2016; Simone, 2004; Utas, 2012); harking back to the way the colonial state and the churches operated a division of labour in organizing education (Poncelet, André & De Herdt, 2010). Concretely, school fees are levied by a variety of state and non-state actors. For example, they are justified as a tithe on pupils at a protestant school, so as to finance the new church. All of these fees, paying both state and non-state actors, come together in the monthly payments due by parents.

These practices are not limited to the education sector. Almost all government services have developed a "*dispositif*" (Li, 2007) or technology of government (Rose, 1999) to raise fees from their users, be it in the education sector (Titeca & De Herdt, 2011), the police (Baaz & Olsson, 2011; Malukisa Nkuku 2017; Thill, this volume), the university (Poncelet et al., 2015), or the organization of public marketplaces (Ayimpam, 2014; Emizet, 1998; ODEP, 2013). In other words, instead of relying solely on public tax income, various sectors also have to rely on fees that are raised and shared by state and non-state actors. Non-state actors are therefore not only raising these fees, but are also involved in using them. For example, school fees finance the catholic school administration and still others finance the state's inspection service.

Estimating the importance of this parafiscal revenue is of course tricky. As far as we know, the *dispositif* works in such a way that a systematic system of budgeting, and reporting on expenses of the revenue thus generated, is rendered virtually impossible. On the basis of our own estimates regarding the education sector (Titeca & De Herdt, 2011), we can roughly determine that it constitutes at least as much as the state's official budget for that sector. The information reviewed by Englebert (2014) suggests non-registered taxes as a whole would more or less double registered government revenue, and a recent study on informal taxes in the DRC came to an estimate of 85% on the basis of tax surveys in a limited number of places (Paler et al. 2016). However imprecise these estimates may be, they do set the importance of international funding in perspective: the state's crucial material basis of survival is not just international, the parafiscal dimension of it could in fact be three times as big. Compared to the rent generated by donor money, the parafiscal revenue is also undoubtedly financing the lower ranks of the state first. It is partly paying (even unregistered and unpaid) lower-level civil servants' salaries, even if a portion of this revenue is percolating up to more senior levels of hierarchy – sometimes all the way to the central state administration. In the case of the education sector, for instance, we estimated that about 5% of school fees filter all the way up from parents' purses across the country to the central level of decision-making in Kinshasa (De Herdt, Marivoet & Muhirigwa, 2015).

The precise way in which this *dispositif* works, and how redistributive it really is, varies between different sectors, services and places. It is nonetheless clear that public services generate a rent that plays an important role in keeping the state together, and in keeping a semblance of public services functioning (Trefon, 2009). It is clear, too, that public services financed in this way are a deeply mixed blessing: the importance of parafiscal revenue in the education sector pushed school managers to cater for ever greater numbers of pupils – which perfectly aligns with the Millennium Development

Goals on education – but to the total neglect of quality of education (De Herdt & Titeca, 2016).

We also think it is useful to distinguish between parafiscal revenue and extortion. Conceptually, the distinction between parafiscal revenue and blatant extortion relates to the object of exchange in return for money. Whereas in the first case, a (supposedly) public service is exchanged for money, in the second, money is paid "in relation to authorizations and rules" (Prud'homme, 1992, p. 5), i.e. in exchange for an authorization that shouldn't be paid for, or for an authorization or an exoneration (of a punishment) that should have been given. Englebert (2014), for instance, estimates the undervaluing of mining rights (by selling them first to shady foreign companies, who then resell these rights at a much higher price to legitimate mining companies) at between \$1 billion and \$1.5 billion per year (or about one third of central government expenses).

Empirically, the distinction between parafiscal revenue and extortion may be difficult to make as, sometimes, the transacting parties are the same. Extortion and parafiscal revenue also have elements in common. To begin with, note that Prud'homme's definition of extortion doesn't invoke the degree of negotiation or threat involved. Indeed, both in the cases of extortion and parafiscal revenue, the terms of the exchange can be, depending on the circumstances, more or less adverse or more or less open to negotiation. Mpiana Tshitenge's analysis (chapter 5) of the practices of the electricity provider demonstrates the space of negotiation between administrators and service users, and the different scenarios when subscribers don't pay their electricity bill in time. The room for manoeuvre generates practical norms that may or may not deviate considerably from legality (De Herdt & Olivier de Sardan, 2015). Furthermore, just like extortion money, most parafiscal revenue will eventually end up in private pockets, complementing administrators' salaries. Finally, it is clear that both extortions and parafiscal revenues are part and parcel of what keeps the state in motion, co-determining what direction it takes and, eventually, what quantity and quality of public services is provided.

To summarize, having a closer look at the ways in which public services are financed allows us to better understand how everyday governance functions. A variety of actors are actively involved – both state and non-state, local, national and international. Talking about Uganda and the involvement of international actors, Klaus Schlichte (2008) describes how what he calls "the internationalization of rule", which causes the idea of the Ugandan state to be "suspended between international agents and local practices and expectations". In doing so, he describes the Ugandan state as "deeply embedded in a conflictive network of agencies that are sometimes at odds and sometimes in line with the idea of unitary statehood" (Schlichte, 2008, p. 380). In other words, this substantially internationalized rentscape provides an additional dimension of institutional complexity to the "weblike society" described by Migdal (1988), multiplying the logics of governance and deepening the heterogeneity in state practices derived from incomplete process of state formation. Yet, as we have shown above, international rents are dwarfed by parafiscal sources of revenue, which are far more important: they are organized at the level of each entity (office, department, function) and ultimately double the flow of rents wielded by "the state". In other words, Schlichte's (2008) descriptions of the practical state as a "conflictive network of agencies", and of the idea of the state being "suspended" between these agencies, is even more accurate in the case of the DRC. In analysing the rentscape of Congolese public services, the "practical" state consists of a variety of actors – not only international actors, but a range of others, each with their own logics and accountability system. It is not that the state doesn't exist anymore. Rather, one has to ask the question why people still refer to this plurality of practices as a singular organizational unit.

So what?

What does this mean for the practical functioning of state institutions, and for the governance processes at stake?

Regulation

First, regulatory processes are profoundly affected. The powers to sanction are not centralized in one institution, and are not part of a hierarchical relation or institutionalized in a systematic relationship between various institutions. There is no monopoly on regulation: neither the state or any other institution has a privileged position or a unique legitimacy to enforce its regulatory monopoly (Bierschenk & Olivier de Sardan, 2003). In other words, local regulatory power is fragmented, consisting of various institutions which have become locally embedded at different times. Regulation is therefore prone to continued change, in which neither the state nor non-state actors (customary chiefs, NGOs, and so on) have a monopoly of regulation. As a result, local-level political arenas are highly fragmented – local governance happens through a "prism of institutions, legitimacies, rules and actors", and is characterized by "feeble regulatory ability" (Bierschenk & Olivier de Sardan, 2003, pp. 156, 159). Institutions have a high degree of flexibility and fluidity, and are characterized by having hazily defined forms of organization that are infrequently written down. Instead, there is a continuous negotiation of competencies and a high level of legal pluralism (Bierschenk & Olivier de Sardan, 2003, p. 159). The access and legitimacy of the various actors also differs considerably. This complexity and fluidity make participation in these activities time-consuming as well as unpredictable (Bierschenk & Olivier de Sardan, 2003, p. 158). Contributing to this situation is the fact that there is little control over the various institutions, with hierarchical bureaucratic state control neither common nor very effective. Non-state actors, such as customary chiefs, also have little hierarchical control.

As a result, the state has a messy, contradictory and tense nature, which is reproduced both in time and space, and around specific events or commodities. A variety of chapters show the incoherent character of state regulation, in which particular rules can be declared legal and illegal at the same time. It also shows how rules are implemented differently in different areas, reflecting both the deep diversity of human interests and the historic ways in which these have found collective expression in regularized patterns of behaviour. Bavinck refers, in this respect, to the "spatially splintered state" or to a "legal patchwork with strongly spatial connotations" (Bavinck, 2003, p. 633). There is a geographical variation in the application of state law, as the state and its public services are differently represented, thereby accommodating themselves to local political settings. Titeca (chapter 10) shows how rules are implemented differently according to different configurations of power in Haut-Uélé. Similarly, Bisoka Nyenyezi and Claessens (chapter 9) show the important engagement of non-state actors in land governance, which nevertheless rely on state symbols to legitimize their practices. Lindstrom (chapter 3) shows how donors reluctantly engage with this "patchwork", in which a variety of actors are present, and in which it is not always clear who holds the power. As she shows, engaging with non-state actors involves a number of challenges for donors, but it is also a necessity if there is genuine concern about the impact of one's interventions in weblike societies.

Lastly, the weblike character of society has implications for our thinking about legitimacy. A reference to a single source of legitimacy is only partly correct, and also entirely misleading, as the hybrid character of it is integral to its essence (De Herdt, 2015). Interestingly, one of the cases discussed by Nyenyezi Bisoka and Claessens (chapter 9) documents how a Big Man allots part of a plantation among interested buyers, justifying the allotment with the distribution of land titles. Is this a case of pre-colonial "bigmanity"? Is it a revival of the concessionary colonial state? Or is it mimicking the modern state-enforced system of individual property? Perhaps it is above all a truly hybrid system incorporating elements of all three types of legitimation. Cases like this demonstrate the problem with analyses built on a dichotomy between state and society. We fully agree, in this respect, with Ferguson's plea to view states as "themselves composed of bundles of social practices that are every bit as 'local' in their social situatedness and materiality as any other" (2006, p. 99).

A multi-level, multi-actor approach

Another implication of the "weblike society" idea is that a view beyond the "political settlements" at the level of the central state and national elites is necessary (Kaiser & Wolters, 2012). First, the very idea of a governing elite, purportedly negotiating social order, needs to be questioned. This becomes particularly clear when looking at the ways in which public services are financed. Given the way in which parafiscal rent is distributed, it seems much more logical to situate the drivers of the system at subnational levels. As our previous work shows, this level holds most power in, for example, deciding whether to implement national-level regulations, or in the appropriation of parafiscal revenue (Titeca & De Herdt, 2011). In the case of the education sector, for instance, we identified school network managers as the dominant actor (Poncelet, André & De Herdt, 2010). Most of them are representing a religious organization rather than the state, and all of them are keeping office at the level of what, from the point of view of the state, one can describe as a sub-district. In other words, the national-level "elite" seems obliged to accommodate the social order arising from below, while the rewards it obtains from doing so come, among other things, in the form of a 5% share in school fees. Charles Tilly's (2004) concept of "brokered autonomy" comes to mind here. According to this concept, leaders of what he calls "trust networks ... yield resources and compliance to rulers in return for significant autonomy within their own domains" (Tilly, 2004, p. 14). In other words, it is not the national state that *brings* social order, the state and the legal system it represents are at most instrumental in strengthening what is already there. This resonates with James

Ferguson's (2006) questioning of the "mythic" vertical topography, whereby the layer of a (weak) national state encompasses society and is in turn encompassed by international actors. For Ferguson, this is a myth, since it leaves out of sight the partial autonomy of "strong" societal actors vis-à-vis the state, the multiple ways in which state representatives can deal with donors, and the independent ways in which societal actors might connect with international actors. The room for manoeuvre at the national level therefore needs to be positioned not only in relation to opportunities for agency the international level, but also *vis-a-vis* the intra-national level.

Understanding the position of societal actors in relation to societal complexity is therefore key. It is, for example, useful to conceive of the levying of parafiscal revenue as chains or networks of actors, from the very local up to the national level, each with their relative holding power and corresponding ability to capture a particular part of the revenue flow. In other words, analyses which focus on the relationships between the "ruling coalition" at the national level and "the rest" of society – for example, the literature on political settlements – are not sufficient. Other levels, such as the sub-national level, are equally important to accurately capture the dynamics generated by the plurality of actors involved in public service provisioning at all levels of decision-making.

The chapters in this volume therefore take an actor-oriented approach, in which specific attention is given to the perspectives and real opportunities of actors that reproduce the state. In particular, the role of ordinary citizens and their routine ways of thinking and acting cannot be ignored when analysing public service delivery. The analysis of street-level bureaucrats (Lipsky, 1972) has a long tradition of ethnographic research in order to better understand the daily functioning of the state. In this volume, Thill (chapter 6) shows how police work and practices are shaped by a multitude of actors and how they reflect an intense process of negotiation, contestation and competition. Perazzone (chapter 4) describes the DRC state as a "composite" of street-level bureaucrats' small acts of everyday statehood. Perazzone uses a popular Congolese phrase to describe this: "*L'Etat ni miye, l'Etat ni weye, l'Etat ni shiye bote*", or "The state is me, the state is you, the state is all of us". This bring us to another central actor: citizens. As Perazzone's quote shows, ordinary citizens play an active role in coproducing the state, and in constructing boundaries over what are considered to be public services. Solhjell's contribution (chapter 8) engages with this question – by analysing waste management in Bukavu, she looks at the perception of public and private spaces, and what it means to be a citizen. Moshonas (chapter 2) also looks at the "little men" behind the scenes. Their distance from the street, however, does not diminish the importance of their interpretations of, and their strategic dealings with, the situation in which they find themselves.

The role of practical norms and the intertwining of formal and informal rules

As the title of this volume suggests, particular attention needs to be given to "negotiation". Almost all the contributions to this issue describe how public services work through an often subtle combination of both conflict and what is termed *"coöp"* in Congo (Nzeza Bilakila, 2004) – an arrangement that suits the parties directly involved. A conceptualization of social arrangements at all levels as cooperative conflicts (Drèze & Sen 1989), the dynamics of which are partly autonomous and partly embedded in the wider social/statal landscape, is the empirical starting point we propose in this volume.

To be sure, we should be careful with what we mean by the word "negotiation". Hagmann and Péclard coined the concept of "negotiated statehood" as a perspective "to better understand how local, national and transnational actors forge and remake the state through processes of negotiation, contestation and bricolage" (2010, p. 544). "Negotiation, contestation and bricolage" sounds in any case more encompassing, though less friendly, and probably more realistic than what mere "negotiation" implies. The space for real processes of negotiation is undoubtedly much more limited than we think (Doornbos, 2010) and the space for contestation and bricolage all the bigger, increasing the probability of a state that is not so much "negotiated", but rather at least provisionally "suspended" (Schlichte, 2008), or even "splintered" (Bavinck, 2003), in the middle of processes of "permanent provocation" (Foucault, 1991; see also: Titeca, De Herdt & Wagemakers, 2013).

Yet, we would argue that the term "negotiated statehood" still merits being used if we don't look at the state as a whole, but instead zoom in on the practical dilemmas faced by public servants. Most of the time a decision is taken by someone on behalf of the state or involving the state, this decision is not a straightforward application of clear formal guidelines, and almost always reflects some local agency. Even if the formal guidelines were unambiguous, they may be contradicted by other formal guidelines, be in tension with other types of norms or, perhaps more obviously, simply be inapplicable because of the lack of resources to implement the decision. How can a school director realistically run a school while fully respecting the constitutional stipulation that education is free, with only one of the teachers on the state's payroll (without necessarily paying them effectively) and without the provision of any functioning costs? How can a police agent, or any other civil servant, do their job, when their salary is far from sufficient? Such gaps between legal principle and reality cry out for practical norms to enable the state to work. In this sense, what ordinary state representatives are facing is quite similar to what other citizens are obliged to do every day, and to what De Boeck (2015) describes in the following way regarding Kinshasa's inhabitants:

> ... to meander successfully through all the contradictions, the impossible possibilities, and the changes of pace and rhythm that urban life constantly generates, to calculate one's chances and to know when to cut one's losses, demands a quality of judgment and a capacity to multitask that Kinois (Kinshasa's inhabitants) commonly refer to as *matematik*. (De Boeck, 2015, p. S147)

Whatever the norms effectively opted for in practice by a state representative, and irrespective of the bumpy nature of the process that led to them, the *matematik* of practical norms can be seen as a pragmatic compromise, possibly between different real or imagined actors to which that representative is accountable to. Compared to official norms, they will rather reflect the "local powers that be". In any case, they will signal what "the state" does, which is why the concept of "negotiated statehood" is fully appropriate.

The existence of a gap between official guidelines and practical norms is a phenomenon that is certainly not restricted to the DRC – even if in the DRC it has developed to an unprecedented level.[1] It is not that either the formal or the informal face dominates, it is the intertwining that determines its logic, dynamics and, ultimately, the space for the transformation of actual practices (De Herdt & Olivier de Sardan, 2015). Such intertwining goes further than a logic of communicating vessels. In the case of the DRC, many observers argue that the extreme level of informalization of the state can be explained by its implosion during the 1990s. But if this was all there was to it, we would witness, in line with the communicating vessels logic, an erosion of informality and a concurrent formalization as a result of the re-emergence of the DRC state in the first decade of the twentieth century (Cassimon et al., 2019). We have demonstrated elsewhere that this is not the case (De

Herdt, Marivoet & Muhigirwa, 2015; Poncelet et al., 2015), something which the various case studies in this book further confirm.
Instead, both "formal" and "informal" dimensions continue to
compose the assemblage of the state in the DRC as if two sides of
the same coin. Here, in what Lund (2006) denotes the "twilight"
character of public authority in sub-Saharan Africa, one sees the
intertwining of the "formal" and "informal" faces of public administration, and how they are negotiated.

This is shown in a variety of chapters within this volume. Moshonas
(chapter 2), for example, shows how administrative reform has been
closely tied to a factional conflict within the ruling coalition, in
which reforms (largely pushed by donors) were closely tied with the
capture of off-budget resources and clientelism. Similarly, Malukisa
Nkuku and Titeca (chapter 7) show how the "revolution of modernity" reform of the transport sector largely failed, as the buses and
their users constitute important vote banks, making formal sector
reforms particularly difficult. Moreover, there were important parafiscal revenue streams attached to it, which were not tackled. Along
similar lines, Mpiana Tshitenge (chapter 5) shows how practical
norms play an important role in the distribution of electricity, but in
close relation to the official norms of the electricity provider SNEL.

Furthermore, these dynamics become clear by looking again at
parafiscal revenue. The arrangements to raise parafiscal revenue
combine both formal and informal elements, as already argued
by Baaz, Olsson & Verweijen (2018) for the case of taxation on the
Congo river. Parafiscal revenue usually rests on an explicit agreement
with formal superiors (as exemplified by the different "ventila-
tions", or overviews of school costs, defined by school managers)
and it may even be quite public – as in the case of school fees, the
justification for which is in many cases also discussed by parent
committees and reported in these meetings' minutes. The practice
of *rapportage*, described by Thill (chapter 6) regarding the case of the
police forces in Bukavu, also illustrates the entangling of the formal
and informal sides of governance. In addition, Malukisa Nkuku and
Titeca (chapter 7) document how, in the case of public transport,
formal regulation is instrumentalized to structure actual practices
that ostensibly deviate from the official guidelines. We come close
here to Ananya Roy's description of what she calls

    ... calculated informality, one that involves purposive action and
    planning, and one where the seeming withdrawal of regulatory
    power creates a logic of resource allocation, accumulation, and

authority. It is in this sense that informality, while a system of deregulation, can be thought of as a mode of regulation. And this is something quite distinct from the failure of planning or the absence of the state. (Roy, 2009, p. 83)

In this case, informality does not indicate the absence of formal regulation, nor of regulation that operates "beyond the framework of the state" (Meagher, 2008, p. 4). Rather, in one way or another, it *suits* state representatives to cultivate an alternative form or regulation. This may be because the formal framework is self-contradictory, because other types of norms would be in tension with the formal rule, or because the formal rules also come with commitments the state is unable to honour. In the latter case, practical norms may allow the state (in actual fact, particular state representatives) to govern with empty pockets (De Herdt & Titeca, 2016). The gap between official norms and actual practices constitutes, for them, the space of the game (Olivier de Sardan, 2015). To the extent their gaming leads to stabilized ways of dealing in this space, their practices acquire a norm-like character – at least they achieve some level of predictability and people can build this into their own *matematik*. In this way, practical *norms* can be seen as an intermediate step, in between actual state practices and the imagined ideal of the state. In a world full of uncertainties, constantly generated by the "changes of pace and rhythm" De Boeck so aptly described, this is already a very important step.

Conclusions

In this introductory chapter, we have introduced the central concepts for the analysis of public services in the DRC. While there is certainly no shortage of original names to denote the state in Africa – whether or not specifically in relation to a particular conjuncture – we propose not to focus on the nature of the DRC state, but rather on how it functions (or not) in Congolese society. The different case studies brought together in this book allow us not just to understand how services are provided in the DRC, but also to look at the state itself. In doing so, they ask the question: what configuration of social processes is involved in its functioning?

We found much value in Migdal & Schlichte's (2005) proposal to distinguish the image of the state, on one hand, and the state as represented in a heterogeneous set of practices, on the other. The gap between the two determines the "space of the game", within which state representatives operate to negotiate the daily governance of public services. This space is also often populated by other state actors, representing other levels or other sectors, and non-state actors, some of whom have partly replaced or complemented the state as service provider. All of these give shape to the "weblike society" of the DRC.

One particularity of the DRC is undoubtedly the importance of off-budget income streams, both relative to on-budget financing of public services and as a driver of the dynamics of public services. This complicated rentscape turns public services into deeply mixed blessings, as the delivery of a public service is dependent on the capacity to collect fees. It is interesting to note this off-budget dimension of statehood in the DRC has hardly been affected by the recent re-emergence of the state during the so-called period of post-conflict reconstruction, and even less so by the substantial increase in external inputs – both financial and otherwise – to strengthen its capacity and performance.

The particular social embeddedness of the DRC state in society plays an important role in explaining its resilience and its relative autonomy from external influence. First of all, elements of governance typically associated with hierarchical bureaucratic control, like the ability to sanction, stand in tension with negotiated statehood. Effective sanctioning implies a monopoly of regulation – a panoply of rules devalues the effectiveness of each of them.

Second, the excess of rules also entails an excess of actors of change. Much in line with Englebert and Tull (2015) or Pype (2016), the different case studies in this book almost all tell stories about new interactions, sudden events, unexpected contestations, and interesting movements. Change is everywhere, but again, the lack of coherence in movements and counter-movements doesn't make it easy to discern in which direction things are going. The space for transformation by external actors, too, seems limited, or in any case far from evident. This is partly because external actors are themselves stakes rather than stakeholders. The ability to act is also conditioned by achieving greater knowledge of what this space for transformation looks like: who operates in it, who could one ally with, how might the balance of forces be tilted? External actors, too, cannot do without their own *matematik*. If anything, this book should be an invitation for further scrutiny of the real governance of public services. People's livelihoods depend on them.

Note

1 The political settlements literature does allow for that distinction, arguing that in pre-capitalist environments, the state is not strong enough to capture and distribute formally enforced rents, and hence it has to resort to informal means to settle conflicts between contending parties (Khan, 2005).

References

Autesserre, S. (2009) Hobbes and the Congo: Frames, local violence, and international intervention. *International Organisation* 63 (2): 249–80.

Ayimpam, S. (2014) Économie de la débrouille à Kinshasa: *Informalité, commerce et réseaux sociaux*. Paris: Karthala.

Baaz, M. E. and Olsson, O. (2011) Feeding the horse: Unofficial economic activities within the police force in the DR Congo. *African Security* 4 (4): 223–41.

Baaz, M. E., Olsson, O. and Verweijen, J. (2018) Navigating "taxation" on the Congo river: the interplay of legitimation and "officialization". *Review of African Political Economy* 45 (156): 250–66.

Bates, R. H. (2008) State failure. *Annual Review of Political Science* 11: 1–12.

Bavinck, M. (2003) The spatially splintered state: Myths and realities in the regulation of marine fisheries in Tamil Nadu, India. *Development and Change* 34 (4): 633–57.

Bierschenk, T. (2010) States at work in West Africa: Sedimentation, fragmentation and normative double-binds. University of Mainz, Department of Anthropology and African Studies. Working Paper 113.

Bierschenk, T. and Olivier de Sardan, J. P. (2003) Powers in the village: Rural Benin between democratization and decentralization. *Africa* 73 (2): 145–73.

Blundo, G. (2006) Dealing with the local state: The informal privatization of street-level bureaucracies in Senegal. *Development and Change* 37 (4): 799–819.

Blundo, G. and Le Meur, P. Y. (2008) *An Anthropology of Everyday Governance: Collective Service Delivery and Subject-making*. Leiden: Brill.

Brandt, C. O. (2017) Ambivalent outcomes of statebuilding: Multiplication of brokers and educational expansion in the Democratic Republic of Congo (2004–13). *Review of African Political Economy* 44 (154): 624–642.

Bosetzky, H. (2019) *Mikropolitik: Netzwerke und Karrieren*. Wiesbaden: Springer.

Bourdieu, P. (1990) Droit et passe-droit. *Actes de la recherche en sciences sociales* 81-82: 86–96.

Callaghy, T. (2001) From reshaping to resizing a failing state? The case of the Congo/Zaïre. In: O'Leary, B., Lustick, I. S. and Callaghy, T. (eds) *Right-sizing the State: The Politics of Moving Borders*. Oxford: Oxford University Press, pp. 102–37.

Cassimon, D., De Herdt, T., Marivoet, W. and Verbeke, K. (2019) From the Executive Board to the classroom: What debt relief means for education in the Democratic Republic of the Congo (DRC). *International Journal of Public Administration*.

Cleaver, F. (2014) *Development through Bricolage: Rethinking Institutions for Natural Resource Management*. London: Routledge.

De Boeck, F. (2015) "Poverty" and the politics of syncopation: Urban examples from Kinshasa (DR Congo). *Current Anthropology* 56 (S11): S146–S158.

De Herdt, T. (2015) Hybrid orders and practical norms: A Weberian view. In: De Herdt, T. and Olivier de Sardan, J. P. (eds) *Real Governance and Practical Norms in Sub-Saharan Africa: The Game of the Rules.* London: Routledge, pp. 95–120.

De Herdt, T., Marivoet, W. and Muhigirwa, F. (2015) Vers la réalisation du droit à une éducation de qualité pour tous. Kinshasa: UNICEF.

De Herdt, T. and Olivier de Sardan, J. P. (eds) (2015) *Real Governance and Practical Norms in Sub-Saharan Africa: The Game of the Rules.* London: Routledge.

De Herdt, T. and Titeca, K. (2016) Governance with empty pockets: The education sector in the Democratic Republic of Congo. *Development and Change* 47 (3): 472–94.

Doornbos, M. (2010) Researching African statehood dynamics: Negotiability and its limits. *Development and Change* 41 (4): 747–69.

Drèze, J. and Sen, A. K. (1989) *Hunger and Public Action.* Oxford: Clarendon.

Emizet, K. (1998) Confronting leaders at the apex of the state. *African Studies Review* 41 (1): 99–137.

Englebert, P. (2009) *Africa: Unity, Sovereignty, and Sorrow.* Boulder, CO: Lynne Rienner.

Englebert, P. (2014) Democratic Republic of Congo: Growth for all? Challenges and opportunities for a new economic future. Brenthurst Foundation. Discussion Paper 6/2014.

Englebert, P. and Tull, D. (2013) Contestation, négociation et résistance: L'État congolais au quotidien. *Politique africaine* 129 (1): 5–22.

Ferguson, J. (2006) *Global Shadows: Africa in the Neoliberal World Order.* Durham, NC: Duke University Press.

Foucault, M. (1991) *The Foucault Effect: Studies in Governmentality.* Chicago, IL: University of Chicago Press.

Hagmann, T. and Péclard, D. (2010) Negotiating statehood: Dynamics of power and domination in Africa. *Development and Change* 41 (4): 539–62.

Hallet, T. and M. Ventresca (2006) How institutions form: Loose coupling as mechanism in Gouldner's patterns of industrial bureaucracy. *American Behavioral Scientist* 49: 908–24.

Hoffmann, K. and Kirk, T. (2013) Public authority and the provision of public goods in conflict-affected and transitioning regions. JSRP Paper 7.

Hoffman, K., Vlassenroot, K. and Marchais, G. (2016) Taxation, stateness and armed groups: Public authority and resource extraction in Eastern Congo. *Development and Change* 47 (6): 1434–56.

Kaiser, K. and Wolters, S. (2012) Fragile states, elites, and rents in the Democratic Republic of Congo (DRC). In: North, D. C. (ed.) *In the Shadow of Violence: Politics, Economics, and the Problems of Development.* Cambridge: Cambridge University Press, pp. 70–109.

Khan, M. (2005) Markets, states and democracy: Patron–client networks and the case for democracy in developing countries. *Democratization* 12 (5): 704–24.

Koddenbrock, K. (2012) Recipes for intervention: Western policy papers imagine the Congo. *International Peacekeeping* 19 (5): 549–64.

Lemarchand, R. (1988) The state, the parallel economy, and the changing structure of patronage systems. In: Rothschild, D. and Chazan, N. (eds) *The Precarious Balance: State and Society in Africa.* Boulder, CO: Westview, pp. 149–70.

Li, T. M. (2005) Beyond the state and failed schemes. *American Anthropologist* 107 (3): 383–94.

Li, T. M. (2007) Governmentality. *Anthropologica* 49 (2): 275–81.

Lipsky, M. (1972) *Street-level Bureaucracy: Dilemmas of the Individual in Public Services.* New York NY: Russell Sage Foundation.

Lund, C. (2006) Twilight Institutions: Public Authority and Local Politics in Africa. *Development and Change,* 37 (4): 685–705.

Malukisa Nkuku, A. (2017) La « gouvernance réelle » du transport en commun à Kinshsasa : La prééminence des « normes pratiques » sur les normes officielles. PhD Dissertation: Institute of Development Policy and Management, University of Antwerp.

Meagher, K. (2008) Informality matters: Popular economic governance and institutional exclusion in Nigeria. Presentation at St Antony's College, Oxford.

Meagher, K., De Herdt, T. and Titeca, K. (2014) Unravelling public authority: Paths of hybrid governance in Africa. IS Academy. Human Security in Fragile States. Research Brief 10.

Migdal, J. (1988) *Strong Societies and Weak States: State–Society Relations and State Capabilities in the Third World.* Princeton, NJ: Princeton University Press.

Migdal, J. and Schlichte, K. (2005) Rethinking the state. In: Schlichte, K. (ed.), *The Dynamics of States: The Formation and Crises of State Domination.* Aldershot: Ashgate, pp. 1–40.

Milliken, J. and Krause, K. (2002) State failure, state collapse, and state reconstruction: Concepts, lessons and strategies. *Development and Change* 33 (5): 753–74.

Mitchell, T. (1991) The limits of the State: beyond statist approaches and their critics. *American Political Science Review* 85 (1): 77–96.

Naseemullah, A. and Staniland, P. (2016) Indirect rule and varieties of governance. *Governance* 29 (1): 13–30.

Nzeza Bilakila, A. (2004) La "coop" à Kinshasa: Survie et marchandage. In: Trefon T. (ed.) *Ordre et désordre à Kinshasa: Réponses populaires à la faillite de l'État.* Tervuren/Paris: Cahiers Africains/L'Harmattan, p. 33–46.

ODEP (Observatoire de la Dépense Publique) (2013) Rapport de l'enquête sur l'évaluation participative de la transparence dans la collecte et l'utilisation des taxes pour l'amélioration du marché central de Kinshasa. Unreleased document.

Olivier de Sardan, J.-P. (2008) Researching the practical norms of real governance in Africa. Africa Power and Politics. Discussion Paper 5.

Olivier de Sardan, J.-P. (2011) The eight modes of local governance in West Africa. *IDS Bulletin* 42 (2): 22–31.

Olivier de Sardan, J.-P. (2015) Practical norms: Informal regulations within public bureaucracies (in Africa and beyond). In: De Herdt, T. and Olivier de Sardan, J. P. (eds) *Real Governance and Practical Norms in Sub-Saharan Africa.* London: Routledge.

Ostrom, E. (1972) Metropolitan reform: Propositions derived from two traditions. *Social Science Quarterly* 53: 474–93.

Paler, L., Prichard, W., Sanchez de la Sierra, R. and Samii, C. (2016) Survey on total tax burden in the DRC, final report. Unpublished.

Poncelet, M., André, G. and De Herdt, T. (2010) La survie de l'école primaire congolaise (RDC): Héritage colonial, hybridité et résilience. *Autrepart* (2): 23–41.

Poncelet, M., Kapagama Ikando, P., De Herdt, T. and Mpiana Tshitenge, J.-P. (2015) A la marge de l'internationalisation de l'enseignement supérieur … mais au coeur du marché universitaire

national: L'Université de Kinshasa
(République Démocratique du
Congo). *Revue Tiers Monde* 223:
91–109.

Prud'homme, R. (1992) Informal
local taxation in developing
countries. *Environment and
Planning C: Government and Policy*
10 (1): 1–17.

Pype, K. (2016) "[Not] talking
like a Motorola": Mobile phone
practices and politics of masking
and unmasking in postcolonial
Kinshasa. *Journal of the Royal
Anthropological Institute* 22 (3):
633–52.

Rose, N. (1999) *Powers of Freedom:
Reframing Political Thought.*
Cambridge: Cambridge University
Press.

Rotberg, R. I. (ed.) (2004) *State
Failure and State Weakness in a
Time of Terror.* Washington, D.C.:
Brookings Institution Press.

Roy, A. (2009) Why India cannot
plan its cities: Informality,
insurgence and the idiom of
urbanization. *Planning Theory* 8
(1): 76–87.

Schlichte, K. (2008) Uganda, or: The
internationalisation of rule. *Civil
Wars* 10 (4): 369–83.

Simone, A. (2004) *For the City Yet
to Come: Changing African Life in
Four Cities.* Durham, NC: Duke
University Press.

Stearns, J. (2013) Helping Congo
help itself: What will it take to end
Africa's worst war? *Foreign Affairs*
92 (5): 99–112.

Tilly, C. (2004) Trust and
rule. *Theory and Society* 33 (1):
1–30.

Titeca, K. and De Herdt, T.
(2011) Real governance beyond
the "failed state": Negotiating
education in the Democratic
Republic of Congo (DRC).
African Affairs 110 (439): 213–31.

Titeca, K., De Herdt, T. and
Wagemakers, I. (2013) God

and Caesar in the Democratic
Republic of Congo: Negotiating
church–state relations through
the management of school
fees in Kinshasa's Catholic
schools. *Review of African Political
Economy* 40 (135): 116–31.

Trefon, T. (2009) Public service
provision in a failed state:
Looking beyond predation in the
Democratic Republic of Congo.
Review of African Political Economy
36 (119): 9–21.

Trefon, T. (2011) *Congo Masquerade:
The Political Culture of Aid
Inefficiency and Reform Failure.*
London: Zed Books.

Utas, M. (ed.) (2012) *African
Conflicts and Informal Power: Big
Men and Networks.* London: Zed
Books.

Veit, A. (2008) Figuration of
uncertainty: Armed groups
and 'humanitarian' military
intervention in Ituri (DR Congo).
*Journal of Intervention and State
Building* 2 (3): 291–307.

Vlassenroot, K. and Raeymaekers, T.
(2008) New political order in the
DR Congo? The transformation
of regulation. *Afrika Focus* 21 (2):
39–52.

van de Walle, N. (2001) The
impact of multi-party politics in
sub-Saharan Africa. *Forum for
Development Studies* 28 (1): 5–42.

Williams, G. and Ghonda, E. (2012).
The political economy of public
financial management in the
Democratic Republic of Congo.
Unpublished manuscript (Dated
22 July).

Young, C. (2004) The end of the
post-colonial state in Africa?
Reflections on changing African
political dynamics. *African Affairs*
103 (410): 23–49.

Zartman, I. W. (ed.) (1995) *Collapsed
States: The Disintegration and
Restoration of Legitimate Authority.*
Boulder, CO: Lynne Rienner.

Part I
Public services and the state

2
Reform of the Public Wage System in the DRC: The Système Intégré de Gestion des Ressources Humaines et de la Paie and Its Prospects[1]

Stylianos Moshonas

The Democratic Republic of Congo (DRC) is frequently depicted as a basket case in terms of "good governance" – the antithesis of a developmental state (Englebert, 2014; Rackley, 2006; Trefon, 2011). Still, since 2001, there have been several undeniable achievements in economic governance, which have succeeded in breaking with the catastrophic situation of the 1990s. These include curbing hyper-inflation, kick-starting growth, and stabilizing the macroeconomic framework; promulgating key pieces of legislation in public finances and investment; and a significant expansion of the state's budget (Herdeschee, Kaiser & Mukoko Samba, 2012). Many of these structural reforms have been promoted by donors – who have made a remarkable comeback since 2001 – via the provision of funding, expertise and technical assistance. One of the salient traits of donor engagement in the DRC has been an emphasis on the reconstruction of state authority as a major solution to the issue of insecurity and war in the East (Autesserre, 2012, p. 212), coupled with capacity-building and expansion of public service provision, the latter heavily bankrolled by external assistance. However, a major paradox of this engagement has been the relative neglect of administrative redress (Moshonas, 2018). This is awkward, given the importance of state personnel for the viability and success of development interventions, and is a problem that poses far-reaching sustainability issues.

Since 2015, the deterioration of Congo's public finances under the weight of external shocks to commodity prices in world markets, as well as the political instability associated with the uncertainty of the electoral cycle, have made painfully clear how fragile achievements in economic governance have been. Considering the sharp contraction of the state's budget since 2015,[2] and given the importance of the wage bill (which absorbs the lion's share – around 40% – of the budget's domestic resources)[3] to it, a look at payroll management and its associated reform is quite timely. After all, a thorough rationalization of payroll management should have a noticeable impact on how state personnel are remunerated, on control of the wage bill and human resource (HR) management, and, in turn, on how civil servants perform their duties, engage in public service provision, interact with public service users, and simply cope and organize their livelihoods. As such, by exploring the complexities of HR management and civil service remunerations, this chapter complements the volume's focus on the organization of public services in Congo, while drawing attention to the scope for reform.

Indeed, the last fifteen years have seen important steps taken with regards to the remuneration of civil servants. A key reform in that respect has been the introduction in 2003 of a computerized, four-step expenditure chain for public spending, which today encompasses the payment of remuneration to civil servants and state personnel (Beaudienville, 2012, p. 22; DRC: MoF & MoB, 2010). Additionally, in August 2011, remarkably without donor involvement, a reform of civil servant's payment modalities was launched, known as *bancarisation*,[4] whereby all civil servants are now paid through the commercial banking system, which has sparked a lot of public debate. Less known is the information-technology (IT) infrastructure on which the payroll operates. The present contribution endeavours to shed light on one component of the new, revised administrative reform that has been underway since 2012, namely the establishment of a computerized integrated human resource and payroll management system, known as the *Système Intégré de Gestion des Ressources Humaines et de la Paie* (SIGRH-P).[5] Insofar as this component forms one of the cornerstones of the revised reform strategy, it can be taken as indicative of its broader chances of success.

This chapter builds on several months of fieldwork conducted between 2010 and 2018,[6] conducted under a broadly qualitative methodology combining extensive analysis of technical documentation with elite interviews of key informants (particularly in the Ministries of Public Service, Budget, Finance, and Health, trade unions, donor officials, consultants, academics, and civil society activists). The key question this chapter raises is how the policy initiative of the SIGRH-P fits within the broader political economy of payroll and civil servant remuneration in the DRC? Where does it sit within a context deeply marked by political struggles within the ruling coalition, bureaucratic tensions across departments and institutions bent on the preservation of vested interests, and where governmental commitment to reform – by no means unanimous –

has been heavily incentivized by donor funding? To explore those issues, the chapter first begins by outlining a conceptualization of the Congolese administration – helped by insights drawn from political settlement analysis literature – to interpret the informal arrangements through which the civil service is governed, stressing the mechanisms of resource capture and rent allocation found at the heart of (re)distributive conflicts within the ruling coalition. Seen through this prism, the abuses associated with payroll management – including the capture of attendant resources – as well as the reforms aiming to address it, are indicative of a wider distributive political conflict fought within the ranks of the ruling coalition, where governmental commitment towards administrative reform should be understood as profoundly ambivalent.

The Congolese administration

Accounts of the wide range of structural reforms introduced in the DRC since 2001 have depicted the process as one of reform failure, whereby aid-promoted reforms have been emptied of their substance, in large part owing to the ruling elite's thwarting of initiatives liable to menace its own political survival (Trefon, 2009, 2011). Such accounts have been broadly in line with neopatrimonialist explanations of Africa's economic predicament, where reforms are subverted insofar as they run counter to the interests of incumbent regimes (Chabal & Daloz, 1999; van de Walle, 2001). Narratives like these, however, have been critiqued from a number of angles. First, they are criticized for their descriptive rather than analytical bent (Erdmann & Engel, 2007; Olivier de Sardan, 2010; Pitcher, Moran & Johnston, 2009). Second, they are seen to lack predictive value (Mkandawire, 2015). Third, from an ethnographic point of view, they are critiqued for their under-specification of bureaucratic dynamics (Bierschenk & Olivier de Sardan, 2014), accounting for what Olivier de Sardan calls "the gap", namely "the difference between a public policy on paper and a public policy as it plays out in reality" (Olivier de Sardan, 2016, p. 119). Critique has also emanated from literature on political settlements (Khan, 2010), which offers a valuable set of entry points for our discussion.

As an approach, privileging analysis of "the politics that underpin particular institutional configurations" – where balance of (informal) power, as well as unequal and conflictual processes of rent distribution are given priority (Lavers & Hickey, 2015, p. 4–5) – foregrounds the importance of exploring the "productivity" of rents under certain circumstances (Khan, 2010, p. 30–31). In Khan's work, political settlements analysis recognizes the salience of patron–client arrangements, essential for the provision of stability insofar as (or as long as) formal institutions are not strong enough to fully respond to the distribution of power in society (Khan, 2010, p. 25). Several contributions have built on Khan's insights (Behuria, Buur & Gray, 2017), and a core preoccupation has formed around understanding the conditions under which economic policies traversed by rent distribution – premised on informal arrangements across horizontal (intra-elite) and vertical (elite–non-elite) groups – can be successful. There are certain limitations to the application of political settlements analysis, as developed by Khan, to our case. In particular, these include a strong focus on "productive sector" policies, and limited attention paid to the role of external actors in shaping the political settlement, or to the way in which ideas influence policy (Hickey, Sen & Bukenya, 2015; Lavers & Hickey, 2015; Yanguas, 2016). Nonetheless, the insights it has brought forward are rich in implications, and far from incompatible with the study of public policies beyond productive sectors, such as public sector reforms (Bukenya & Yanguas, 2016; ESID, 2016).

This contribution falls short of a full-fledged application of political settlement analysis to the DRC, which arguably only makes sense at the macro-political level, rather than that of sectoral policy-making (Behuria, Buur & Gray, 2017, p. 9). However, taking the idea that formal institutions hardly correspond to the distribution of power in society, Khan's insights can help us conceptualize resource capture through rent allocation and (re)distribution as an important facet of the way in which informal arrangements governing the public sector are organized.[7] As the following discussion suggests, such resource capture can be seen as characterizing Congo's financial windfalls associated with payroll leakages, as much as the flow of external aid in the form of development projects. Before expanding on this, a few remarks on the specificities of the Congolese administration are in order.

A cursory look at Congo's civil service, indeed, shows it resonates strongly with Khan's outlook of political competition and clientelism in developing countries (Khan, 2005, 2010). The Congolese civil service, since independence, has undergone a protracted process of decline, particularly accentuated by the late years of the Mobutu regime, when economic duress, structural adjustment-inflicted retrenchment, state disintegration in the 1990s, and the Congo wars severely eroded its functionality (Moshonas, 2018, chapter 3). In 2001, as outlined in a consultant's report, clientelism, predatory behaviour towards service users, moonlighting, patronage-fuelled recruitment outside official procedures, accompanied by numerous inadequacies in remuneration, equipment or functioning expenses, was rife (Nasser Niane, 2003). This situation is broadly consistent with that of a decade later. There have been improvements, for example in scaling up remuneration,[8] or, with donor support, in improving the capacity of the Ministry of Finance. However, the capacity of the bulk of administrative services remains emaciated.

Lemarchand's analysis, sketched in the 1980s, of patronage and prebends in African public sectors – to which Zaire was no exception – is still of wide relevance today: "personal benefits [being] drawn from the appropriation of public office", where the state emerges "'as a market' where officeholders compete for the acquisition of material benefits" (Lemarchand, 1988, p. 153). Or, to cite more recent accounts, the state functions much like an "arena" or a set of "parcels of power", where each administrative position offers not only a salary, but also an opportunity for appropriation (De Herdt, Marivoet & Muhigirwa, 2015, p. 49). In this sense, the state is partly understood as a resource, not only among central political elites, but also along the lower rungs of the administrative hierarchy (Englebert & Kasongo, 2016, pp. 24–5), which scholars working on 1980s Zaire termed the "privatisation of the state" (Newbury, 1984; Lemarchand, 1986; Gould, 1980). In addition, as noted by Englebert and Tull, Congo's political economy is premised on the multiplication and acquisition of rents (including development rents), and the privileging of transactions over production, in large part guided by short-term distributive politics to the detriment of longer-term accumulation (2013, pp. 14–17).

Appointments in the higher echelons of the civil service, particularly for strategic areas associated with revenue generation, as Trefon notes, are far from selected haphazardly, but are "decided at the top of the political pyramid and respect clearly defined paternalistic logic and patron–client patterns" (Trefon, 2010, pp. 713–14). The logic of co-option, patronage, and clientship-based recruitment and appointment also extends to other spheres of the civil service, where political relations, ethnicity and kinship, financial exchange as well as other affinity-based networks, play a role. This is attested to by a raft of anecdotal and field-based observations and interviews, as well as the widespread use of the term of *parapluie*,[9] denoting the protection of a patron. Equally important, even as public service provision by the state remains very meagre (Trefon, 2007), the proceeds from the appropriation of the spoils of office tend to be redistributed, whereby a portion of generated revenue is channelled upwards, in effect a "payment" in return for appointment – a practice referred to as *rapportage*[10] (Englebert & Kasongo, 2016, pp. 23–4). This practice is quite widespread, and extends as much to the central administration as to specific sectors, such as health, education (De Herdt & Titeca, 2016, pp. 486–7) or the police (Baaz & Olsson, 2011; Malukisa Nkeka, 2017).

Taken together, these points can help us articulate the following conceptualization. First, the state as a plural arena of power; a disputed terrain where competing claims over resources, authority and legitimacy are permanent, within, outside and between state and social actors (Englebert & Tull, 2013, p. 17; Olivier de Sardan, 2005, pp. 70–71; Schlichte, 2008); and where much of this terrain is held together by the sort of informal arrangements described above, bearing the mark of clientelist politics. Second, within this plural arena of power, the implementation of an ambitious administrative reform package (including payroll rationalization), towards which the ruling coalition in power is, at best, deeply ambivalent. Third, the roots of this ambivalence, as well as the rocky implementation of payroll reform, derive from an institutional conflict fought over jurisdictional turf between the Ministry of Public Service (MPS) and Ministry of Budget (MoB), underneath which rest different types of rents, most notably related to payroll (mis)management and development assistance. It is this chapter's contention that to understand the prospects of payroll reform, rent distribution must be analysed across both its horizontal dimension (within the ranks of the ruling coalition) and its vertical diffusion (within the bureaucracy) in light of the broader political context in which it unfolds. The following sections, then, flesh out empirically the identification of these types of rent, the political and bureaucratic pressures they produce, and the resistance they occasion.

The political economy of payroll and its stakes

To understand the ongoing struggle surrounding payroll reform, an outline of current procedures – including the underlying practices characterising the payment of remunerations – is in order. A computerized, four-step expenditure chain was introduced in 2003, when the "super-ministry" of Economy, Finance and Budget, which had managed to achieve substantial progress with regards to structural reforms, was broken up at the beginning of the transition to accommodate the patronage demands of the 1+4 coalition government (Beaudienville, 2012, p. 5). Since 2003, then, the payment of wages and salary supplements (*primes*) in the DRC operates through a complex circuit linking several institutions, as highlighted in the following table:

Table 2.1 – The four stages of the remuneration expenditure circuit[11]

Institution	Role in the circuit
Line ministries	Preparation of the elements required to calculate their payroll, passed on to the MPS, as well as ex post controls and verification of received payments
Ministry of Public Service (MPS)	Commitment of spending, passed on to the MoB
Ministry of Budget (MoB)	Validation of the expenditure, passed on to the MoF
Ministry of Finance (MoF)	Issuing of the payment order to the Central Bank
Central Bank	Execution and report of the payment, carried out in part via commercial banks or Caritas since 2013

In practice, there are numerous distortions to this official procedure,[12] the key one being that the MPS has long ceased to play its role. The official mandate of that ministry, aside being tasked with civil servants' remunerations, encompasses several responsibilities. These include the elaboration and application of the civil service general statute, the management of civil servants' careers (including recruitment modalities), the study of administrative methods and implementation of civil service reforms, and the management of retired personnel.[13] In reality, after decades of administrative malpractice, its hold over the careers of civil servants is rather theoretical: there is no longer any control over recruitment, with line ministries by-passing the MPS and recruiting autonomously, the latter's role being limited to ex-post registration and issuing of badge numbers (*numéros de matricule*) which are needed for incorporation into the payroll. Moreover, the MPS is unable to keep track of movements of personnel, until recently being entirely devoid of a single computerized database (Camaly & Tudienu Magenga, 2008, p. 26).

Thus, the MPS places the total number of civil servants at 793,615, including litigious cases and *Nouvelles Unités* (that is, appointed but unregistered state workers) (DRC: MFP, 2015a).[14] At the same time, the MoB's payroll data from October 2015 places the total number of remunerated state personnel at 1,288,168 (DRC: MFP, 2017, p. 37).[15] Finally, as far as the four-step remuneration expenditure circuit is concerned, line ministries, instead of passing on to the MPS the elements required to calculate their payroll – as stipulated by current legislation – tend to deal directly with the MoB's Payroll Department. Notification to the MPS by line ministries regarding the movements of their personnel is effectively side-stepped, not least due to that ministry's inability to play its role of manager of the state's human resources, de facto excluding it from participation in the payroll procedure (Morganti, 2007, p. 24). This marginalization of the MPS lies at the root of the institutional conflict that pits it against the MoB.

This circumvention of the MPS in the payroll procedure does not mean, however, that this ministry has become irrelevant. To understand the real strategic importance of the MPS in the political economy of HR management, a closer look at civil service registrations is required. As we saw, recruitment in the civil service occurs at all levels, outside the control of the MPS, but the latter, by its capacity to allocate badge numbers (a necessary but not sufficient condition for a civil servant's incorporation in the payroll, and therefore to receive a salary), is a neuralgic point upon which tremendous amounts of political pressure are applied. Indeed, recruitment and regularization of one's situation in the civil service is a strategic tool of patronage, particularly for the building up of political constituencies during electoral periods. For registrations, the principal pressure points are at the level of the minister of the MPS and his cabinet. Until 2012,[16] each successive minister upon arrival in office proceeded to register *Nouvelles Unités* into the civil service (that is, recent recruits lacking a badge number). This was done not only for the sake of the minister's own party, but also followed a logic of political exchange of favours and clientelism frequently involving other parties, as well as catering for the interests that supported him.[17] A good example is that of MPS minister Dieudonné Upira (in position from 2010 to 2012 under the Muzito II and III governments), under whose leadership 73,951 agents saw their situation regularized in 31 successive ministerial decrees (Ndondoboni Nsankoy, 2014).

Badge numbers (*numéros matricule*) for civil servants, it is worth noting, are an absolute prerequisite for integration in the payroll, and therefore to receive one's salary, but they are not necessary to receive a salary supplement. As such, they may appear as a merely symbolic issue, but in fact are highly sought after. Even though some agents' salary supplements vastly dwarf their low salary, this is not the case for all personnel. Indeed, many are deprived of significant salary supplements. This is the case for teachers, and (rural) health sector workers without university qualifications, which account for vast swathes of public service workers. Second, a badge number is a strong guarantee of job security, as it removes the precariousness of being an unrecognized civil servant (a *Nouvelle Unité*), and provides certain statutory entitlements (including the hope of retiring one day, should the administrative reform process move forward).

To return to the political economy of payroll management, we have seen that, in principle, for inclusion into the payroll (*mécanisation*) and to receive his or her salary, a civil servant requires a badge number. As such, the MPS regularly supplies lists of registered civil servants under its jurisdiction with a badge number for incorporation to the Payroll Department. In that department, officials have at their disposal long lists of names which are awaiting incorporation, but which have not yet been approved, due to the financial constraints of the state's budget. However, the state's wage bill is "dynamic" – that is, there is fluctuation based on movements of personnel, deaths, revocations, transfers, and so on. This means that despite the tight constraints of the wage bill envelope, there is nevertheless some latitude available for the Payroll Department to incorporate civil servants therein. This phenomenon, known as *"les prises en compte"*,[18] refers to the process whereby particular civil servants manage succeed in having themselves added to the listings for wages or supplements. In practice, this requires networks and financial resources, as well as proximity to Kinshasa, and tends to favour the already advantaged. Such practices are facilitated by dysfunctions within the payroll procedure, in particular the inability of the MPS to play its role, by-passed as a result by line ministries which prefer dealing unilaterally with the Payroll Department at the MoB. As already noted, salary supplements, in contrast to the low-based salaries harmonized across the civil service, can climb very high for some categories of staff, rendering this prerogative even more important.

Overall, because of the weak capacity of the MPS and line ministries to control and verify information, the MoB's Payroll Department has acquired a high-stake position deriving from the weaknesses in HR and payroll management. Today, this is where integration in the payroll is decided, and, as numerous accounts attest,[19] it is a prime locale for informal influence-peddling and financial exchange in return for inclusion.[20] Over the years, this has created a set of vested interests around the status quo, constituting a major source of rents, and is essentially a jealously-guarded prerogative of the Payroll Department and the MoB. An indication of the importance such issues can muster can be gauged from recent control procedures, launched in June 2015 by minister of budget Michel Bongongo, whereby, with the help of trade unions, misappropriations totalling $11.7 million were discovered in the city of Kinshasa in three ministries related to the health and education sectors. Control missions were then extended to five provinces for these same sectors (DRC: MFP, 2016, p. 17–24).[21]

To return to our conceptualization of HR and payroll management as underpinned by forms of rent distribution, we therefore have, on the one hand, a ministry in charge of human resource management that is all but by-passed in the expenditure chain but which retains the ability to regularize the situation of unregistered civil servants, essentially a powerful patronage device; and on the other hand, the Payroll Department within the MoB, which because of the deficiencies in human resource management, retains the capacity to oversee integration in the payroll, whether for salaries or supplements, and which finds itself at the crux of entrenched interests capitalizing on malpractice and abuse, whence important financial bonanzas are derived.

The ongoing struggle around payroll reform

It is now time to turn to the reform that is aiming to introduce an integrated human resource and payroll management system (*Système Intégré de Gestion des Ressources Humaines et de la Paie*, SIGRH-P). Given the challenge it poses to the extremely opaque remuneration system in place, how has it fared over time, what political arrangements have sustained it, how are these articulated to the different types of rent present in the MPS and MoB, and finally, what are its prospects of success?

In 2004, following an audit by the French cooperation of the DRC's manual payroll system, two recommendations were made. First, the establishment, in the long run, of an integrated payroll management system allowing for budgetary control over the wage bill; and second, in the short run, as a palliative measure, the introduction of a Simplified Transitory Procedure (*Procédure Transitoire Simplifiée* or PTS), capable of computerized management of civil servants' remuneration. This system, introduced in 2007, had the objective of rationalizing, centralizing and automating payroll management through the creation of a single payroll database maintained by the Payroll Department at the MoB, enabling computerized calculation and payroll verification (DRC: MoF & MoB, 2011; World Bank, 2008, p. 144). This information technology system was progressively extended to various categories of personnel from July 2007 onwards, and even when the French withdrew from the project in 2009,[22] the MoB continued supporting the system through local expertise (DRC: MoB, 2010, p. 2). Eventually, the PTS came to incorporate most paid personnel, and, as we shall see, was operational until June 2015, when for technical reasons it was replaced by a new piece of software, at the initiative of the MoB's authorities. The PTS system and its successor, as the IT infrastructure upon which the payroll operates, have been managed by the MoB. In the meantime, the second phase envisaged in payroll reform (the introduction of an integrated human resource and payroll management system, known as SIGRH-P) only started being implemented from 2014 onwards. Importantly, the implementation of the SIGRH-P is a major component of the new, revised civil service reform strategy underway since 2012, piloted by the MPS cabinet. As such, it is embedded in and forms the cornerstone of a wider, interdependent architecture of reform, which includes a policy of retirement and rejuvenation through recruitment based on competitive exams, ministerial restructuring, and especially the creation of new human resource departments in each ministry (DRC: MFP, 2015a). Besides being MPS-led, this wide-ranging reform initiative, strongly incentivized through the provision of a World Bank $77 million retirement and rejuvenation project (PRRAP) in 2013, has also benefited from solid support provided by prime minister Augustin Matata Ponyo, in office from April 2012 to November 2016. Before delving into the importance of the SIGRH-P initiative for payroll management and the difficulties it has encountered, it is worth pausing to consider the political arrangements that have underpinned it, the types of rent they are linked to, as well as the broader context of the period under consideration.

Firstly, it is worth noting that the present round of administrative reform (since 2012) came about in the wake of the 2011 elections, with the establishment of the Matata I government, widely perceived as being composed of technocrats (Nyenyezi Bisoka, 2015, p. 82). Under the leadership of Jean-Claude Kibala (a politician of the *Mouvement Social pour le Renouveau* party of Pierre Lumbi, which has held the MPS since 2007), the revised and World Bank-supported reform strategy was launched. If Kibala's role was instrumental in reviving the reform process, his dynamism and unilateral methods at points fostered frustration among his colleagues in priority ministries.[23] The MoB was headed by Daniel Mukoko Samba, another so-called technocrat,[24] though this did not help the long-standing jurisdictional conflict regarding to payroll management between the MPS and MoB from abating when donor funds rekindled the reform process. While the manoeuvring space for prime minister Matata was somewhat curtailed with the 2014 governmental reshuffle, particularly with regards to his control over public finances (Nyenyezi Bisoka, 2015, p. 82), the appointments of Michel Bongongo (an ally of senate president Kengo-wa-Dondo) at the MoB and Pascal Isumbisho at the MPS did not put a halt to the activities linked to payroll reform. In fact, Isumbisho, although a newcomer in politics, continued pushing forward with reform, having been given the tacit signal "not to stir things up with regard to donor support".[25]

Second, it is worth noting that this political configuration, as explored below, is only partly linked with the different types of rents that co-exist with the operations of payroll. If the political leadership of the MPS drew significant advantages from (ab)using the process of large-scale civil service registrations, this type of practice receded between 2012 and 2016, and the strategic value of the MPS was reinforced by an external source of finance – the World Bank funds that are the primary reason why there is a reform today. The creation and staffing of reform structures, such as the *Cellule de Mise en Oeuvre de la Réforme de l'Administration Publique* (CMRAP/PRRAP),[26] the recruitment of experts, of consultants, the organization of events, workshops and activities associated with reform, the disbursement of per diems, are far from negligible in that respect as sources of rent and patronage. That is not to say that they are incompatible with progress on reform initiatives. Even if the extent to which change is substantive can be debated, it has at the very least given them visibility. In the case of the MoB, however, it is far from clear that its political leadership is systematically linked to payroll (mis)management as a form of rent.[27] The irregularities, abuses and leakages characterizing wage payment appear to be far more importantly tied to bureaucratic actors. Our analysis suggests they are often the result of a convoluted payroll procedure replete with openings, whereby each actor in the circuit who is in a position to do so exploits available loopholes.[28]

Third, the above considerations cannot be dissociated from the broader context in which the politics of payroll reform play out, which conditions both the externally enabled drive for payroll reform,

as well as the bureaucratic resistance it occasions due to the interests it threatens. Even if the current phase of administrative reform
since 2012 has benefited from much stronger government ownership
(certainly compared to previous rounds of reform between 2003 and
2011. See: Moshonas, 2014), it also occupies a rather ambivalent
position in relation to the ruling coalition in power. On the one hand,
even though President Joseph Kabila never ceases to nominally
pledge his commitment to reform as a precondition to administrative redress, there are no concrete indicators of this being a priority.
On the other hand, this reform is also an important legitimizing
tool for the display of governmental commitment to aid-promoted
reforms, not least due to the necessity of maintaining operative relations with donors, which if anything has only gained in importance
over recent years. At the same time, if under the successive Matata
governments administrative reform featured steadily on the horizon,
since late 2016 the political uncertainty associated with the vagaries
of the electoral calendar has meant that a sensitive issue such as
payroll reform has become a far more distant possibility.

To return to the focus on payroll management, the aim of the
SIGRH-P is to improve HR data management and fully integrate
it within payroll procedures, through the electronic interfacing and
reconciliation of the MPS personnel database with the payroll database held by the Payroll Department. The SIGRH-P will also allow
the management of both HR and payroll information through an
automated, computerized procedure, and put an end to the communication deficit between the institutions involved in the payroll,
restoring the official circuit. It is hoped that this will rationalize
the system, eliminate the phenomenon of ghost workers, close the
loopholes arising from the disconnection and fragmented procedure across a multiplicity of institutions and actors, and restore
the principle of budgetary control over the wage bill, including
adequacy of HR management to the needs of public service. The
implications of the SIGRH-P, as such, are far-reaching, as they have
the potential to profoundly alter the current configuration around
which HR management and the payment of remunerations takes
place, which, as described above, has clustered around a set of vested
interests settled around the Payroll Department. In other words, the
SIGRH-P envisions nothing short of a displacement of the sources
of rent within payroll management.

However, its establishment faces uncertain prospects, particularly
considering the ongoing struggle between the MPS and the MoB
over control of the payroll, insofar as effective implementation would

strip the MoB's Payroll Department of its current prerogatives. Indeed, a latent confrontation has been underway between those two ministries for some time concerning the control of the payroll. As far as senior officials at the MPS are concerned,[29] the MoB's Payroll Department is nothing more than a technical structure, and should be exclusively executing orders, rather than assuming an expansive role far beyond its mandate.[30] The drive by the MPS to reclaim its prerogatives is also evident from civil service reform documentation. The MPS's October 2015 administrative reform strategy clearly lays out the disposition according to which the MPS is in charge of spending commitments for remuneration, and envisages the creation of a new HR department in every ministry, which will include a division dealing with payroll commitments (DRC: MFP, 2015a, p. 81). Former MPS minister Kibala had stoked the fire of that confrontation, having turned the SIGRH-P, in the words of close observers, into "a personal affair" (*une affaire personnelle*).[31] Sanguine declarations such as the one below left little ambiguity:

> In preparation of the SIGRH-P, a structure of the MPS will be in charge of the remuneration of civil servants and state personnel, and we are already working on this. We therefore will have the control of salaries for all civil servants, and we shall be better placed to answer the challenge of their social condition.
> (J. C. Kibala, cited in DRC: MFP, 2014, p. 43)

Officials at the MoB, however, acknowledge the role of the MPS as far as the initiation of spending commitments for base salaries is concerned, but deem the management of salary supplements an affair for the Payroll Department, upon instruction from line ministries. This is partly justified, according to MoB informants, because of the MPS's loss of control over HR management, which renders many civil servants recipients of a supplement without a base salary due to the lack of clear instructions or required updates emanating from the MPS.[32] As far as they are concerned, the MPS has de facto excluded itself from payroll management. In other words, the current configuration around payroll management – where the MoB's Payroll Department has come to assume an expansive role, in tandem with line ministries which deal unilaterally with it, especially for salary supplements – constitutes an important blockage point as far as the implementation of the SIGRH-P is concerned. To understand the rocky road of the SIGRH-P in its course of implementation, as well as its associated bottlenecks, two parallel developments need to be specified, each of which are bound up with different types of rents. The first concerns the steps taken to implement the SIGRH-P itself, under the auspices of the MPS-led, World Bank-funded, civil service reform programme; the second concerns an MoB-introduced home-grown initiative to upgrade the PTS software system upon which payroll management was based to date.

As already stated, the SIGRH-P reform has been underway since 2014. The company charged with implementation following the award of the procurement contract – Tunisian consultancy firm SIMAC – has completed feasibility studies, installed the server hosting the SIGRH-P, and various forms of data are being integrated and harmonized to populate the database.[33] However, operationalization stalled after 2016, with few signs of progress since then. At around the same time, at the MoB's Payroll Department, a new software system was introduced to replace the PTS. The reason behind this initiative, taken by former minister of budget Daniel Mukoko Samba, was largely technical, having to do with the limited capacity of the previous PTS software to deal with the ever-growing amounts of payroll entries.[34] This could potentially be a serious problem, because in the case of severe payroll malfunctions, the threat of massive strikes loomed large. To replace the PTS, the MoB contracted a Congolese consultant and his company (BSC-ERCTool) to migrate the database onto a new system, known as the *Système de gestion centralisée de la paie des agents et fonctionnaires* (SYGECPAF),[35] which became effective in June 2015. As we shall see, this initiative, although largely justified in its intentions, added a further layer of complexity to the inter-ministerial struggle pitting MPS against MoB on the issue of payroll management. The current stand-off regarding the SIGRH-P can be viewed through two inter-related issues, both linked to the themes addressed in the chapter thus far. First, the inter-ministerial struggle across two ministries, each driven by its own incentives – on the one hand, the MPS-led, World Bank-supported civil service reform initiative; on the other, the MoB and its Payroll Department, whose home-grown initiative with regards to upgrading software is bent on the defence of its *de facto* prerogatives. Second, and closely linked to the first, the high stakes surrounding control over the political economy of payroll, which have come to constitute a strong set of vested interests.

As explained above, the SIGRH-P consists of an integrated HR and payroll management system, introduced under the auspices of the MPS, with the explicit aim of rationalizing both career and payroll management. In principle, it is envisioned as functioning in parallel to the home-grown MoB payroll software system, SYGECPAF, until it eventually absorbs the latter. However, for the reasons set out above, there has been strong, mostly bureaucratic, resistance to its implementation, from within the MoB but also beyond. To begin with, for the SIGRH-P to become effective its database needs to be populated with payroll data, and as such the transfer of the SYGECPAF database to the Tunisian consultancy firm SIMAC (in charge of the SIGRH-P) is essential. However, even though the SYGECPAF database had been requested by the MPS as early as July 2015, and explicit orders had been provided by the prime minister's office to the MoB, and in turn by the budget minister himself to his services, the payroll department only provided the list to SIMAC in February 2016, a situation resolved only via the intervention of the prime minister's office. The tensions between the MPS and MoB have extended to the two consultant cabinets respectively working on SIGRH-P and SYGECPAF. On the one hand, the Congolese consultancy company BSC-ERCTool, working on the latter, has been involved in delaying the transfer of the database to SIMAC, and obviously has a stake in the continued use of the software it established. On the other hand, due to the very sensitive nature of the work undertaken by SIMAC, the team of international consultants working on the SIGRH-P has reportedly been exposed to a difficult working environment, including at times open hostility. Another telling indication of bureaucratic resistance to the changes introduced by the SIGRH-P is that certain sectors had also eschewed providing their database, such as the education sector managed via SECOPE, or the police. Obviously, these sectors are reluctant to see their own prerogatives regarding the remuneration of their personnel recuperated by the MPS.

As can be inferred from the above discussion of the political economy of payroll in the DRC, there are numerous reasons why this is a highly sensitive and high-stake matter. The SYGECPAF data provided to SIMAC in February 2016 contains all the payroll information for the month of January 2016, and rather expectedly presents its own set of problems. Indeed, prior to receiving the entire SYGECPAF database for January 2016, SIMAC was provided with a portion of the October 2015 payroll data, which were then compiled in a single file for analysis. Some of these detailed results are quite revealing: out of 1,288,168 entries (including widows, pensioners, orphans, *nouvelles unités* without a badge number, etc.), there are 1,067,561 registered badge numbers, of which only 799,571 are unique. More precisely, the analysis revealed that 115,171 badge numbers appeared at least twice – some of them even appeared four-teen times, suggesting the reliability of controls in the MoB's payroll procedure is extremely weak (SIMAC, 2015).

Unsurprisingly, therefore, the current struggle between the MPS and the MoB seems closely tied to a set of forces which render the latter's Payroll Department very reluctant to relinquish, or even share, control over the payroll. For all practical purposes, this department at present wields the power to decide matters of inclusion within the wage payroll, albeit on the basis of requests submitted by the MPS for public sector workers who have been admitted into the civil service through the many *arrêtés sous-statut* (status decrees), and within the bounds of the current financial law. It also manages the payment of salary supplements, which are dealt with without the involvement of the MPS, whereby ministries and services send their requests directly to the Payroll department. This constitutes a jeal-ously guarded prerogative, with important financial interests at stake, as hinted at by the SYGECPAF data cited above. The "black box" of the payroll system is certainly hard to peer into, even more so since it rests on a cumbersome expenditure circuit replete with openings, where, beyond the MoB's Payroll Department, other actors (such as ministerial departments dealing with HR by-passing the MPS) equally command influence. Collusion, opacity and allegations of 'mafia networks' permeating the civil service are its inevitable result.

Conclusions

The introduction of IT infrastructures in Congo is by no means a new phenomenon. In 1972/73, Mobutu had introduced an admin-istrative reform premised on rationalization of the civil service, flagging efficiency as its rationale, to be achieved via modern mana-gerial techniques – the computer was to be its banner (Vieux, 1974, p. 91). Salary administration for teachers was centralized through the instalment of computers in the 1970s. As a first-hand observer of noted, however, even a superficial analysis of the process suggested that it supplied numerous avenues for enrichment, and even facil-itated "centrally-controlled corruption on a mass, computerized scale" (Gould, 1979, p. 96–7).[36] While Gould's hypothesis cannot be fully discounted, forty years later, the Congolese administration shows that the introduction of computerized wage payment systems does not warrant appraisals that solely stress malpractice. After all, if one considers the PTS or the SYGECPAF software on which the payroll has operated, for a large proportion of civil servants, wages and supplements *are* paid, and the software infrastructure has even provided the basis on which the flagship reform of *bancarisation* has been built. In the scholarly literature which addresses the question of why information technology reforms fall short of their aims in Africa, the issue has been framed either in terms of committed but marginalized reformers pitted against "spoilers" in a context of organizational weakness (Peterson, 1998), or through the lens of settings pervaded by neopatrimonial relations tied to the colonial legacy and authoritarian decision making (Berman & Tettey, 2001). This chapter follows a different route. The introduction of the SIGRH-P to rationalize the payroll circuit was analysed as part of a broader initiative – administrative reform – which sits rather ambiguously within the ranks of the ruling coalition. The capture of off-budget resources and clientelism within the arrangements that govern civil servants' remunerations, as well as the World Bank funding which has enabled the drive towards payroll reform, are both different types of rent which have fed into a latent confrontation between the MoB and its Payroll Department on the one hand, and the MPS and its cabinet on the other.

The question remains, though, of what allowed the SIGRH-P to move forward to the point it did? The short answer, and the only one we feel confident enough to advance at this point, is that advances were permitted insofar as they enabled the continuation of vital donor support for an embattled regime, and to the extent they have not (yet) threatened the stability of existing arrangements. The latter are indeed far reaching in scope, as can be glimpsed from the types of rent associated with HR and payroll management. On the one hand, the rent derived from donor funding for civil service reform appear to us rather peripheral – the sort of politico-financial windfall ceded to a coalition minister (and his party). On the other hand, the financial returns tied to payroll system abuses, for their part, may appear quite localized, but the possibility that a large chunk of the proceeds are siphoned upwards the political command chain (in line with the system referred to as *"rapportage"* in the DRC) is a strong one. Last but not least, the function fulfilled by the MPS in terms of patronage-based recruitment via civil service registrations should not be underestimated. In pre-electoral contexts, its strategic significance is huge, and its political returns reach far beyond the MPS minister alone. All of this suggests the balance of forces is currently heavily tilted against implementation, especially when mobilization of funds and votes is of paramount importance.

Finally, it should be noted that the SIGRH-P's prospects are closely tied to the other administrative reform initiatives with which it is intermeshed, which have generated substantial amounts of resistance. The displacement of staff working in departments targeted by restructuring, the fate of irregular personnel such as the *Nouvelles Unités*, the competitive exam-based recruitment through which rejuvenation is pursued, are all cases in point. Deep-seated feelings of unease pervade the wider corps of civil servants, uncertain about their place in an overhauled administration. As such, in the longer run, whether the SIGRH-P results in effective implementation or partial, watered-down operationalization under the weight of compromises struck within both the political and bureaucratic command chains, remains an open question.

Notes

1 The author would like to thank DFID, Atos and Integrity Global for the permission to make use of some of the information presented in this chapter, which is partly drawn from an EACP/DFID research report on pay issues in the DRC's health sector, for which the author served as lead researcher. The support provided by these organizations, along with the help of researchers Hermès Karemere and Ali-Ben Kapeta, is gratefully acknowledged. Of course, the views expressed here do not in any way reflect those of DFID.

2 The state's budget underwent a marked contraction of almost 50% between 2015 and 2017, going from around $9 billion to $4.6 billion (DRC: MoB, 2015 & 2017), before prime minister Bruno Tshibala declared the state was working towards a budget of $7.8 billion – announcements, however, many considered out of touch with reality (Le Potentiel, 2017).

3 Between 2009 and 2013, 41% of the total domestic budget was devoted to the wage bill, which has risen on average by 30% per annum during the last decade (World Bank, 2015, p. 6–7).

4 Literally "bank-ization".

5 The Integrated Human Resource and Pay Management System.

6 Fieldwork was conducted in May–August 2010, April–June 2011, March–April 2016 (when the author served as a lead researcher for an EACP/DFID study on remuneration issues in the DRC's health sector), April–October 2017, and May–July 2018. The field research conducted in 2016 made use of a methodology whereby interviewees provided information under strict conditions of anonymity; as such, in this chapter, wherever interview-related information is used, the citation only lists the city and month.

7 As such, the terms of formal/informal should be seen as part of the political settlement analysis framework that informs the argument, and not as an assumed empirical dichotomy. The latter would be problematic insofar as, in a context of legal pluralism such as the one considered here, distinguishing between different shades of formality and their underlying practices in terms of a dyad would make little sense.

8 In 2001, wages ranged from $4 for a *huissier* to $35 for a *Secrétaire Général*. They have since been

progressively scaled up. Yet the bulk of remuneration continues to be composed of salary supplements *primes permanentes*, literally "permanent bonuses") (Herdeschee, Kaiser & Mukoko Samba, 2012, p. 34).

9 Literally "umbrella".

10 Literally "reporting".

11 A fuller account of the current payroll procedure can be found in a number of sources (World Bank, 2008, p. 144; DRC: MoF & MoB, 2010; SIMAC & PRCG, 2014; DRC: MoB, 2014).

12 It should be noted that the MPS is only responsible for civil servants under its jurisdiction, governed by the general statute of the civil service. Over time, the civil service has fragmented into a multiplicity of special and specific statutes (Morganti, 2007, p. 3), meaning numerous other sectors (such as the army, police, teachers, etc.) manage their personnel separately.

13 As outlined in the Ordonnance n°80-215 of 28 August 1980, which re-instated it.

14 These figures are those of the census of civil servants, which was launched in 2005.

15 These discrepancies are due to a variety of reasons, the main one being that there are many registered civil servants without a base salary and/or salary supplement, and therefore absent from the payroll database; whereas the payroll contains all paid personnel, whether they receive a base salary, a salary supplement, or both. Equally, the fact that the census of civil servants initiated in 2005 lasted nine years, was carried out without necessary external controls, and to a large extent excluded teachers, renders MPS' figures unreliable.

16 In 2012–13, new registrations of civil servants by issuing badge numbers (via *arrêtés d'admission sous-statut*, or decrees of status admission) were formally proscribed by order of prime minister Matata Ponyo, except for graduates of the *École Nationale de l'Administration* or for the World Bank-funded Young Professionals scheme, a decision broadly respected until 2017.

17 Interviews. Kinshasa (4 & 5 April 2016).

18 Literally "considerations" or "awareness".

19 A cartoon in the official MPS publication *Journal du fonctionnaire* (DRC: MFP, 2015b), which has been a donor-funded output of the administrative reform strategy since 2012, provided a humorous illustration of the process, focused on the travails of a recently hired civil servant.

20 Interviews. Kinshasa (April 2016 & April–October 2017).

21 There were wide echoes of this in the press (e.g. RFI, 2015). A few months before that, controls on the doctors' payroll had been made which led to the discovery of severe irregularities regarding their *prime de risque* (i.e. risk bonus) (Radio Okapi, 2015). The repercussions in the MoB were serious enough that minister Bongongo, in April 2015, just before the finalization of the SYGECPAF (*Système de Gestion Centralisé de la Paie des Agents et Fonctionnaires de l'État*), decided to replace a good portion of the Payroll department (including allegedly around half of its IT personnel, several chefs de division liquidation and its director), and led to him being questioned in parliament (Le Soft International, 2015).

22 This withdrawal was in large part caused by the delays occasioned by the census launched in 2005, on which the success of the second round of payroll reform was conditional. From: Interview. Kinshasa (18 June 2010).

23 Interviews. Kinshasa (April 2016 & 2017).

[24] Daniel Mukoko Samba came from the UNDP; he was propelled to the position when prime minister Matata vetoed the other names on the list of ministerial candidates of the *Parti Lubumbiste Unifié*, a party which had held the ministry since 2007.

[25] Interviews. Kinshasa (April 2016).

[26] Unit for the Execution of the Reform of Public Administration.

[27] After all, as the ministry responsible for the elaboration of the state's budget, and the allocation alongside the MoF of budgetary lines to line ministries, there are ample opportunities for other types of rent-generation, which we believe play a much greater role insofar as the minister and his cabinet are concerned.

[28] The fact that the government authorized trade unions to undertake controls of the payroll for certain sectors, as noted above, tends to corroborate this point.

[29] Interviews. Kinshasa (April 2016 & May 2017).

[30] Regulatory confusion has amplified this situation. Both the old 1981 General Statute of the civil service, and its 2016 successor, affirm that in terms of remuneration of civil servants, the MPS retains a key, defining role with regards to salaries and supplements, even if the latter leaves some uncertainty over the precise roles of the MoB and MoF in the case of salary supplement definition.

[31] Interviews. Kinshasa (30 March 2016 & 4 May 2017).

[32] Interviews. Kinshasa (15 & 16 April 2016).

[33] These sources of data include the figures of the 2005 census, the figures of various sectoral censuses, and recently, the SYGECPAF database.

[34] To be more precise, the PTS system functioned under MS-Access, but its processing ability encountered growing problems as payroll entries approached the one million mark. The new piece of software introduced, the SYGECPAF, operates on the basis of MS-SQL Server 2012, superseding the limitations of the previous software and coming closer to the production of a unified database. From: Interview. Kinshasa (16 April 2016).

[35] Centralized System for the Payment of Agents and Functionaries.

[36] Similarly, a decree in 1983 was issued with the aim of establishing a central computerized database of civil servants, which came apart "after saboteurs planted a virus in the system" (Moloi, 2010, p. 77).

References

Autesserre, S. (2012) Dangerous tales: Dominant narratives on the Congo and their unintended consequences. *African Affairs* 111 (443): 202–22.

Baaz, M. E. and Olsson, O. (2011) Feeding the horse: Unofficial economic activities within the police force in the Democratic Republic of Congo. *African Security* 4 (4): 223–41.

Beaudienville, G. (2012) Public financial management reforms in fragile states: The case of Democratic Republic of the Congo. ODI Research Report.

Behuria, P., Buur, L. and Gray, H. (2017) Studying political settlements in Africa. *African Affairs* 116 (464): 1–18.

Berman, B. and Tettey, W. J. (2001) African states, bureaucratic culture and computer fixes. *Public Administration and Development* 21 (1): 1–13.

Bierschenk, T. and Olivier de Sardan, J.-P. (eds) (2014) *States at Work: Dynamics of African Bureaucracies.* Leiden: Brill.

Bukenya, B. and Yanguas, P. (2013) Building state capacity for inclusive development: The politics of public sector reform. Manchester: ESID Working Paper 25.

Camaly, O. and Tudienu Magenga, F. (2008) *Analyse Institutionelle et organisationelle du Ministère de la Fonction Publique: Rapport final de mission.* Kinshasa: Möbius & CTB.

Chabal, P. and Daloz, J. P. (1999) *Africa Works: Disorder as a Political Instrument.* Oxford/Indiana: James Currey/Indiana University Press.

De Herdt, T., Marivoet, W. and Muhirigwa, F. (2015) Vers la réalisation du droit à une éducation de qualité pour tous. UNICEF Research Report.

De Herdt, T. and Titeca, K. (2016) Governance with empty pockets: The education sector in the Democratic Republic of Congo. *Development and Change,* 47 (3): 472–94.

DRC: MoB (Democratic Republic of Congo: Ministry of Budget) (2010) Rapport de l'execution de la mise en service de bout en bout de la Procédure Transitoire Simplifiée de Paie (PTS) à Kinshasa.

DRC: MoB (Democratic Republic of Congo: Ministry of Budget) (2014) Le nouveau circuit de la paie des agents et fonctionnaires de l'État selon la réforme (PTS).

DRC: MoB (Democratic Republic of Congo: Ministry of Budget) (2015) Budget citoyen 2015: Chiffres, politiques publiques, actions et mesures en condenses. Available from: www.budget.gouv.cd/2012/budget2015/budget_citoyen_2015.pdf [Accessed 23 November 2018].

DRC: MoB (Democratic Republic of Congo: Ministry of Budget) (2017) Budget citoyen 2018: Chiffres, politiques publiques, actions et mesures en condenses. Available from: www.budget.gouv.cd/2012/budget2018/budget_citoyen_2018.pdf [Accessed 23 November 2018].

DRC: MoF & MoB (Democratic Republic of Congo: Ministry of Finance and Ministry of Budget) (2010) Manuel des procédures et du circuit de la dépense publique. Circuit rationalisé.

DRC: MoF & MoB (Democratic Republic of Congo: Ministry of Finance and Ministry of Budget) (2011) Atelier sur 'les procédures d'exécution de la paie des agents et fonctionnaires de l'État'. Thème: État de mise en oeuvre de la Procédure Transitoire Simplifiée de la Paie.

DRC: MFP (Democratic Republic of Congo: Ministère de la Fonction Publique) (2014) *Journal du Fonctionnaire 1.*

DRC: MFP (Democratic Republic of Congo: Ministère de la Fonction Publique) (2015a) Cadre stratégique général de la réforme et modernisation de l'administration publique.

DRC: MFP (Democratic Republic of Congo: Ministère de la Fonction Publique) (2015b) *Journal du Fonctionnaire 3.*

DRC: MFP (Democratic Republic of Congo: Ministère de la Fonction Publique) (2016) *Journal du Fonctionnaire 4.*

DRC: MFP (Democratic Republic of Congo: Ministère de la Fonction Publique) (2017) Cadre stratégique général révisé de la réforme et modernisation de l'administration publique, 2017–2021.

Englebert, P. (2014) Democratic Republic of Congo: Growth for all? Challenges and opportunities for a new economic future. Brenthurst foundation. Background paper 6/2014.

Englebert, P. and Kasongo, M. E. (2016) Misguided and misdiagnosed: The failure of decentralization reforms in the DR Congo. *African Studies Review* 59 (1): 5–32.

Englebert, P. and Tull, D. M. (2013) Contestation, négociation et résistance: L'Etat Congolais au quotidien. *Politique africaine* 129: 5–22.

Erdmann, G. and Engel, U. (2007) Neopatrimonialism reconsidered: Critical review and elaboration of an elusive concept. *Commonwealth and Comparative Politics* 45 (1): 95–119.

ESID (2016) Public sector reform in Uganda: Behind the façade. ESID Briefing 23.

Gould, D. J. (1979) The administration of underdevelopment. In: Gran, G. (ed.) *Zaire: The Political Economy of Underdevelopment.* New York, NY: Praeger, pp. 87–107.

Gould, D. J. (1980) *Bureaucratic Corruption and Underdevelopment in the Third World: The Case of Zaire.* New York, NY: Pergamon Press.

Herdeschee, J., Kaiser, K.-A. and Mukoko Samba, D. (2012) Rapport de Synthèse. In: J. Herdeschee, Kaiser, K.-A. and Mukoko Samba, D. (eds) *Résilience d'un géant Africain: Accélerer la croissance et promouvoir l'emploi en RDC. Vol. 1.* Kinshasa: MediasPaul, pp. 1–91.

Hickey, S., Sen, K. and Bukenya, B. (2015) The politics of inclusive development: Towards a new conceptual approach. In: S. Hickey, Sen, K. and Bukenya, B. (eds) *The Politics of Inclusive Development: Interrogating the Evidence.* Oxford: Oxford University Press, pp. 3–32.

Khan, M. (2005) Markets, states and democracy: Patron–client networks and the case for democracy in developing countries. *Democratisation* 12 (5): 704–24.

Khan, M. (2010) Political settlements and the governance of growth-enhancing institutions. London: SOAS.

Lavers, T. and Hickey, S. (2015) Investigating the political economy of social protection expansion in Africa: At the intersection of transnational ideas and domestic politics. ESID Working Paper 47.

Lemarchand, R. (1986) Bringing factions back into the state. In: Nzongola-Ntalaja, G. (ed.) *The Crisis in Zaire: Myth and Realities.* Trenton, NJ: Africa World Press.

Lemarchand, R. (1988) The state, the parallel economy, and the changing structure of patronage systems. In: Rothschild, D. S. and Chazan, N. (eds) *The Precarious Balance: State and Society in Africa.* Boulder, CO: Westview, pp. 149–70.

Le Potentiel (2017) Projet de Budget 2017: Tshibala n'a pas convaincu. Available from: www.lepotentielonline.com/index.php?option=com_content&view=article&id=17064:projet-de-budget-2017-tshibala-n-a-pas-convaincu&catid=85&Itemid=472 [Accessed 14 August 2017].

Le Soft International (2015) Michel Bongongo fait part d'une opération de bancarisation réussie. Available from: www.lesoftonline.net/articles/michel-bongongo-fait-part-d%E2%80%99une-op%C3%A9ration-de-bancarisation-r%C3%A9ussie [Accessed 4 June 2017].

Malukisa Nkuku, A. (2017) La « gouvernance réelle » du transport en commun à Kinshsasa : La prééminence des « normes pratiques » sur les normes officielles. PhD Dissertation: Institute of Development Policy and Management, University of Antwerp.

Mkandawire, T. (2015) Neopatrimonialism and the political economy of economic performance in Africa: Critical reflections. *World Politics* 67 (3): 563–612.

Moloi, D. (2010) Headcount: Lessons learnt from the DRC public service census project. *Service Delivery Review: A Learning Journal for the Public Service* 8 (1): 76–85.

Morganti, T. (2007) Democratic Republic of Congo: Reforming the

public service wage system. World
Bank report.

Moshonas, S. (2014) The politics
of civil service reform in the
Democratic Republic of Congo.
*The Journal of Modern African
Studies* 52 (2): 251–76.

Moshonas, S. (2018) *Aid Relations
and State Reforms in the Democratic
Republic of the Congo: The Politics
of Mutual Accommodation and
Administrative Neglect*. London:
Routledge.

Nasser Niane, S. (2003) Cadre
stratégique de la réforme de la
fonction publique en République
Démocratique du Congo
(Programme d'Actions Prioritaire
18–24 mois). PNUD/DESA Projet
ZAI/00/004.

Ndondoboni, Nsankoy (2014)
Consultance sur le contrôle de
la conformité des arrêtés pris
depuis 2010 par le Ministère
de la Fonction Publique. RDC
Primature. Rapport Final.

Newbury, C. M. (1984) Dead and
buried or just underground?
The privatization of the state in
Zaire. *Canadian Journal of African
Studies/Revue canadienne des etudes
africaines* 18 (1): 112–14.

Nyenyezi Bisoka, A. (2015)
Chronique politique de la RDC,
2014–2015. In: Reyntjens, F.,
Vandeginste S. and Verpoorten M.
(eds.) *L'Afrique des Grands Lacs:
Annuaire 2014–2015* (pp. 79–106).
Antwerp: University of Antwerp
Press.

Olivier de Sardan, J.-P. (2005)
*Anthropology and Development:
Understanding Contemporary Social
Change*. London: Zed Books.

Olivier de Sardan, J.-P. (2010)
Le culturalisme traditionaliste
africaniste: Analyse d'une
idéologie scientifique. *Cahiers
d'études Africaines* 198-199-200
(2-3-4): 419–53.

Olivier de Sardan, J.-P. (2016)
For an anthropology of gaps,
discrepancies and contradictions.
Anthropologia 3 (1): 111–31.

Peterson, S. B. (1998) Saints,
demons, wizards and systems: Why
information technology reforms
fail or underperform in public
bureaucracies in Africa. *Public
Administration and Development* 18
(1): 37–60.

Pitcher, A., Moran, M. H.
and Johnston, M. (2009)
Rethinking patrimonialism and
neopatrimonialism in Africa.
African Studies Review 52 (1):
125–56.

Rackley, E. B. (2006) Democratic
Republic of the Congo: Undoing
government by predation. *Disasters*
30 (4): 418–32.

Radio Okapi (2015) Détournement
des primes des médecins:
La direction de la paie agit
seule, affirme Félix Kabange.
Radio Okapi. Available
from: www.radiookapi.
net/actualite/2015/06/03/
detournement-de-la-paie-des-
medecins-le-ministre-kabange-
exige-des-sanctions-severes
[Accessed 13 June 2017].

RFI (2015) RDC: Le scandal
du détournement massif de
la paie des fonctionnaires.
Radio France Internationale.
Available from: www.rfi.fr/
afrique/20151117-rdc-fraude-
massive-paiement-fonctionnaires
[Accessed 27 Janurary 2017].

Schlichte, K. (2008) Uganda, or: The
internationalization of rule. *Civil
Wars* 10 (4): 369–83.

SIMAC (2015) Résultats des
analyses effectuées sur les fichiers
livrés par SYGECPAF.

SIMAC and PRCG (2014) Étude
préalable, critique de l'existant
et description de l'ensemble du
système proposé.

Trefon, T. (2007) Parcours
Administratifs dans un Etat
en faillite: Récits populaires
de Lumumbashi (RDC).
Tervuren/Paris: Cahiers
Africains/L'Harmattan.

Trefon, T. (ed.) (2009) *Réforme
au Congo (RDC): Attentes et*

désillusions. Tervuren/Paris: Cahiers Africains/L'Harmattan.

Trefon, T. (2010) Administrative obstacles to reform in the Democratic Republic of Congo. *International Review of Administrative Sciences* 76 (4): 702–22.

Trefon, T. (2011) *Congo Masquerade: The Political Culture of Aid Inefficiency and Reform Failure.* London: Zed Books.

van de Walle, N. (2001) *African Economies and the Politics of Permanent Crisis, 1979–1999.* Cambridge: Cambridge University Press.

Vieux, S. A. (1974) *L'administration zaïroise.* Paris: Berger-Levrault.

World Bank (2008) Democratic Republic of Congo: Public Expenditure Review (PER). World Bank, Government of the Democratic Republic of Congo and DFID.

World Bank (2015) RDC: Revue de la gestion des depenses publiques et de la responsabilisation financiere. World Bank Report 96172-ZR.

Yanguas, P. (2016) The role and responsibility of foreign aid in recipient political settlements. ESID Working Paper 56.

3
Neighbourhood Chiefs in Urban DRC: "The State is Me, the State is You, the State is All of Us"

Stéphanie Perazzone[1]

"Mboka Ebebi": State absences

In Kinshasa, "Mboka ebebi" ("the country is spoiled" in Lingala) is often heard among Congolese of all social backgrounds – the low-level civil servant, the well-heeled businessman, the taxi driver, the local barber, the marginalized widow, the middle-class lawyer, the politician, the military officer. As they go about their daily life, most refer to the Congolese state's many ailments; from inefficient bureaucratic services to routinized corruption and rampant insecurity. Sharing a morning tea in a blue plastic cup with fellow street-level bureaucrats at the district office's[2] *malewa*,[3] state officials and ordinary citizens alike criticize state governance, waving their arms in protest. "Ah! If only the state provided us with the resources to work!" an old civil servant awaiting retirement lamented to me.[4] Acute poverty and material scarcity are striking in the poorest districts of Goma, Kinshasa and Lubumbashi, where I conducted fieldwork for seven months. A few newly built or remodelled high-level political offices may catch the eye, mainly in Kinshasa, where the government has indeed sought to "rewrite the mythologies of power" (Mbembe, 2001, p. 108). By contrast, the sites of "lower politics" (Bayart, Mbembe & Toulabour, 2008) and the realms of interpersonal relations often display the signs of decades of government neglect, societal conflict and war. That is to say, whether in streets, homes, local markets, *malewa*, police posts or local state offices, services and infrastructure such as street lights, tarred roads, efficient sewage system, and trash collection are all absent. In addition, the absence of digital and electronic technologies, appropriate furniture, and basic office stationery in most administrative offices often convey a sense of abandonment. Sometimes seemingly frozen in their old colonial guise, some present the image of "the ruins of modernity" (Hell & Schönle, 2010). Decaying infrastructure and equipment[5] are not the only instances of state absences. Illustrating the discrepancies between the neat image and messy practices of the state, Congolese state agents seem at a loss for meaningful professional activity adhering to a coherent, legal-rational apparatus of formal state authority. On a quest to probe public service provision in the Congo, the casual observer would indeed remark that many spend their time negotiating unofficial "motivation fees", sit idle on plastic chairs, rest at their desk, or watch local TV programs. To those forced to navigate the Congolese state, the prevalence of informal activities renders attempts to make an appointment, see the right official, fill out paperwork, or pay a bill, an endless stream of improvised complications.

Well acquainted to the rhythm of these absences, city residents for their part lament the gigantic potholes everywhere in sight or recurrent issues of *délestage*,[6] while grabbing an evening beer with neighbours and friends in a dimly-lit *nganda*:[7]

> It is true our government doesn't do good governance, especially among the political elite. Because it's high politics, we cannot change this at our local level. Our chief, President Kabila, doesn't do anything. When we tell him we suffer, he says we're lying. Here, everyone is unemployed.[8]

These words are a local rendition of a broader political narrative typically encapsulated in the diagnostic discourses of state weakness, defined mainly by the characteristics of "poor governance" (see De Herdt & Titeca, this volume). Evidently, Congo's colonial and postcolonial history is fraught with extreme violence and protracted crises. The past three years have only buttressed this image as renewed state-sanctioned violence accompanying the unfolding electoral crisis has once again cast a menacing shadow over the last decade's timid successes in establishing both a fragile peace and institutional reforms. Poor governance in the Congo, considered typical of many African states, prompted policy and academic circles alike to craft political remedies. Forming the building block of "negative interpretations" (Mbembe, 2001, p. 1) of African social organization, the absence of material infrastructure, modernized bureaucratic practices and economic integration in increasingly globalized market forces, act as blinding glares within international political inquiry. They do so by obscuring the complexity of myriad state–society relationships that continue to generate the (global) image of the state (Schlichte, 2005) and to enact what is seen as its key prerogatives.[9]

Although this chapter concurs that many of sub-Saharan Africa's ailments might be grounded in "poor governance", it moves away from a normative and prescriptive agenda that still sees the post-colonial African state as a weaker or failing version of its presumably better Western counterpart (Perazzone, forthcoming). In an attempt to "pay due attention to the observed heterogeneity in real governance and its modernity" (De Herdt & Olivier de Sardan, 2015, p. 4), this text argues the (colonially inflected) Congolese state is revived and consolidated through daily processes of collective "meaning-making" and "socio-material practices" that cut-across upward institutionalization and states' traditional areas of governmentality such as health care, education, democratic rights and land tenure. The study of the state I present below thus draws from my analytical and methodological "localizing" of its heterogeneous dynamics. First, using ethnographic tools, I localized the various manifestations of the state within the realms of the personal, mundane and routinized habits of everyday life. Second, I reconstructed patterns of state formation within the circulation of collective imaginaries and the deployment of socio-material practices among street-level bureaucrats (Lipsky, 2010) and other ordinary urbanites. Mundane practices, being the processes by which people make sense of the state, are solidly threaded within quotidian sites of interactions, relationships and discussions. These, I suggest, provide critical analytical leverage for capturing and informing the constant redeployment of the state (Hibou, 1998, 2013), a phenomenon that extends far beyond the conclusions that African bureaucracies "exist solely to carry out the orders of the executive and, in petty ways, to oppress citizens" (Rotberg, 2004, p. 7). In evidencing this claim, this chapter asks a set of three imbricated questions. How is the state performed, transformed and reactivated in the Congo? More specifically: what micro-level, socio-material practices and meaning-making processes enacted among ordinary citizens and neighbourhood chiefs can be identified in urban Congo, and how do they generate broader "state effects" (Foucault 1977; Mitchell, 1991)?

In concrete terms, I argue that the Congolese state's existence is not due to a plethora of parasitic state agents and victimized urban residents. It survives instead because many entertain connections, practices and collective sense-making that potentially re-legitimize the state both at the micro- and macro-levels of analysis. Operating in the shadow of an overbearing political elite, hundreds of thousands of low-level state agents continue, against all odds (without salaries, infrastructure and technological means), to make the state a very real and lived experience in the Congo, both in its ideational and performative dimensions. The state thus derives from a set of socio-material (that is, both human and non-human) practices, which produces in turn larger state effects, two of which are discussed here in further detail: distantiation and humanization.[10] While the former results from patterns of subtle violence and procedural routines, the latter emerges from ordinary problem-solving activities. The (global) idea and the concrete presence of the state, then, are in a persistent conflictual relation – the state appears in its unitary, coherent guise as the aggregated[11] effect (Mitchell, 1991; Trouillot, 2003) of myriad routinized encounters enacted daily between street-level bureaucrats such as neighbourhood chiefs (and their subordinates) and ordinary urbanites living in Kinshasa, Lubumbashi and Goma. In the Congo, what is done, and how, both matter.

I answer these questions in two stages. Firstly, I briefly present the analytical and conceptual footing for understanding the realm of everyday life as the production site of "state effects". This draws on academic perspectives that seek to interrogate traditional conceptualizations of state domination and have, therefore, contributed towards capturing the inherent ambiguities of the state. In this respect, I reflect upon the potentials of engaging with an ontology of the state, by which the researcher's attention is not drawn to that which might be theoretically missing in comparison to a Western model, but instead to investigating the experiential nature of the state as a provider of public services and creator of meaning. Secondly, I provide concrete illustrations of the processes through which the distantiation and humanization effects emerge in urban DRC. This is done, in particular, through analysing the lives of low-level public figures such as neighbourhood chiefs, who, as the official mediators and disciplinary agents of the state, devise activities, employ discourses, and thread relationships that produce patterns of public authority in urban settings.

Everyday life and state effects

Critiques of the worldviews summarized above have long emerged. Some have shown how polities in the global south, including in the Congo, develop multiple coping mechanisms to alleviate institutional weakness and create new conduits for establishing order. Grassroots and non-governmental organizations, bus drivers, local residents, traders, educators and churchgoers (Titeca, De Herdt & Wagemakers,

2013); all have devised ingenious strategies to circumvent corrupt state authorities, access public services, and earn a living (Kabamba, 2015). In so doing, these studies have avoided taking the state for granted in conceptual terms in order to probe, empirically, how state and society interact, intersect and mutually constitute each other on a daily basis. Similarly, classical state theoreticians have shown that state and society, public and private spheres, do not evolve as distinct entities, but rather compose each other in both so-called "failed states" and Western democracies.[12] Rejecting reified interpretations of Max Weber's sociology and challenging conventional epistemologies in political inquiry, some have encouraged researchers to craft a political "ontology of the state" (Hay, 2014; Jessop, 2014). The latter hopes to grasp the inherent "difficulty of studying the state" (Abrams, 1977) as a neither real nor fictitious, but rather an "as if real", phenomenon (Hay, 2014). Put simply, an ontology of the state works both as a heuristic device and as a theoretical tool to provide analytical space for noticing invisible ordering mechanisms, and for further problematizing the distinction between the state and society (Mitchell, 1991, 2006).

In this view, concepts that follow an explanatory avenue stressing inappropriate or absent norms tend to depict only one facet of a much more complex social reality. This is especially problematic since other approaches – such as anthropological explorations of the "everyday state" (Corbridge et al., 2005) – have long unveiled the existence and maintenance of functional "practical norms" (De Herdt & Olivier de Sardan, 2015) and the broad implications of "real governance" (Titeca & De Herdt, 2011). Moving beyond academic and popular narratives that assume either extreme differentiation between Western and non-Western societies, or a progressive "Westernization" of the latter (see also Bilgin, 2008; Owen, Heathershaw & Savin, 2018), many across African studies and related fields have endeavoured to nuance and interrogate these reified accounts of the story of African states (among others: Bierschenk and Olivier de Sardan, 2014; Hagmann & Péclard, 2010; Lund 2006, 2016). Building on these scholarly works, the material presented here seeks to unveil the sites where mundane state–society interactions generate relatively strong patterns of state authority in delivering collective services and exerting social control, precisely as the state in the Congo and elsewhere, remains politically contested, theoretically ambiguous and institutionally brittle. Drawing from the concept of "everyday state" (Corbridge et al., 2005), "state effects" (Foucault 1977; Mitchell, 1991), and "assemblage" theory (DeLanda, 2006), this text offers an understanding of the state as a practical and ideational composite that cuts across institutions, rights, civil society and other institutions. This scholarship crucially problematizes the relationship between the individual, the state and society as a multiple qualitative reality in which "agency – the capacity to act – is everywhere ... in individuals, groups, states, ideational structures and non-human actants" (Salter, 2013, p. 2). Applied to the ambiguous and fluid characteristics of the state, as always under construction (Lund, 2006), this connects to the idea, as Hagmann and Péclard argued (2010), that the state is indeed negotiated, and, as such, is a relational, ideational and ambivalent phenomenon. As just one of social reality's various "wholes constructed from heterogeneous parts" (DeLanda, 2006, p. 3), the state is simultaneously coherent and multiple, fragile and stable, mundane and high-level.

In further conceptual terms, the study of the state detailed below entails three foundational elements: a) micro socio-material practices; b) collective meaning-making; and c) state effects. Firstly, the phrase "socio-material practices" refers to the large set of governing techniques, regardless of their formal or informal status, that emerge from the intertwined relationships between street-level bureaucrats, objects and citizens. Inspired by the idea of tracing "the total dynamic – human and non-human – of a public setting" (Amin, 2008, p. 8), my study of the state starts with the theoretical premise that agency (located in practices, people, things and relations) can occur everywhere and anywhere, including in contexts where power relations are particularly unequal. Located within myriad places and things, practices then, are not the mere product of social relationships – they are also material (Latour, 2005). Social interactions among humans are critical, but they are mediated, supported and altered by the regular usages of objects and things. Looking at the role they play in preforming administrative tasks and shaping cognitive processes of interpretation, I term the various objects and artefacts discussed here "ordinary state objects". This leads us to meaning-making.

The association of people and things in enacting the state daily, tends to produce stable patterns of collective meaning-making[13] vis-à-vis the state: what the state is for, what it ought to do, what is wrong with it. Paying attention to "meanings" leads us to the idea that the state is generative not just of practices, but of its own ideational dimension. The state practices at work in the Congo (re)produce some of the formal aspects of the Weberian state

and engage in a state/society co-production of a system of significance that allows individuals – whether state and non-state – to
voice grievances and imagine the state in both local and Western
state registers. Finally, the perspective I develop here draws on
the works of Trouillot (2003) and Mitchell on the "state effect"
(1991, 2006). Defining it, Mitchell noted state theory should not
attempt "to separate the material forms of the state from the ideo-
logical, or the real from the illusory", but understand instead that
"the phenomenon we name 'the state' arises from techniques that
enable mundane material practices to take on the appearance of an
abstract, nonmaterial form" (1991, p. 170). In concrete terms, these
three constitutive elements of state formation aim at fleshing out
the dynamics underlying such enabling processes. The combination
of "matter of habit, accretion and bricolage" (Li, 2007, p. 276), local
repertoires of practical knowledge and systems of significance, form
the sites where the ideal-typical image of the state is simultaneously
eroded by wars, neoliberal policies, or widespread corruption, and
is still actively reinvented as an important provider of public goods
and shaper of collective adherence to officialism, historical symbols
and procedural modes of governance.

   Although closely inspired by existing notions of negotiated
statehood, state effects, and related terms, this analysis seeks to
address two additional dimensions of stateness. Firstly, it strongly
adheres to the political stand that "the mundane matters" (Enloe,
2011), and uses daily life to critique the idea of the state forming
primarily via bottom-up/top-down patterns of institutionalization
and legitimization. This perspective, because of its non-deterministic
characteristics, highlights the networked patterns of state formation,
as building vertically from top-down and bottom-up dynamics, as
well as emerging horizontally in unpredictable ways that transcend
and displace the verticality/encompassment binary of the state form.
Ferguson and Gupta (2002) argue that grassroots politics, and therefore the everydayness of real governance (De Herdt & Olivier de
Sardan 2015), can call into question traditional understanding of the
state as either distinct from (Evans, 1995; Mann, 1984), in (Migdal
2001), or standing above society. Secondly, the theoretical approach
put forward in this chapter construes the ambiguities of the state
as enabling multiple sites/possibilities for political transformation,
rather than mere constraints on the definition and methodological
capture of the realities of the state.

Neighbourhood chiefs and the contested terrain of public authority

Distantiation

As explained above, the conceptual and methodological approach developed here implies the coexistence of several "states". It emerges in forms that echo the concrete absence resulting from institutional and administrative weakness in the words of my own informants, and others that recreate strong performative and ideational state attributes in its struggles for social control and public service delivery. The police, for instance, often epitomize failure and subsequently fall under considerable scrutiny by the individuals they abuse, harass or ignore (see Baaz & Olsson, 2011; Thill, this volume). Many Congolese, including police officers themselves, recognize and complain about the systemic lack of adequate material, training and human resources needed in order to provide security as a true public good. Laurie, for instance, who inhabits Masina, near Kinshasa's international airport, once explained: "There is no trust between the police and us. When I lived in Binza, some bandits were active there, next to the police station, but the police there, they did nothing! ... They let the people fend for themselves."[14]

A few days later, I asked Angélique,[15] a resident of one of Kinshasa's southern districts, whether the police scare her. She answered, "Not really, but at night, yes. I don't trust them at night. Because, I am sorry to use this term, but they are thieves. They patrol the streets to steal from us, our things; not to protect us."[16]

While investigating the daily workings of districts and neighbourhoods in all three cities, I noticed police stations habitually stood next to the neighbourhood chiefs' offices and, as such, I investigated the relations they nurtured with one another. In practice, while tensions often run high, the police nonetheless cooperate with local residents, chiefs, the district mayor and community leaders on various security-related matters. Indeed, the chiefs who compose the *cadre de base*, for instance, are formally tasked with looking after the population living within the territorial boundaries of their administrative units: neighbourhood, block, street, and "ten houses". A block chief once reported her formal attributions as follows:

> We supervise the population; we ensure peaceful community relations and we guarantee security to the people and their property. We also help the neighbourhood chief to conduct the annual census because he rarely has enough agents. We have to

avoid disorders and tensions among neighbours and to do this, we give them counselling and advice when they come to us.[17]

By contrast, as she began thinking of her own neighbourhood chief, Angélique conceded: "I do not know my neighbourhood chief's formal attributions. I often see him on the bus, right? ... But I don't know what he does."

These short excerpts speak volumes about the absences, low capacity and poor governance (stereo)typical of places like the DRC. In line with the concept of real governance mentioned above, an ethnographic exploration of state agents and ordinary citizens in action reveals much more nuanced accounts of the dynamics that make and unmake the state. The section below thus presents the various activities of *cadre de base* chiefs, as they engage in exercises of census-taking and official registration, produce paper-trails, use symbolic state artefacts such as stamps, signatures and letter heads, and cultivate regular documenting habits to their hierarchy. While deciding upon who gets access to administrative services and state recognition, these low-level civil servants contribute to composing the state's disciplinary apparatus by exerting social and ideational control. This is done mainly through the tropes of subtle and hidden bureaucratic violence and, in Foucauldian terms, governmentality and discipline (Foucault, 1977). Insofar as the state's disciplinary power consists of "particular ways of managing and organizing multiplicity" (Foucault, 2007, p. 12), the various micro-techniques documented here, of counting, bureaucratizing, and reporting – often informally practiced – engender a distantiation effect. Distantiation encapsulates the various moments at which state officials, auxiliaries of the state and private citizens alike engage on a daily basis in mental and behavioural adherence to officialism – that is, the strict obser- vation of formal rules and procedures within a professional field. Although state practices and narratives reveal normalized recourse to bargaining, gift-giving, or illicit behaviour, much of the dynamics at work are blended with recurring usages of administrative proce- dures, red tape, bureaucratic rituals, or "ordinary state objects". This confers on the state its ambiguous, yet concrete, "autonomous" status (Evans, 1995) as seemingly distanced from the rest of society.

Now consider the typical work day of a neighbourhood chief.[18] Chiefs often hold other professional occupations outside of their formal civil servant status, primarily to make ends meet in the absence of a steady and adequate salary. From owning and renting a bus to selling soft drinks, beers or phone credit, the chiefs organise their schedules around office hours and tending to their economic activities. Often up by 5:30am, they may first say their morning prayer before washing up, and, if available, prepare tea and eat a piece of bread for breakfast. Many neighbourhood chiefs are female, such as the woman I encountered, who is here referred to as "Henriette" for the purposes of anonymity. In the morning, she would tend to her youngest children and prepare tea for every family member, and sometimes her neighbours as well. Leaving their home around 6:30am, they either take a bus or walk to their first order of business. One of the chiefs I met owned and rented out a taxi-bus in the public transportation system, and would meet with the conductor before heading to her office. On her way, she would typically make several stops through her neighbourhood and chat with friends, greet acquaintances, delivering pieces of advice or inquiring about their problems. Embodying the state in this context grants her the authority to act in her official capacity as she records problems. Far from being invisible in the public sphere, chiefs are always recognized as such within the vicinities of their homes or offices. "Yes, I know our chief. We are often together," Angélique recalled. "When we moved to this neighbourhood, people told us about him, showed him to us saying 'this is our chief'. We always greet each other. He's the chief, everyone greets him."

Chiefs may formally go on "neighbourhood patrols", during which they take note of their residents' grievances and complaints, and participate therefore in surveillance activities. During those patrols, they may heed to security-related issues, including theft, murder, trespassing, family feuds or land disputes. Should serious crimes such as murders and rape have occurred, they would refer the victims directly to a police officer working with them so they might initiate a formal investigation. As Angélique confirmed: "Our neighbourhood chief can direct us, help us file complaints with the local police, because they work next to one another." Since most Congolese do not trust the police for carrying out justice, I examined the matter further, asking: "You said earlier the police were useless. Why would you go to them then?" She answered:

> Because when we have a problem, we cannot stay idle, and do nothing. We have to go to the police even though they may not help us. Also, some of them do their jobs properly so we could get lucky. The others there, they don't work well. If people continue to cause you problems, we can have them punished through the police, they're the ones with the authority to punish.

Similar statements recurred across the interviews and informal discussions I conducted in all three cities. Police work involves violent practices that ignore the principles of the rule of law and institutional accountability, and target political activists, local residents, children or prostitutes in the hopes of securing a few bribes and favours. The information retrieved from fieldwork and secondary sources reveal other activities, including guarding private houses and personal cars at night, investigating instances of popular justice, participating in communal works, securing neighbours and family members, collaborating with motorbike taxis in cases of lethal car accidents, and organizing public transportation parking lots and fees.

Ambivalent attitudes towards police officers and neighbourhood chiefs suggest the coexistence of conflicting sentiments, by which ordinary citizens simultaneously see state agents as both useful and trustworthy, and unreliable and dishonest. Ambiguity, however, is not just a symptom of poor governance, it is also an analytical vehicle for studying processes of collective meaning-making. Residents and state agents alike often express meaning through political grievances and expectations. Low-level bureaucrats have often voiced lassitude as they "wish [they] could do a better job" in the face of increased pressure by other non-state providers of political order and public services (churches, NGOs, armed groups etc.), who, as they entertain ambiguous relations with state authorities, lay competing claims to public authority.

Alongside dealing with (petty) crime, administrative and surveillance exercises of counting and categorizing citizens occupy a central role in the chiefs' daily tasks. While they must be informed of any deaths, weddings and births occurring in their quarters before people file paperwork at the district office, a census also occurs every year in urban DRC. This period of the year is thus usually quite busy in the small offices where a handful of census takers travel from home to home with a mission order, as well as state forms demanding money and information. Seen as another opportunity to indulge in corruption schemes, the census is carried out nonetheless, figures are reported down on paper, and results sent out to the hierarchy for further surveillance and security purposes.

Evidently, categorizing residents by gender, age, profession and location is not aimed merely at delivering services (many of which do not materialize). It also forms part of routinized, traditional bureaucratic work. A neighbourhood chief in Lubumbashi described his reporting habits as follows:

> The report has four or five categories, like Administration, State
> of Mind, Politics, Security, Economy, Finance and Socio-Cultural
> ... For security, we report on the sanitary situation, petty crime
> ... When someone dies or when someone is born, we add it here,
> under Socio-Cultural ... The Finance category is often empty
> because we never receive funding from the higher authorities. We
> tend to keep 10% of daily transactions, fines, document fees and
> so on for ourselves, as administrative fees.[19]

As they count and categorize, order and impose rules, state agents
leave behind (and circulate) an endless trail of bureaucratic red tape,
which, in line with Gupta's analysis on the politics of writing (2012),
contributes further to subjugating ordinary people in contexts of
widespread illiteracy and resistance to the burden of legal paperwork. Adherence to official procedures, conventional tasks and
ceremonial practices thus do not work to create a facade of state
administrative power. Rather, it serves the hegemonic purpose of
recreating the state's autonomous sphere of action and authority.
As writing and reporting create an almost physical distance between
state and citizens, the practices of counting, securitizing and categorizing bolsters the state's capacity to exert its power of injunction.
State–society relations become effectively bureaucratized even in a
context in which informal practices have become the norm.

Distantiation is then further enacted via the use of voids, spaces
and material objects that punctuate everyday life and routinized
practices. Civil servants are confronted with a lack of office stationery
and technologies (computers, office phones, printers) and rely at
times on objects such as personal cell phones, stamps, hand-drawn
maps, and *convocations*[20] they print out themselves. In producing
and using these ordinary objects they seek to re-formalize more
informal, negotiated practices of governance (see examples below)
that respond to informal logics of public service provisions. To get a
more vivid image of what this means, it is worth quoting one of my
interlocutors at length:

> We do it in a systematic way. Not with technical devices or with
> lots of personnel, but through our everyday tasks. Our people
> in the neighbourhood, they have my personal phone number,
> the police works here with me, we solve criminal issues together,
> we have to collaborate constantly even though [local] politics,
> the private interests from our hierarchy, it breaks collaboration
> sometimes! ... People come to me; they call me, or my assistant,

whenever something bad happens. They bring their land disputes to me, their property issues. When this happens, we send out an invitation to all family members, and all the parties to the dispute. I ask that they bring all the documents they possess and I will look in my own archives see if I have old property titles that might clarify the situation. If we manage to solve the issue here, it is good, if not, I send them to court. That's how we get information. People call us, they come here, our census takers ask questions, and we also use the block and "ten houses" chiefs who know everyone and all their problems at their own level. We can share this with the intelligence services, the police, the mayor this allows the authorities to know whether or not the population is calm and where there is insecurity.[21]

The micro-techniques of government enumerated here continue to go largely unnoticed within conventional political theory. This is particularly problematic because an empirically-grounded analysis shows the routinized tasks that hundreds of neighbourhood chiefs and their colleagues perform daily allow the state to make count-less appearances in a) crafting social control, and b) bureaucratizing state–society relations. Furthermore, this happened not in spite of personal ties and clientelist relations, but rather through them. The information thus retrieved from my data points towards a distanti-ation effect, whereby officialism and procedural routines not only surface from physical artefacts (documents, red tape, objects) but emerge from the collective recognition (i.e. the construction of a system of significance) that these state agents are still in charge of organizing and controlling the public sphere. Despite widespread recognition of the gross inadequacies of the state in providing public goods, and of its being consistently plagued by corruption ("we keep 10% … for ourselves")[22] the state continues to appear as a critical political force standing above society.

In bureaucratizing state–society relations at the lowest but broadest levels of social interaction, street-level bureaucrats serve as the eyes and ears of the state, perpetuating the commonly accepted idea that citizens are an "object of governance" (Jessop, 2015, p. 34). Under the benign claim to be "securing our people", state agents surveil and subdue potential sites of political dissent. They also aim to impose popular abdication to state authority as they organize censuses and civil registries, notify their hierarchy, summon local residents, give orders, and monitor discontent. In bypassing material scarcity, the neighbourhood chiefs, local police and other official and unofficial state personnel, manage and organize control within their jurisdiction.

Humanization

Simultaneously, attending to other aspects of their daily works, neighbourhood chiefs actively engage in another, albeit contradictory, humanization effect, whereby the state is brought ever closer to, and is strongly intertwined with, the lives of ordinary citizens. This effect emerges from a large range of activities aimed at solving problems, reaching compromise and settling issues. Mediation, in this view, renders state–society relations intimate, prompting neighbourhood chiefs to embody an otherwise cold, bureaucratic and exclusionary state apparatus at the micro-levels of governance. Let us return to the neighbourhood chiefs' typical workday. As mentioned above, many tour the neighbourhood once a week. When I asked about their administrative territorial boundaries, the chief named "Henriette" brought her own map out of her desk drawer. Like her counterparts in Goma and Lubumbashi, she had sketched it by hand, and with a pen, showed me her habitual patrolling itinerary. She then directed me to the police station next door so I could see the hand-made map they use. I soon discovered that the objective of using maps was not only to control and bureaucratize, but to devise formal and informal problem-solving avenues. People recognizing her passing by the streets would use her patrols to discuss their problems with her:

> Two days ago, by the stadium, some people ran up to me to complain about other residents who have been throwing away trash in the street. They were complaining about the bad smell this caused. Then I sent out convocations to those who throw their trash in the streets. We have convocation booklets you know.[23]

Echoing the processes of distantiation mentioned above, these booklets exist because Henriette prefers receiving formal complaints at her desk, so she summons the parties to a dispute to visit her by appointment. She demands they bring everyone involved in the dispute along, in the hope of brokering an amicable arrangement. If one of the parties refuses to show up, she sends out another one of these invitations, after which, they usually show up. On many occasions, the issues were settled. Due to their formal aspect, such as their language, format, title, and ministerial seal, I at first assumed the government had provided these invitation booklets. I quickly understood, though, that she had had them printed out in a nearby shop at her own expenses, in order to give her daily activities a more procedural guise. Once her patrol finished, Henriette, like the other chiefs I interviewed, would go to the office and question her assistant and secretary about what had happened in the morning, and determine if any urgent matters where thus to be tended to immediately. She would then receive visitors at her desk and alternately reconcile neighbours if their children had been fighting, dispense administrative advice, or settle land and inheritance disputes among family members. "Papa Louis!" she once shouted to her secretary through the door, "Hand me the minute book of last week's family council we convened here at the office. Also look for that other minute book number 119, in which we decided to divide the land plot."

But settling disputes is only one aspect of the job. She also regularly offers guidance to many on how to navigate state services and departments at the higher levels when one of her residents needs special authorizations or legal documentation. These tasks are mediated through the use of various "ordinary state objects". Phone calls, and their loud ringtones emanating from all over the office and its courtyard, would sometimes cut off our interviews as state agents tended to their personal businesses or made appointments. The census takers, secretary, assistant-chief, the police and visitors are often involved in long conversations about on-going private and professional matters. All chiefs told me their phones rang constantly, because their residents can reach them at any time, day or night. Apart from a small stack of invitation booklets, Henriette's office displays a combination of work and personal objects. While an old microwave and ironing board stand in a dusty corner, hundreds of cadastral archives – some dating from the 1930s, 40s and 50s she confided – are organized chronologically, next to her old wooden desk. Between pictures of herself and her children hangs a large framed portrait of President Joseph Kabila, and the walls are painted blue. "The colours of the Congolese flag," she clarified.

Although she continuously deplores her "terrible working conditions" and the prevalence of petty corruption, she takes pride in being a representative of state authority. "Who is the state?" she asked me. "The state is us [the chiefs]. We represent the state. If we are not respected, it's only in instances where we are not ethically proper." Along with their maps, convocations, stamps, signatures, reports and other symbols and artefacts, she and her colleagues provide the state with human and familiar faces. This "embodied state" (Garmany, 2009) takes shape via listening, counselling and mediating. It makes interactions intimate against otherwise less palpable higher-levels of government. Angélique, among others, confirmed this tendency: "We go to the chief because he is the one we have appointed chief. Some people try to solve their issues among themselves, but when it doesn't work, it's best to consult the chief, because he can report our griev-ances to his hierarchy, he can help us go to the district office or advise us on how to settle our problems." Months later, in Kinshasa, I met with two young Kinois students, who declared:

> Yes, they're very important the neighbourhood chiefs. They're like the fathers in the family … what I mean is that the chief's role is very important, he's the chief, he's our number one guide. You bring your problems to them: 'Mama … we have a problem with a funeral, with documents, with inheritance' … she will help us. She will counsel us, tell us what to do, invite us to her office. If the mama can't do it, she'll bring it to the district mayor on our behalf … I already went to see her! She is our mama. [They smile.] She is our mama. We often go visit her at home and at her office.[24]

It is common knowledge in the streets of Kinshasa, Lubumbashi and Goma that these street-level bureaucrats come to soothe daily struggles and soften the edges of the saying "*mboka ebebi*". System-atic popular recourse to local chiefs' mediation skills generates another layer in the Congolese system of significance that many indi-viduals connect to the state. Once again, the chiefs of the *cadre de base* interacting with each other and their residents shape yet another state effect. Again, socio-material and broader structural constraints result in a double, ambivalent effect. While they reinforce a sense of absences in the postcolonial state, the liminal position of neigh-bourhood chiefs, being both tied to the higher levels of the state and embedded in society, gives them leverage to devise a syncretic blend of organic and procedural mechanisms to governing, which creates a sense of stability and promotes peaceful coexistence.

"L'Etat ni miye, l'Etat ni weye, l'Etat ni shiye bote": Ambivalence and state presence

This chapter presented a brief overview on the intimate lives and relationships of a number of individuals involved in the making, however ambivalent, of the state and state authority. Perhaps the most critical insights we may gather from this text lie in the fact that fine ontological and ethnographic explorations of state–society relations do not speak to a reading in which the state exists mainly in spite of, or via, predatory schemes of governance, or thanks to international principles of internal and external sovereignty. Of course, it has long been established across African studies that there is no such thing as a purely informal or purely formal practice – these are inherently syncretic. There remains a bias, however, towards conceptualizing adherence to officialism – verbal or otherwise – on the part of state agents as consisting of a mere facade for debilitated state governance. Although it is unclear whether these micro-techniques of government directly affect, and to what extent, the highest levels of the state, a more systematic analysis of practices, meaning-making and their associated state effects can turn the otherwise invisible Congolese street-level bureaucrats and ordinary residents into essential components of the state. In this view, the socio-material practices analysed here generate a sense of steadiness, both within the subtle violence of maintaining state control over an agitated and often dissatisfied citizenry, and in ensuring networks of solidarity (Olivier de Sardan, 1999) are nurtured and reproduced. The state therefore surfaces both from the countless sites of formal and informal associations of human and non-human agencies, and through the construction of a collective system of significance. In this system, not only is it often understood that street-level bureaucrats do what they can given the limited choices accruing to them, but reiterated again and again was the collective sense that the discipline and mediation practices should retain their public character, and therefore be performed by the state. In the words of Laurie, for instance:

> The Chiefs must inform people, ask them to denounce crimes and abuses in the neighbourhood. They are also in charge of census and must ensure their residents' personal safety the neighbourhood. The chief should also know about pretty much all migrations and movements and report to the district mayor. They also are in charge of the neighbourhood's hygiene … At night, in cases of loud noises, music and drunks, he should be able to ask people to stay quiet.[25]

On police brutality, she added nuance, saying: "They are not really paid though. This is why they have such a negative attitude. What are they supposed to do with 50 dollars a month? He has a wife and children, how is he supposed to take care of them? It isn't good what the state is doing, abandoning them like this."

Interestingly, analysing the translation of sense-making and social practices into broader effects shows that key dimensions of the official attributes of the state are recreated through attempts at formalizing bureaucratic tasks and modes of governance from various points in time, spaces, actors and practices that transcend top-down or bottom-up modes of analysis. An informal "game of the rules" (De Herdt & Olivier de Sardan, 2015), however, often comes to complement, rather than weaken, formal state structures, in cases where, like in the Congo, acute logistical, financial and infrastructural shortages challenge countless low-level state agents and their constituents to engage with one another in relationships that are not exclusively driven by predatory and abusive behaviour (Baaz & Olsson, 2011). On the contrary, while civil servants might be deemed "notoriously inefficient" in popular local narratives (Olivier de Sardan, 1999, p. 34), they also compose, along with their local constituencies, an expansive and dynamic web of narratives and activities that sustain both a public space and, to a degree, a cooperative social organization. Based on daily encounters, the words – "She is our mama" – of the two Congolese students mentioned above act as another mundane rendition of the popular Congolese phrase "*L'Etat ni miye, l'Etat ni weye, l'Etat ni shiye bote*" (The state is me, the state is you, the state is all of us). Beyond the territorial borders of the Congo, this captures the ambivalent characteristics of the state as being enacted, performed and imagined by all of us – academics and students, writers and informants, citizens and civil servants.

To be sure, although relatively omnipresent, the distantiation and humanization effects thus dissected are not carved in stone. This is because, first, states are not ahistorical apparatuses defying time and epochal change; and, second, because the societal and material agencies they are composed of are constantly in the making. The broad structural impacts of neoliberal policies, economic inequalities and international development assistance, for instance, can alter the generative micro-processes these effects have emerged from. The state, however, continues to exist in the Congo in both its ideational and performative dimensions. This, in turn, materializes the "as-if-real" character (Hay, 2014) of the state–society distinction I problematized along with other existing texts in this chapter.

Simply put, the daily relationships that tie low-level bureaucrats and ordinary residents together act as the connective tissue of the state, even as state agents espouse the characteristics of the "petty sovereign" (Butler, 2004). Through intimate interactions that humanize an otherwise abstract entity, the personalization of power by local civil servants and their residents does not always work to disintegrate state legitimacy or fuel corruption schemes. Instead, it reinforces its authority from localized state practices to its larger system of significance, and participates to the (re)formalization of sometimes informal and spontaneous practices such as mediation. As Li put it, minute social interactions "seldom reform the world according to plan, but they do change things" (2007, p. 276). The goal here, albeit modest, was to capture the idea that state ambiguities are, in fact, a realm of possibilities for change and transformation, rather than a practical impediment to grasping its content and contours. It also places Mitchell's theoretical conversation on "state effects" on a stronger ethnographic and empirical footing, narrating the real-life stories that have been historically effaced in the study of the state and (global) politics. This may be a significant step towards "repopulat[ing] international politics with human life and recreat[ing] the dramatic milieu of everyday experience" (Vrasti, 2013, p. 62).

As such, the state in the Congo may indeed show signs of institutional weaknesses and unaccountability, but it simultaneously re-emerges both as a coherent force flowing through and above society in the Congo, and a tangible element of life consolidated through the routinized and performative work of its agents and peoples. Lending theoretical value to the broader effects of assemblages, compositions and multiplicity in studying practices and processes of collective meaning-making, new avenues are opened towards a more pressing interrogation: do we want to remain stuck with the modern state as the single political form of government promoted by and through our international system? Indeed, as history and current events around the world painfully remind us, the state – an inescapable reality of social life and politics, both in the Congo and globally – lies at the heart of political violence, exclusion, human suffering and death, regardless of its form of government, geographical location and historical origins (see also: Arendt, 1958; Bauman, 1989; Ferguson, 1990; Gupta, 2012; Scott, 1998).

Regarding the state as a mobile composition of practices, narratives and wider effects, Louisa Lombard thoughtfully argued: "That people desire a state is not a bad thing." But international, regional and local "insistence on the state form" come "to smother any organic state-making initiatives", including those shaping accountable and inclusionary politics "while staying agnostic on the ultimate administrative shape of things" (Lombard, 2016, p. 3). This is mirrored in the practices I have scrutinized above. While bureaucratizing state–society relations may support the internationally recognized role of the state as the formal guarantor of social organization and control, it also, perhaps ironically, may cast a shadow on critical collaborative practices, such as mediation, that have cemented urban social life and may have proved significantly more effective as a collective service for communities and disempowered individuals.

Notes

1 I would like to extend my thanks to Tom De Herdt and Kristof Titeca for their kind encouragement and their thoughtful comments, which rendered this chapter's writing process smooth and productive. I also wish to extend my thanks to the anonymous reviewers for their careful reading and helpful feedback on the manuscript. I cannot thank enough all my informants, friends and acquaintances in the DRC who have relentlessly sought to assist me in conducting fieldwork in the safest possible conditions. Finally, I would like to express my greatest appreciation to Jonathan Austin and Sorina Crisan for reading the draft versions of this text and providing me with insightful comments.

2 Formally, Congolese cities are divided into administrative units. At the higher levels of urban governance stands the city mayor (*maire*). In Kinshasa, being a city-province, one finds the governor. This oversees the districts (*communes*). The district is located mid-level between the mayor's authority and the neighbourhoods (*quartiers*) and is headed by a district mayor (*bourgmestre*). He, in turn, oversees the local chiefs who form the so-called *cadre de base* (baseline group). The latter is organized along a pyramidal administrative model, headed by neighbourhood chiefs (*chefs de quartier*). These are official entities and are recognized by law. Their subordinates act at the levels, in descending size, of block (*cellule*), street (*avenue*), and "ten houses" (*nyumba kumi*, in Goma, not Lubumbashi or Kinshasa. This does not always contain exactly ten houses). These entities are not enshrined in law, nor can they be registered at the Ministry of Internal Affairs.

3 A street restaurant.

4 Informal conversation. Congolese civil servants. Kinshasa (October 2015). Translations from French always mine.

5 For a dynamic discussion on the Congolese government's lack of political will in reinforcing public services and infrastructure, see Stearns et al. (2017).

6 Organized system of electric outage in certain streets, housing units and general areas, for a time lapse ranging from a few hours to three or four days, so other areas, housing or streets can get electricity instead.

7 Popular area where people congregate around a bar or a restaurant.

8 Interview. Neighbourhood residents and street chief. Kinshasa (19 March 2016).

9 As Habermas and Cronin put it: "The historical type of state that emerged from the French and American Revolutions has achieved global dominance. This fact is by no means trivial" (1998, p. 397). Deeply entrenched in international history and, as in our case, violent patterns of colonization, the (Western) state has become a transnational idea and institution, the product of a mystified Westphalian world order (Caporaso, 2000; Grovogui, 2001)

and capitalist expansion (Weber, 1978).

10 Humanization is not conceived here as within anthropological works on cultural processes, nor is it opposed to processes such as politicization. It merely refers to the actions that grant a more intimate, humane dimension to the otherwise procedural, abstract entity that is the state.

11 The theoretical premises underlying the potentially broad ramifications of individuals' aggregated understanding of the social world on producing large webs of intersubjective (and thus collectively shared, contested and produced) meanings, emerged long before post-structuralist works, and was debated at length within (micro-)sociology. See the works of Erving Goffman, Harold Garfinkel, Pierre Bourdieu or Alfred Schutz among others.

12 For further reading on these issues, see, inter alia, Bayart et al., 2008; Frödin, 2012; Jessop, 2015; Migdal, 2001; Müller, 2012.

13 See also the works of Clifford Geertz on "webs of meaning" (e.g. Geertz, 1973).

14 Interview. Congolese citizen. Kinshasa (7 October 2015).

15 All names have been changed for the purposes of anonymity.

16 Interview. Congolese citizen. Kinshasa (22 October 2015).

17 Interview. Block chief. Lubumbashi (12 November 2014).

18 Of course, this may vary from one neighbourhood or chief to another, and depends on the current tasks or issues at hand. This is an aggregated collection of information gathered while interviewing and following them around in all three cities.

19 Interview. Neighbourhood chief. Lubumbashi (20 November 2015).

20 A written invitation by which someone is summoned to the office.

21 Interview. Neighbourhood chief.

Lubumbashi (20 November 2015).

22 For a nuanced account on corruption, see Olivier de Sardan (1999).

23 Interview. Neighbourhood chief. Kinshasa (15 October 2015).

24 Interview. Local residents. Kinshasa (30 March 2016).

25 Interview. Congolese citizen. Kinshasa (7 October 2015).

References

Abrams, P. (1977) Notes on the difficulty of studying the state. *Journal of Historical Sociology* 1 (1): 58–89.

Amin, A. (2008) Collective culture and urban public space. *City* 12 (1): 5–24.

Arendt, H. (1958) *The Human Condition*. Chicago, IL: University of Chicago Press.

Baaz, M. E. and Olsson, O. (2011) Feeding the horse: uunofficial economic activities within the police force in the Democratic Republic of the Congo. *African Security* 4 (4): 223–41.

Bauman, Z. (1989) *Modernity and the Holocaust*. Ithaca, NY: Cornell University Press.

Bayart, J.-F., Mbembe A. and Toulabour, C. (2008) *La politique par le bas*. 2nd ed. Paris: Karthala.

Bayart, J.-F. (2006) *L'Etat en Afrique*. 2nd ed. Paris: Fayard.

Bierschenk, T. and Olivier de Sardan, J.-P. (2014) *States at Work: Dynamics of African Bureaucracies*. Leiden: Brill.

Bilgin, P. (2008) Thinking past "Western" IR? *Third World Quarterly* 29 (1): 5–23.

Butler, J. (2004) *Precarious Life: The Powers of Mourning and Violence*. London: Verso.

Caporaso, J. A. (2000) Changes in the Westphalian order. *International Studies Review* 2 (2): 1–28.

Corbridge, S., Williams, G., Srivastava, M. and Véron, R. (2005) *Seeing the State: Governance and Governmentality in India*.

Cambridge: Cambridge University Press.

De Herdt, T. and Olivier de Sardan, J.-P. (2015) *Real Governance and Practical Norms in Sub-Saharan Africa: The Game of the Rules.* Abingdon: Routledge.

DeLanda, M. (2006) *A New Philosophy of Society.* New York, NY: A&C Black.

Enloe, C. (2011) The mundane matters. *International Political Sociology* 5: 447–50.

Evans, P. (1995) *Embedded Autonomy: States and Industrial Transformation.* Princeton, NY: Princeton University Press.

Ferguson, J. (1990). *The Anti-politics Machine.* Minneapolis, MN: University of Minnesota Press.

Ferguson, J. and Gupta, A. (2002). Spatializing states: Toward an ethnography of neoliberal governmentality. *American Ethnologist* 29: 981–1002.

Foucault, M. (1977) *Discipline and Punish* (trans. A. Sheridan). New York, NY: Pantheon.

Foucault, M. (2007) *Security, Territory, Population: Lectures at the Collège De France, 1977–1978.* New York, NY: Springer.

Frödin, O. J. (2012) Dissecting the state. *Journal of International Development* 24 (3): 271–86.

Garmany, J. (2009) The Embodied State. *Social & Cultural Geography,* 10 (7): 721–39.

Geertz, C. (1973) *The Interpretation of Cultures: Selected Essays.* New York, NY: Basic Books.

Grovogui, S. N. (2001) Sovereignty in Africa: Quasi-statehood and other myths in international theory. In: Dunn, K. C. and Shaw, T. M. (eds) *Africa's Challenge To International Relations Theory.* London: Palgrave Macmillan, pp. 29–45.

Gupta, A. (2012) *Red Tape: Bureaucracy, Structural Violence, and Poverty in India.* Durham, NC: Duke University Press.

Habermas, J. and Cronin, C. (1998)

The European nation-state. *Public Culture* 10 (2): 397–416.

Hagmann, T. and D. Péclard (2010). "Negotiating statehood: dynamics of power and domination in Africa." Development and change 41(4): 539-562.

Hay, C. (2014) Neither real nor fictitious but "as if real"? A political ontology of the state. *The British Journal of Sociology* 65 (3): 459–80.

Hell, J. and Schönle, A. (2010) *Ruins of Modernity.* Durham, NC: Duke University Press.

Hibou, B. (2013) Introduction. La bureaucratisation néolibérale, ou la domination et le redéploiement de l'État dans le monde contemporain. In: Hibou, B. (ed.) *La bureaucratisation néolibérale.* Paris: La Découverte, pp. 7–20.

Hibou, B. (1998) "Retrait ou redéploiement de l'Etat?" *Critique internationale* 1 (1): 151–68.

Jessop, B. (2014) Towards a political ontology of state power. *The British Journal of Sociology* 65 (3): 481–6.

Jessop, B. (2015) *The State: Past, Present and Future.* Oxford: John Wiley & Sons.

Kabamba, P. (2015) In and out of the state. *Anthropological Theory,* 15 (1): 22–46.

Latour, B. (2005) *Reassembling the Social.* Oxford: Oxford University Press.

Li, T. M. (2007). Governmentality. *Anthropologica* 49 (2): 275–81.

Lipsky, M. (2010) *Street-level Bureaucracy.* 30th Anniversary ed. New York, NY: Russell Sage Foundation.

Lombard, L. (2016) *State of Rebellion: Violence and Intervention in the Central African Republic.* London: Zed Books.

Lund, C. (2006) Twilight institutions: Public authority and local politics in Africa. *Development and Change* 37: 685–705.

Lund, C. (2016) Rule and rupture: State formation through the production of property and citizenship. *Development and Change* 47: 1199–228.

Mann, M. (1984) The autonomous power of the state: Its origins, mechanisms and results. *European Journal of Sociology* 25 (2): 185–213.

Mbembe, A. (2001) *On the Postcolony*. Berkley, CA: University of California Press.

Migdal, J. (2001) *State in Society*. Cambridge: Cambridge University Press.

Mitchell, T. (1991) The limits of the state: Beyond statist approaches and their critics. *American Political Science Review* 85 (1): 77–96.

Mitchell, T. (2006) Society, economy, and the state effect. In: Sharma, A. and Gupta, A. (eds) *The Anthropology of the State: A Reader*. Oxford: John Wiley & Sons, pp. 169–86.

Müller, M.-M. (2012) *Public Security in the Negotiated State: Policing in Latin America and Beyond*. New York, NY: Springer.

Olivier de Sardan, J.-P. (1999) A moral economy of corruption in Africa? *The Journal of Modern African Studies* 37 (1): 25–52.

Owen, C., Heathershaw, J. and Savin, I. (2018) How postcolonial is post-Western IR? Mimicry and mētis in the international politics of Russia and Central Asia. *Review of International Studies* 44 (2): 279–300.

Perazzone, S. (forthcoming) "Shouldn't you be teaching me?" State mimicry in the Congo. *International Political Sociology*.

Rotberg, R. I. (2004) Failed states, collapsed states, weak states: Causes and indicators. In: Rotberg, R. I. (ed.) *State Failure and State Weakness in a Time of Terror*. Washington, D.C.: Brookings Institution Press, pp. 1–25.

Salter, M. B. (2013) Introduction. In: Salter, M. B. and Mutlu, C. E. (eds) *Research Methods in Critical Security Studies: An Introduction*. Abingdon: Routledge, pp. 1–23.

Schlichte, K. (2005) *Der Staat in der Weltgesellschaft: Politische Herrschaft in Asien, Afrika und Lateinamerika*. Frankfurt: Campus.

Scott, J. (1998) *Seeing Like a State: How Certain Schemes to Improve the Human Condition Have Failed*. Durham, NC: Yale University Press.

Stearns, J., Vlassenroot, K., Hoffmann, K. and Carayannis, T. (2017) Congo's inescapable state: The trouble with the local. *Foreign Affairs*. Available from: www.foreignaffairs. com/articles/democratic- republic-congo/2017-03-16/ congos-inescapable-state [Accessed November 10, 2018].

Titeca, K. and De Herdt, T. (2011) Real governance beyond the "failed state": Negotiating education in the Democratic Republic of Congo. *African Affairs* 110 (439): 213–31.

Titeca, K., De Herdt T. and Wagemakers, I. (2013) God and Caesar in the Democratic Republic of Congo. *Review of African Political Economy* 40 (135): 116–31.

Trouillot, M.-R. (2003) *Global Transformations*. London: Palgrave Macmillan.

Vrasti, W. (2013) Travelling with ethnography. In: M. Salter and C. E. Mutlu (eds) *Research Methods in Critical Security Studies*. Abingdon: Routledge, pp. 59–62.

Weber, M. (1978) *Economy and Society: An Outline of Interpretive Sociology*. Berkley, CA: University of California Press.

4

Donors and a Predatory State: Struggling with Real Governance

Camilla Lindstrom

Widespread disillusionment with "failed state" perspectives on African governance has drawn attention to new forms of order emerging on the ground in areas where the presence of the state is weak. The term "hybrid governance" emerged in reference to these new organizational arrangements that incorporate local institutions and popular organizations in order to fill gaps in state capacity (Meagher, De Herdt & Titeca, 2014, p. 1). The idea that there are forms of order beyond the state is nothing new. Hybrid arrangements incorporating non-state institutions into formal governance arrangements have been well documented in Africa since colonial experiences of indirect rule. What is new is the move from state-based ideals of postcolonial order to a more practical emphasis on local non-state arrangements already operating on the ground in fragile areas of Africa (Meagher, De Herdt, & Titeca, 2014, p. 1). This signals what Crook and Booth have called a paradigm shift from the "good governance" orthodoxy to a focus on "arrangements that work" (2011, p. 97). Instead of fixing failed states, one might "work with the grain". That is, work with local institutions that are already operating on the ground (Crook & Booth, 2011; Kelsall, 2008, 2011), and acknowledge that the state is not the only actor organizing governance. Instead, the state shares its authority with a number of non-state actors, such as community groups, militias, local Big Men (they rarely tend to be women), and customary chiefs. These actors sometimes exercise more influence than state officials, and are often seen by the population as being more legitimate than state actors.

The hybridity can be seen as a kind of co-production in which a range of actors "co-produce" services (Olivier de Sardan, 2011). While some authors accept such hybridity as a practical response to weak states and encourage donors to more actively engage with this reality on the ground (see for example: Boege, Brown & Clements, 2009, p. 19), others critique it for reasons related to legitimacy, transparency and accountability (see for example: Hilhorst et al. 2010; Meagher, 2012). Whatever one's position on hybrid states, they pose important normative and practical questions for donors as to what kind of state-building to support and who to negotiate with. Should one strengthen or move towards more Weberian organizations? And who, given the strong presence of alternative forms of authority, should one engage with and whose ownership is one trying to cultivate? Despite the fact that researchers have shown that many of the fragile states that donors are trying to build state capacity in are indeed hybrid forms of governance, we know relatively little about how donors[1] are dealing with it, and how it may affect aid negotiations regarding state-building in fragile states. Do they involve these actors in their discussions and negotiations on issues related to state-building? If not, how does this affect the complex relationship and linkages that often exist between the non-state actors and the state? There is some research on the topic, such as the work by De Herdt, Titeca and Wagemakers on the education sector in Congo (2012); Baaz and Stern's work (2013) on the security sector reforms in the DRC; and Denney (2013, 2014) on DFID's interaction with informal institutions in Sierra Leone. While these studies offer some insights, they also underscore the difficulties donors have grappling with issues of "real governance" and hybrid institutions on the ground.

The fact that the relationship with the government has been a challenge for the donors, and that many of them see the Congolese state as being predatory, makes it especially interesting to see how donors have managed to recognize and respond to this real governance and hybridity on the ground. Have they kept their state-centric lenses on, or has their acknowledgement of the predatory nature of the state pushed them to identify and work with other actors involved in the complex "weblike society" in the DRC?

In this chapter, I will review how real governance is functioning in the health and justice sectors, and how the state co-exists with non-state actors like Faith-Based Organizations (FBOs) and customary chiefs. I will then analyse how the donors have reacted to these manifestations of real governance. The two sectors were chosen because they are key sectors in public service provision. In addition, they were likely to differ in a number of aspects and thereby be more interesting to compare. The justice sector, for example, is more at the core of the state and likely to be more sensitive for national sovereignty than the health sector. The actors "co-producing" services in the two sectors also differ, with the health sector having more engagement from FBOs, whilst the justice sector is dominated by traditional authorities alongside state institutions. This is likely to have an effect on how the donors engage with real governance.

I will demonstrate in this chapter that there is a growing recognition of how real governance functions, but that donors still struggle regarding how to work with it. This, I argue, is related to four main factors:

- First, donors' somewhat limited understanding of the context.
- Second, donors' tendency to analyse the situation through a state-centric lens.
- Third, normative considerations that make some non-state actors difficult for donors to deal with.
- Fourth, political considerations that affect whether it is feasible or not for donors to work with actors other than the state.

These factors, to varying degrees, make it more challenging for donors to fully embrace real governance.

The chapter draws both on my own experience, having worked for a bilateral donor in the DRC in 2011–13 and 2016, as well as on extended field research carried out in the country 2014–16 for my PhD. In total, I interviewed 117 people, including those working for donor agencies, Congolese officials, academics, consultants and representatives from Civil Society Organizations (CSOs) and Faith-Based Organizations.

Donors and state-building in the DRC

Donors started to engage in the DRC on a large scale after the peace-agreement in Sun City in 2002. In 2016, the DRC received over $2.1 billion in Official Development Assistance (ODA) (OECD, 2016). This should be viewed in relation to the government's budget for 2016, which was around $4.53 billion (DRC: MoB, 2015, pp. 6–7).[2] Due to the prolonged crisis in the east, the DRC is also one of the world's biggest recipients of humanitarian assistance, and the UN has one of its largest peace-keeping operations in the country, with around 18,000 uniformed staff members (UNSC, 2018, p. 10).

Although the DRC is a major recipient of aid, it is far from a "donor darling". The levels of aid per capita it receives are, for example, far less than those provided to neighbouring Rwanda and Uganda. The country receives neither budget support nor sector-budget support, due to donors' lack of trust in the government and the high fiduciary risks. The relationship between the donors and the government are often fraught by tensions that occasionally erupt into open confrontation.

Much of the development assistance in fragile and conflict-affected states has in the past bypassed the state, instead focusing on short-term results and mainly working through the UN system and international non-governmental organizations (INGOs). However, following the so-called War on Terror, state-building in conflict states has increasingly become one of the key priorities for the international community (Marquette & Beswick, 2011, p. 1704). The donors have been accused of having a state-centric focus and of ignoring non-state actors (Kurz, 2010). One reason why donors have often failed to consider non-state service providers as potential partners in post-conflict reconstruction and state-building is due to a perceived disjunction between service-provision through non-state actors and the objectives of state-building (Allouche, 2013). Donors have feared that by building on non-state institutions they might undermine state authority, and that the failure to support direct state delivery of essential services might negatively affect the legitimacy of the state (Mcloughlin, 2015; OECD, 2010). However, as research has pointed out, there are multiple pathways to post-conflict state-building. As a consequence, while policy-makers and donors may see state-building as institution building of and by state actors, it might be more helpful to think of state-building initiatives in a multi-institutional, or hybrid, context (Allouche, 2013).

Real governance in the health sector

It is hard to believe when one looks at the health sector today that the DRC at the beginning of the 1970s was seen as a role model for community health care in sub-Saharan Africa. Today, the health system is in a sad state with, for example, one of the highest maternal mortality rates in the world and recurrent outbreaks of epidemics such as yellow fever and Ebola. The health sector has virtually disappeared from the Congolese state budget. Government spending on health is extremely low, with a mere 4.95% of the 2015 budget spent on health (USAID, 2018). Current health expenditure per capita is $34, which can be compared with Rwanda and Uganda where expenditures are, respectively, $143 and $139 per capita (USAID, 2018). Most of the budget remains at the central level, which leaves the provincial and health zone levels – where responsibility for service delivery – resides, with very few resources (DFID-DRC, 2018, p. 6). The health sector is the second largest sector for donors in the DRC, with 23% of official aid going to health (OECD, 2016).

As mentioned by De Herdt and Titeca in the introduction to this volume, many sectors in the DRC, instead of solely relying on public tax income, depend on user fees. This is very much the case for the health sector, where user fees are financing a large part of the health system. The fees are used to pay staff at the health centres, as the majority of them don't receive salaries.[3] The user fees also finance administrative staff who do not have access to patients and there-fore have limited possibilities of extracting money. This is what the Congolese refer to as the "ventilation system" and can be described as a form of alternative taxation, or in the words of De Herdt and Titeca, a "parafiscal" revenue. The exact figures that flow through the system from the patient all the way up to the Ministry of Health are hard to get, but studies have shown that 5–10 % of the health centres' revenues from the patients move up the ladder to finance staff at the health zone, provincial and central level (DRC: MoH, 2009, pp. 6–7; Weijs, Hilhorst & Ferf, 2012). The high poverty rates combined, with high user-fees, have left the population to a large extent without any affordable qualitative care, forcing people to rely instead on self-medication, traditional healers or simply doing nothing about sicknesses and diseases.

Much of the health care that is being provided is delivered by FBOs. Church organizations, such as the Catholic Church and the Protestant Church, have been heavily involved in the provision of health care ever since colonial times (Seay, 2013). It is estimated that the FBOs own and manage 50% of the health centres, and that they co-manage, together with the state, around 40% of the health zones (Baer, 2007, p. 1). That FBOs play a major role in providing health care at the community level is quite frequent in Africa. However, what makes the situation in the DRC differ from other countries is that, in addition to providing direct services, the FBOs are also in principle co-managing health zones together with the state. Hence, the relationship between the state and the FBOs can best be described as a form of hybrid organization whereby both parties are closely inter-linked with each other in a complex set of negotiations. Hence, just as in the education sector, through its collaboration with the FBOs the state can be present in the health sector, despite its empty pockets.

The hybridity of the system manifests itself in various ways, the first example being the complex system of co-management of the local health zones. Although in principle co-management has been forbidden since 2007, it is still happening.[4] Co-management takes different forms, but basically means that the health system at the local level is co-managed by the state and the FBOs. For example, the health zone manager, who leads the administration of the health zone, is often appointed by the state. However, in certain cases, especially when the FBO is also in charge of the health zone's main hospital (the reference hospital), the health zone manager may be appointed by the FBOs.[5] In other cases, the state tries to find a health zone manager that is at least acceptable to the churches. When a consensus cannot be reached it sometimes leads to situations where the health zone manager is literally chased from the reference hospital by the FBOs.

The co-management is also manifest in the fact that the FBOs often provide key staff members to be part of the health zone team (*Équipe Cadre de Zone de Santé*), which is the local management unit that oversees the health centres. Another case in point is that a number of health staff working in health centres run by FBOs are paid by the state but follow the rules and regulations established by the FBOs (DRC: MoH, 2007, pp. 2–3).

Secondly, the relationship between the state and the Church organizations is regulated by a *"convention"*[6] (written agreement) that, according to one of my interviewees, dates back from colonial times, when the Belgian king signed the paper and sent it to his administrator in the country.[7] The Convention has been re-negotiated several times and is another indicator of the hybrid character of the Congolese state, in the sense that the FBOs and the state are working together in close symbiosis. Basically, the Convention underlines that the state should facilitate the functioning of the FBO-run health centres, and that it should respect the independence of the FBOs (DRC: MoH, 2007). It also states that the FBO-run centres should follow national health policies, and offer the government-established minimum and maximum packages of services at their centres and hospitals.[8]

The close links between the government and the FBOs can also be observed in their attitudes towards each other. Some people in the government see the FBOs as part of the government system. "They are a part of us" was something that some of my key government informants in the health sector insisted on.[9] That this attitude was rather common was confirmed by interviewees within CSOs and implementing agencies as well.[10] It was also recognized that the FBOs were the ones who, to a large extent, kept the health sector going and that partnering with the FBOs was the only way to improve the governance and coverage of the health sector (Bwimana, 2017, p. 1481). The fact that many of the senior level health professionals have been trained by the FBOs also facilitates a more collaborative approach between the government and the FBOs (DFID-DRC, 2013, pp. 25–6).

Despite the Convention and the recognition, both from the state and from the FBOs, that they need each other, there is nevertheless some tension between them, as well as among the FBOs themselves. For example, the FBO-managed centres have historically had better access to resources, which has meant that they have been able to pay salaries to a larger extent than the state. They are also better organized and usually have better-trained staff. As a consequence, where people have a choice, they generally prefer to go to FBO-run centres. This creates some jealousy amongst people in the centres that are run by the state.

The FBOs often complain that the state does not always facilitate their work, as it should according to the Convention. A common area of conflict is the collection of taxes. The FBOs are exempted from some taxes, but not all, which creates confusion and opens doors for predation by state officials. It is, for example, not uncommon for state officials to try to collect taxes on medicines and equipment that the FBO centres have received free of charge from donors. This sometimes results in absurd situations where, for example, a thermometer that costs around US$1 at the market can be taxed by up to US$5 by state officials.[11] Sometimes this predation puts people's lives at risk. To illustrate, the hospital in Katoka health zone, managed by the Catholic Church, at one point had to cease operations as tax authorities had claimed tax for equipment at the laboratory. When the hospital refused to pay, the lab was simply closed down by the tax authorities. As it is impossible to run a hospital without a laboratory, the whole hospital closed down and the population found itself without its main hospital for weeks. The conflict ended when the governor stepped in and paid the requested tax himself, which also shows the limited power that governors have over tax authorities.

The power balance between the state and the FBOs is constantly changing. Many of my informants stated that in the past the FBOs often wanted to operate independently from the state, whereas there now seems to be a better understanding that they both need each other. One reason for the churches' willingness to work closer with the state is likely linked to the fact that they receive less funding from abroad than they used to.

Real governance in the justice sector

In the justice sector, the state system plays an even smaller role than in the provision of health care. It is estimated that up to 80% of cases involve alternative conflict mechanisms (Sida, 2011, p. 4). Many of these are handled by the customary chiefs. However, other mechanisms – such as the Barza inter-community mediation system, conflict resolution through FBOs, as well as through international and local NGOs – exist as well (see for example: ISDR-Bukavu, 2017). There is great variation amongst the provinces as to who provides conflict resolution. The state system is not well understood by the population, being usually far away and expensive (see also Titeca, this volume). Courts also have a punitive approach that is in many ways foreign to the way that many people in Congo perceive justice, which they see as being about the restoration of social order and relationships.[12] People's confidence in the customary system is higher than it is for the state system. The joint UNDP/Harvard Humanitarian Initiative, which regularly measures people's perceptions of security in the eastern part of the country, found that 65% had little or no trust in the formal court system, whereas for the customary justice system the figure was 34% (Vinck & Pham, 2014, p. 65).

As in the health sector, the government is trying to provide justice with empty pockets. The state budget for the justice sector is very small, and the system relies on various fees to operate. Nonetheless, the government seems determined to build courts all over the country in order to replace alternative conflict mechanisms.[13] This seems unrealistic, considering that the state only invests a minimal amount in the infrastructure system (such as courts and prisons) and instead fully relies on the donors to finance these costs. Between 98% and 100% of the cost for construction and re-building of the justice infrastructure is currently financed by donors.

In contrast to the health sector, where there was a certain level of collaboration between the FBOs and the state, there were clear tensions and competition between the government and the customary chiefs. As one judge put it: "once the traditional chiefs are gone, we have won".[14] According to the judge, the relationship was basically a zero-sum game where one loses and the other one wins. This attitude of a zero-sum game seems to have permeated the relationship between the customary chiefs and the state for a long time, hindering effective collaboration between the two systems. Mobutu had already tried in the 1960s to undermine the authority of the customary chiefs. His plan was to build local courts all over the country and, once there was a local court in a territory, the customary chief would no longer be authorized to handle cases. However, the progress on establishing the formal courts, from the point of the government, has been rather disappointing. Out of the around 180 courts that were envisaged to cover the whole country almost 50 years ago, only around 50 are so far up and running (Ilac, 2009; Tekilazaya, Fataki Wa Luhindi & Wetsh'okonda Koso, 2013a, p. 23).

Despite this, in 2013 the government went ahead with more or less forbidding the involvement of customary chiefs. The law in 2013 regarding the organization of the justice sector says nothing about the customary chiefs (DRC, 2013). This has widely been interpreted as customary chiefs no longer having the right to solve problems of justice within their territories.[15]

Considering the slow rollout of the formal system and the challenges it is facing, many people were worried about the government's hard-line approach towards alternative justice mechanisms, in particular the customary chiefs. This was clearly expressed by a senior judge from Equateur:

> People can't turn to the formal system because it does not
> exist, and they can't turn to the customary chief as normal,
> because he is forbidden to rule so they are left in a vacuum. I am
> deeply worried. What will people do? Will they turn to personal
> vendettas?[16]

Other people are worried about the negative consequences the ban could have on the social contract between the state and its citizens. They are concerned about how it could affect people's perceptions about the state when they don't trust the formal system and might not understand why the state is not allowing customary chiefs to intervene. Even if there were a functioning court in the territory, people usually wouldn't trust it, and they would often be geographically a distance away, considering the size of the country. One key informant who had just been visiting a remote area in South Kivu voiced his concern by saying:

> The state imposes itself on people and they are sending judges to
> areas where they don't speak the local languages. Nobody asks the
> people what they want. The justice system alters the social contract
> between the people and the state, and you have to mitigate the
> negative impact of it. To forbid the traditional system to operate
> will severely undermine people's confidence in the state.[17]

So, there is a clear worry amongst observers about the abolishment of the customary system that relates both to what consequences it could have for people seeking justice, as well as the negative effects it could have on the social contract between the population and the government.

In brief, the close collaboration – although marred by competition – which characterized the health sector, does not exist in the justice sector. Instead, competition and exclusiveness seem to be the guiding forces. The government is clearly not pleased with sharing its authority and legitimacy on issues related to law enforcement with other actors, and tries to hinder the real governance apparent on the ground.

Having established some of the main characteristics of real governance in both sectors, I will now turn to how donors have reacted to it.

Donors' struggles with real governance

As I will show in this section, the donors more easily engaged with the FBOs in the health sector than with the alternative providers in the justice sector. However, even in the health sector they tend to engage more with the state than with the FBOs, especially regarding the discussion of policy issues and the development of programme proposals. I will argue that the donors' engagement with real governance on the ground was partly impeded by a mix of the four following factors: a) lack of understanding of the context; b) state-centric lenses; c) normative considerations; and d) political considerations.

Lack of understanding of the context

An obvious challenge for donors is that fragile states are almost by definition extremely complex to understand. It might be almost impossible for donor staff that are normally in a country for only a few years to fully grasp the complex nature of the interactions between the state and the non-state providers, and the multiple linkages between them. Effective engagement with these different actors requires an in-depth understanding of how, and in what ways, they provide services; how they exercise power within communities; and what kind of legitimacy they draw upon. To complicate matters further there might be subnational variations in how legitimate an actor is perceived to be (Risse & Stollenwerk, 2018).

My interviews with donor representatives involved in health reforms revealed that in general they had good knowledge of the important role FBOs had in health care provision and that the churches had a high degree of legitimacy in Congo. It was also widely recognized that they were working in collaboration with the state, and that faith-based organizations were managing a large percentage of the health centres. However, a deeper understanding of the complexity and inter-linkages between the state and the FBOs (i.e. the hybridity or real governance) was often neither very well understood, nor taken into account in the programming of development aid. Some of the donors I interviewed were, for example, not aware of the Convention between the state and the churches, and how deeply involved the churches are in the management of the health zones. Neither did they seem aware that they might accidentally undermine the FBOs to the advantage of the state by focusing mainly on the state in their interactions on state-building in the health sector. However, compared to the justice sector, there was a more open attitude amongst the donors towards working with non-state actors in the health sector. DFID, for example, in their health programme,[18] decided to implement the programme through FBOs rather than INGOs. This change was motivated by the fact that the FBOs would be staying in the country even after the donors and the INGOs would have left (DFID-DRC, 2013, p. 1).[19] Even in this programme, however, it was mainly representatives from the state that were involved in the discussions on how to set up the programme.

Most of the donors in the justice system that I interviewed were well aware of the limitations of the formal system, and that actors other than the state solved most of the justice cases. From perceptions studies being conducted by UNDP and Harvard Humanitarian Initiative, there was also an understanding that people had more confidence in the customary system than in the formal state structures. Nonetheless, moving from this realization to actually working with the real governance on the ground seemed to be a leap too far for most of them, for reasons that I will explore below. There were only a few NGOs, for example the Belgian organization RCN Justice et Démocratie, working with alternative forms of justice, such as various forms of mediation and collaborating with customary chiefs. Some donors, however, tried to include minor activities regarding customary chiefs within their overall justice reform programmes. This was especially the case in programmes that included land disputes, such as the EU's Uhaki Safi programme. However, the overall objective of donor- funded programmes was still very much on strengthening the formal system.

In sum, while there was some basic understanding of real governance, it seemed that it was a step too far to move from this to accepting and actively working with real governance, especially in the justice sector. Part of the problem was the state-centric view that many donors had, which I will analyse next.

State-centric lenses

That donors usually have a state-centric view has been highlighted by a number of scholars (IDS, 2010; Kurz, 2010). Such state-centric lenses make it difficult for the donors to look beyond the state in their support for public services. This mind-set was evident most clearly in the justice sector, which most donors see as a key function of the state. The Swedish aid agency, for example, justified its support to the formal justice sector by stating that: "We cannot contribute to increased access to justice if there are no courts, no prisons with adequate standards and no Ministry of Justice building to enter into." (Sida, 2014, p. 4)

In documents like the New Deal on Engagement with Fragile States (OECD, 2011), the introduction of a system based on the rule of law has been seen as a crucial step to stop violence in fragile states. It has also been viewed as a cornerstone for the establishment of democracy as well as being a prerequisite for economic development. These viewpoints don't fit easily with a system that is in many ways characterized by a very personal type of justice, based on unwritten laws. Most of the donors I interviewed simply could not imagine how a justice system could work if it was not based on a formal state-system with written rules and clear regulations. In the health sector, the donors more intuitively seemed to understand that the government didn't have to be the only one providing health care, perhaps because it is not always the state that provides health care in their own countries. However, as we saw above, they still struggled to understand the complex relationship between the FBOs and the state, and as a consequence how to engage with it.

Few of the donors worked directly with the FBOs, and neither were the FBOs to any great extent involved in the conceptualization of donor programmes. The engagement with them was often limited to offering them the opportunity of taking part in training courses and other capacity-building activities. According to some of the FBO representatives that I interviewed, the donors and the government tended to forget to invite FBOs to policy discussions on health-related matters, as the following representation indicates: "Sometimes we are invited to meetings with the donors and the government, but other times we just seem to be forgotten and the support we get from external sources is very small. I don't know why they forget us."[20]

Considering that the health centres managed by FBOs are regarded as offering better care, and that the FBOs enjoy higher legitimacy in comparison to the state, it is not clear that such a weakening of the FBOs will produce better health care and improve the social contract between the state and the population. That the state, fully aware of the complexity of the arrangement, nonetheless preferred to keep the FBOs outside their discussions with the donors is not surprising, considering the competition that exists between them. By leaving the FBOs outside the main discussions, the government gets the upper hand and can try to control donor resources.

Normative considerations

Working with non-state actors also poses difficult questions as to what kind of actors donors are willing to engage with. Engaging with non-state actors can mean dealing with unsavoury characters involved in dubious activities, such as various rebel groups or deeply conservative informal institutions (Denney, 2013, p. 17). As pointed out by, for example, Meagher and Hilhorst, there is a need for a nuanced discussion regarding the merits or otherwise of building on informal and local structures. They rightly argue that the idea of development from below builds on an overly simplistic idea of communities as homogeneous, and that it ignores processes of inequality and exclusion within communities and local structures (Hilhorst, Christoplos & Van Der Harr, 2010; Meagher, 2012). For example, women and members of ethnic minority groups might find it difficult to get their voices heard and might find themselves excluded from certain services. Donors also need to be careful not to legitimize actors that enjoy very little recognition amongst the local population.

Working with customary chiefs in the justice sector is not without difficulties and risks for donors. The role and the legitimacy of the customary chiefs has diminished in some parts of the country (Vlassenroot, 2012, pp. 4–5; Verweijen, 2016). In urban areas, like Kinshasa, they have more or less lost their influence.[21] Much depends on the individual chief and what legitimacy he has amongst his population. Some of them have moved away from the villages and have lost contact with their population.[22] In addition, some of them are actively fuelling conflicts in their territories by, for example, selling land without informing the communities (ICG, 2013; Vlassenroot, 2012, p. 4).

In the health sector there were also concerns regarding normative issues when dealing with the FBOs. For example, the UK's decision to involve FBOs more actively in their health programme was not without controversy. Some people within the DFID country office, as well as within the Swedish International Development Cooperation Agency (Sida – which financed a minor part of the programme), questioned whether it was a good idea to work with FBOs when issues regarding sexual and reproductive rights were involved. It was feared that they would not guarantee women's and adolescents' right to reproductive health (Sida, 2013, p. 11).

Political considerations

Engaging with non-state actors that sometimes openly challenge the authority of the state can be very sensitive, and can be seen as interference in domestic affairs (Derks, 2012, p. 22). Donors need to assess whether their relationship with the government is strong enough to withstand the potential fallout from supporting non-state security and justice actors, who may be perceived as competitors to the state (Allouche, 2013).

In the justice sector, the reaction of the government was clearly a factor that needed consideration by the donors. It would have been hard for them to support a system that had more or less been pronounced illegal by the government. In addition, the relationship between the donors and the government had often been tense, and the donors faced major obstacles in moving their programmes on justice reforms forward. This made them, understandably, cautious of challenging the government, fearing this might make the government even more uncooperative.

In interviews, some donor representatives recognized it was not realistic to believe the government would be able to cover the whole country with formal courts. As a consequence, they believed that it would be necessary to involve, and build on, the customary system. However, because of resistance from the government, donors found it hard to officially raise the issue. One illustration of this was the organization of the *États Généraux de la justice* in 2015. This was the first meeting held in years to discuss justice reforms and some donors suggested that customary chiefs should be invited. The government had shown limited interest, and when the Terms of Reference for the event were finalized, the customary chiefs were not mentioned amongst the 24 different groups to be invited (DRC: MoJ, 2015). Hence, at the largest conference ever in the country to discuss the future of the justice sector, the actors that deal with the majority of cases were largely excluded. Another example where the donors tried to engage with real governance was the EU-funded PARJ programme, where a study on alternative justice providers had been mooted but was cancelled due to lack of interest by the Ministry of Justice.[23]

The willingness of the donors to work with the customary system seems, however, to have increased lately as a direct result of the increased political instrumentalization of the justice sector by President Kabila. He has in various ways used the justice sector to postpone the elections and silence the opposition. One example of this is the verdict by the constitutional court in May 2016, stating that Kabila wouldn't have to step down on 19 December 2016, which, according to the constitution, should have been his last day in power. Another case in point was when a judge in Lubumbashi was pressured to convict Moïse Katumbi, a presidential candidate and former governor of Katanga, to a three-year prison sentence (Reuters, 2016). As a consequence, some donors have started to look into the possibility of more actively engaging with alternative forms of justice such as mediation by NGOs, but also by finding linkages between the formal and informal system, for example by providing training for customary chiefs. According to some of my interviewees, the Ministry of Justice had started to open up to the idea, apparently recognizing that the move to the state system perhaps had gone too quickly and that there might still be a role for the customary chiefs in solving disputes.[24]

In the health sector, donors didn't need to take the same political considerations into account. The Ministry of Health considered the FBOs to be more or less part of the government, and although there was some competition between them, it was minor compared to the hostility that characterized the justice sector. The cooperation between the donors and the Ministry of Health was also much more amicable.

To summarize, my assessment is that donors are aware of the real governance on the ground, with the FBOs and the customary chiefs playing an important role in the provision of health and justice services to the population. However, they were clearly struggling to fully understand the nuances of the complex relationships between the state and non-state actors. In the health sector, both the donors and the government were willing to engage with the FBOs, but they were being left out from some of the policy discussions. I would argue that this has mainly to do with the state-centric lenses that the donors are carrying and which makes them overlook the full importance of the FBOs. There is also some reluctance related to normative issues, such as worries that FBOs will not adhere to sexual and reproductive rights supported by donors. This might be a short-sighted way of looking at the issue, because considering the high legitimacy the FBOs have in Congo, significant advances could be made by working together. In the justice sector there was a clear reluctance to accept the reality on the ground, both amongst donors and by the government. This can be explained by normative considerations related to working with customary chiefs, donors' state-centric lenses, as well as political considerations.

Conclusions

As research has shown, many fragile states have never had a functional state (in the Weberian use of the term). Despite this, most haven't turned into complete anarchy. Instead they are being governed by a mixture of local forms of order and authority. Development assistance to these countries has increased substantially during the last decade, and is likely to continue increasing. By 2030 it is estimated that 50% of the world's poor will be living in fragile states (IDA, 2017, p. 41). Despite this, we only have limited accounts of how donors are trying to take into consideration real governance in countries where services are often being provided in a complex arrangement between the state and non-state actors.

As this chapter has shown, the donors have reacted to this real governance in different ways. In the health sector, they acknowledge that the FBOs are playing an important role, and have been keen to involve FBOs in their activities. However, they often do not involve them in policy discussions and in the formulation of project proposals. This leaves the FBOs feeling ignored, and misses the opportunity of building on a system that has managed to produce results even during challenging times. Considering the FBOs' strong legitimacy and in-depth knowledge regarding health care, there could be clear advantages for the donors to work more closely with them. The donors' focus on the government has contributed to the strengthening of the state at the expense of the FBOs. In the justice sector, the donors have more or less ignored the customary chiefs, focusing their state-building effort on the formal justice system. A more balanced approach, considering the lack of judges and court buildings, would have been to try to build linkages between these two systems, and to make them work in synergy with each other.

This chapter has highlighted some difficulties the donors are struggling with when encountering real governance and in working with the grain. One of these is the state-centric view that many donors have and their difficulties in understanding a context that is so far from their own reality. This was particularly obvious in the justice sector, where many of the donors simply couldn't understand how a justice system could work unless there was a formal system. Other hindrances are of a normative character: not all non-state actors (or state actors for that matter) are uncomplicated to work with. For example, customary chiefs often have traditional views on gender equality, and FBOs might work against donor agendas on sexual and reproductive rights. In addition, even systems that have proved valuable to solve local disputes in the past might come under pressure by, for example, conflicts and urbanization, and might lose legitimacy. Finally, political considerations matter. For example, in the justice sector donors feared their fragile cooperation with the Ministry of Justice could break down if they insisted on working with the customary chiefs.

More critical thinking is needed to explore the nature of the state and the nature of governance. If the interlinkages between state and non-state actors are considered, there would be clear benefits to stretching the idea of the state in donors' state-building efforts to incorporate more non-institutional models, and to carefully analyse which actors are deemed legitimate according to the local population, and to then build from that.

Notes

1 Donors is a notoriously imprecise label that tends to homogenize differences between official aid agencies. Donors is nevertheless a convenient and almost unavoidable term for describing the relationship between the donor community and the government. Despite the fact that donors have different approaches and work in different sectors, they broadly follow the same policy guidelines issued by the OECD Development Assistant Committee (DAC). This plays an important role in homogenizing donor discourse and actions (Whitfield, 2009). In addition, donors attend the same donor coordination meetings at the country level, and are thereby, to a certain degree, harmonizing their viewpoints.

2 This was the part of the budget that got executed. The initial budget was higher.

3 The percentage of staff salary varies from province to province. DFID found that, for example, out of 4,773 health workers identified in Kasaï Central, only 10% received a salary, whereas 24% received a salary supplement (DFID-DRC, 2018, p. 23).

4 Interview. Implementer. Kinshasa (5 March 2015); Interview. FBO representative. Kinshasa (26 May 2015).

5 Interview. Implementer. Kananga (9 March 2015); Interview. FBO representative. Kinshasa (1 June 2015).

6 Each church signs it individually with the state, although the text is the same.

7 Interview. Implementer. Kinshasa (3 June 2015).

8 The health package is based on the government's norms for what services and standards the health centres should provide.

9 For example: Interviews. Government official. Kinshasa (24 April 2015 & 24 November 2016).

10 For example: Interview. Multilateral donor. Kinshasa (30 March 2015); Interview. CSO representative. Kinshasa (9 April 2015).

11 Interview. Two FBO representatives. Kananga (17 April 2015).

12 Interview. Law professor. Kinshasa (15 June 2015). See also Tekilazaya et al. (2013b).

13 Speech heard in person. Minister of Justice. Goma (11 May 2015).

14 Interview. INGO representative. Kinshasa (2 March 2015).

15 Interview. Government official. Kinshasa (28 May 2015).

16 Interview. Judge. Kinshasa (27 April 2015).

17 Interview. Consultant. Kinshasa (30 June 2015).

18 Accès aux soins de Santé Primaires (ASSP).

19 Also: Interview. Donor representative. Kinshasa (20 March 2015).

20 Interview. FBO representative. Kinshasa (1 June 2015).

21 Interview. Law professor. Kinshasa (25 November 2016).

22 Interview. INGO representative based in Bukavu. Via Skype (19 May 2015).

23 Interview. Implementer. Kinshasa (27 May, 2015).

24 Interviews. Donor officials. Kinshasa (16 November 2016 & 1 December 2016).

References

Allouche, J. (2013) The role of informal service providers in post-conflict reconstruction and state-building. In: Weinthal, E. et al. (eds.) *Water and Post-conflict Peace-building.* Abingdon: Routledge, pp. 31–42.

Baaz, E. M. and Stern, M. (2013) Willing reform? An analysis of defence reform initiatives in the DRC. In: Bigsten, A. (ed.) *Globalisation and Development: Rethinking Interventions and Governance.* Abingdon: Routledge, pp. 193–213.

Baer, F. (2007) FBO health networks and renewing primary health care. Published online. Available from: www.sanru.org/reports/FBOs_and_Renewing_PHC.pdf [Accessed 23 November 2018].

Boege, V., Brown, M. A. and Clements, K. P. (2009) Hybrid political orders, not fragile states. *Peace Review* 21 (1): 13–21.

Bwimana, A. (2017) Heath sector network governance and state-building in South Kivu, Democratic Republic of Congo. *Health Policy and Planning* 32 (10): 1476–83.

Crook, R. C. and Booth, D. (2011) Conclusion: Rethinking African governance and development. *IDS Bulletin* 42 (2): 97–101.

De Herdt, T., Titeca, K. and Wagemakers, I. (2012) Make schools, not war? Donors' rewriting of the social contract in the DRC. *Development Policy Review* 30 (6): 681–701.

DRC (Democratic Republic of Congo) (2013) Loi organique n°13/011-B, n°13/011-B du 11 avril 2013 portant organisation, fonctionnement et compétences des juridictions de l'ordre judiciaire.

DRC: MoB (Democratic Republic of Congo: Ministry of Budget) (2015) Budget 2015, ESB des depenses par fonction et sous fonction, exécution au 31/12/2015 (published 22 January 2016).

DRC: MoH (Democratic Republic of Congo: Ministry of Health) (2007) Convention-cadre de Partenariat No 1250/CAB/MIN/SP/009/2007 du Septembre 2007 entre le gouvernement de la Republique Democratic du Congo et le comite permanent des eveques du Congo asbl, portant sur la collaboration dans le domaine de la sante.

DRC: MoH (Democratic Republic of Congo: Ministry of Health) (2009) Stratégie de renforcement du système de santé.

DRC: MoJ (Democratic Republic of Congo: Ministry of Justice) (2015) Termes de reference etats-generaux in Kinshasa April/May 2015.

Denney, L. (2013) Liberal chiefs or illiberal development? The challenge of engaging chiefs in DFID's Security Sector Reform Programme in Sierra Leone. *Development Policy Review* 31 (1): 5–25.

Denney, L. (2014) Justice and security reform: Development agencies and informal institutions in Sierra Leone. Abingdon: Routledge.

Derks, M. (2012) Improving security and justice through local/non-state actors: The challenges of donor support to local/non-state security and justice providers. Clingendael research paper.

DFID-DRC (2013) Business Case and Intervention Summary. United Kingdom Department for International Development, DRC office.

DFID-DRC (2018) Annual review access to primary health care. United Kingdom Department for International Development, DRC office.

Hilhorst, D., Christoplos, I. and Van Der Harr, G. (2010) Reconstruction 'from below': A new magic bullet or shooting from the hip? *Third World Quarterly* 31 (7): 1107–24.

ICG (International Crisis Group) (2013) Understanding conflict in Eastern Congo: The Ruzizi Plain. Africa Report 206.

IDA (2017) Towards 2030: Investing in growth, resilience and opportunity. International Development Association and World Bank Group. IDA18 Final Replenishment Report.

IDS (2010) An upside down view of governance. Institute of Development Studies, Centre for the Future State, University of Sussex. Research Programme Summary Report.

Ilac (International Legal Assistance Consortium) (2009) Rebuilding courts and trust: An assessment of the needs of the justice system in the Democratic Republic of Congo. International Legal Assistance Consortium and International Bar Association report.

ISDR-Bukavu (Institut Superieur de Developpement Rural du Bukavu) (2017) Personnes deplacees et provision de la justice en République Démocratique du Congo.

Kelsall, T. (2008) Working with the grain in African development. *Development Policy Review* 26 (6): 627–55.

Kelsall, T. (2011) Going with the grain in African development? *Development Policy Review* 29 (s1): s223–s1.

Kurz, C. P. (2010) What you see is what you get: Analytical lenses and the limitations of post-conflict statebuilding in Sierra Leone. *Journal of Intervention and Statebuilding* 4 (2): 205–36.

Marquette, H. and Beswick, D. (2011) State building, security and development: State building as a new development paradigm? *Third World Quarterly* 32 (10): 1703–14.

Mcloughlin, C. (2015) When does service delivery improve the legitimacy of a fragile or conflict-affected state? Service delivery and state legitimacy. *Governance: An International Journal of Policy, Administration and Institutions* 28 (3): 341–56.

Meagher, K. (2012) The strength of weak states? Non-state security forces and hybrid governance in Africa. *Development and Change* 43 (5): 1073–101.

Meagher, K., De Herdt, T. and Titeca, K. (2014) Unravelling public authority: Paths of hybrid governance in Africa. IS Academy. Human Security in Fragile States. Research Brief 10.

OECD (2010) The state's legitimacy in fragile situations: Unpacking complexity. Paris: OECD.

OECD (2011) A new deal for engagement in fragile states: International dialogue on peacebuilding and statebuilding. Available from: www. pbsbdialogue.org/media/ filer_public/07/69/07692de0-3557-494e-918e-18df00e9ef73/ the_new_deal.pdf [Accessed 23 November 2018].

OECD (2016) Statistical data on public finance. Worldwide, for period 2014–2016. Available from: public.tableau. com/views/OECDDACAi-dataglancebyrecipient_new/ Recipients?:embed=y&:display_count=yes&:showTabs=y&:tool-bar=no?&:showVizHome=no [Accessed 29 November 2018].

Olivier de Sardan, J.-P. (2011) The eight modes of local governance in West Africa. *IDS Bulletin* 42 (2): 22–31.

Reuters (2016) Congo opposition leader sentenced in absentia to three years in prison. *Reuters Africatech*. Available from: af.reuters.com/article/africaTech/ idAFKCN0Z828C [Accessed 23 November 2018].

Risse, T. and Stollenwerk, E. (2018) Legitimacy in areas of limited statehood. *Annual Review of Political Science* 21: 403–18.

Seay, L. E. (2013) Effective responses: Protestants, Catholics and the provision of health care in the post-war Kivus. *Review of African Political Economy* 40 (135): 83–97.

Sida (Swedish International Development cooperation Agency) (2011) Assessment memo Uhaki Safi (December). Document provided on request.

Sida (Swedish International Development Cooperation Agency) (2013) Sida appraisal of support to DFID Access to Primary Health Care. Document provided on request.

Sida (Swedish International Development Cooperation Agency) (2014) Background paper to appraisal of additional support to PARJ. Document provided on request.

Tekilazaya, K., Fataki Wa Luhindi, D. and Wetsh'okonda Koso, M. (2013a) Le secteur de la justice et l'Etat de droit Un Etat de droit en pointillé Essai d'évaluation des efforts en vue de l'instauration de l'Etat de droit et perspectives d'avenir. Johannesburg: AfriMap and Open Society Foundations.

Tekilazaya, K., Fataki Wa Luhindi, D. and Wetsh'okonda Koso, M. (2013b) République démocratique du Congo – Le Secteur de la justice et l'Etat de droit – document de Synthèse (Document de Synthèse). Open Society Foundations.

UNSC (2018) United Nations Security Council Resolution 2409 (27 March).

USAID (2018) Key indicators. Health sector, Congo (Kinshasa). Available from: idea.usaid.gov/cd/ congo-kinshasa/health [Accessed 23 November 2018].

Verweijen, J. (2016) Between "justice" and "injustice": Justice populaire in the Eastern DR Congo. *JSRP Policy Brief* 4.

Vinck, P. and Pham, P. (2014) Searching for lasting peace:

Population-based survey on perceptions and attitudes about peace, security and justice in Eastern Democratic Republic of the Congo. Harvard Humanitarian Initiative & UNDP.

Vlassenroot, K. (2012) Dealing with land issues and conflict in Eastern Congo: Towards an integrated and participatory approach. Conflict Research Group, Egmont (University of Ghent), Humanity United and UK Aid.

Weijs, B., Hilhorst, D. and Ferf, A. (2012) Livelihoods, basic services and social protection in the Democratic Republic of the Congo. Secure Livelihoods Research Consortium, ODI London. Working paper.

Whitfield, L. (ed.) (2009) *The Politics Of Aid: African Strategies for Dealing with Donors*. Oxford: Oxford University Press.

Part II
Case studies

5
The Public Electricity Service in Kinshasa: Between Legal Oversight and Autonomy

Jean-Pierre Mpiana Tshitenge

Introduction

In the Democratic Republic of the Congo (DRC) public services are, in many respects, an observatory into where the failure of the state meets the poverty of the population. They betray the inability of the public authorities to meet the needs of the population and, at the same time, the difficulties experienced by the latter in accessing services due to their destitution. This convergence becomes apparent, in particular, in public health structures, where the dilapidation of infrastructure and the quality of healthcare delivered go hand-in-hand with the difficulties sick persons have getting treated.

One of the features of these services is the devastated character of their material substratum, the expression of the public authorities' disengagement, and the primacy of the informal as the capacity for self-regulation held by the agents charged with administering them. Through arrangements, negotiations, understandings, cooperation and so on, the agents also make the services work on the basis of principles other than the established regulations. Thus, public services in the DRC find themselves on the intersection of restrictive institutional regulations (legal oversight) and the regulations invented by the agents (autonomy), or, to put it in another way, they are subject to "hybrid governance" (Malukisa Nkuku, 2017a).

From an analytical perspective, this configuration can be approached by the concept of "semi-autonomous regulation", to adopt a phrase coined by Sally Falk Moore (2000, p. 5), also termed "joint regulation" (Reynaud, 2003), or "entangled logics" (Olivier de Sardan, 2007). The value of this conceptualization within the framework of this study is that it provides "analysis tools of the relationship between the games of the actors and the rules of the game" (Ayimpam, 2014, p. 289) in the situation of the provision of electricity by the Société Nationale de l'Électricité (National Electricity Company) (SNEL) which we have observed in the city of Kinshasa.

On the basis of investigations carried out through a socio-anthropological approach in the districts of Kasa-Vubu, Kisenso, Limete, Masina and N'djili in Kinshasa,[1] this study analyses the forms of the regulation of the public electricity service on the basis of the ways in which the Kinshasa population ensures its energy survival in a context where the SNEL has accumulated bad performance after bad performance for several years.

The daily observation in the neighbourhoods and districts of Kinshasa shows that the persistence of below-par performances by SNEL has led to the emergence of often informal, alternative modes of electricity delivery and access. These alternatives take the form of arrangements, negotiations and bricolages which the SNEL agents and the users[2] have established, and which co-exist alongside the company's regulation. They respond to other forms of regulation, which Jean-Pierre Olivier de Sardan (2008) calls "practical norms".

The current study questions the context of the establishment of these alternative modes of the provision of electricity in the city of Kinshasa, the principles and the logics which underpin them, as well as the grounds for their acceptability. It is based on the idea according to which in "the space of the game" (De Herdt & Olivier de Sardan, 2015) – in this case the public electricity service – the practical norms which regulate the supply of electricity function on the basis of logics of action, resulting from a realization of the precarity in which the SNEL functions and in which both the agents and the population live. This context of precarity, in the eyes of the actors, legitimizes the practical norms regulating the delivery of electricity. As was said by an agent of a Kasa-Vubu agency over the course of the interviews:

> If we strictly apply all the norms of access to electricity, too few households would have access to this service. But if don't apply them even partially, nobody would fulfil their obligations. On the one hand, we too (SNEL) are aware that we do not supply electricity as it should be, we cannot be too rigorous either. Anyway, the subscribers and ourselves, we understand each other.[3]

The study is based on a rapid collective inquiry for the identification of conflicts and strategic groups (ECRIS)[4] carried out in the five aforementioned districts of Kisenso, Masina, N'djili, Kasa-Vubu and Limete. The investigation took place from 12 July to 30 August 2016. Over 45 days it mobilized eight researchers, who carried out 296 individual comprehensive interviews (Kaufmann, 1996). The comparative design of the socio-anthropological strategy determined the choice of these five communes in order to capture the heterogeneity in practices, representations and logics of inter- action between the agents of SNEL and the users of electricity. More in particular, it is important to stress that the communes of Kisenso, Masina and N'djili (the part that was surveyed) are all "self- constructed" areas that emerged during the postcolonial decom- position of the state and of its economy and where electricity is very irregular, whereas the communes of Kasa-Vubu and Limete (the residential area) are of colonial origin, they benefit from rela- tively appropriate electricity infrastructure. Starting from the idea that the SNEL agencies are arenas, that is, "local spaces in which concrete confrontations and clashes take place between social actors around shared issues" (Olivier de Sardan, 1995, p. 178–9), it targeted subscribers (168), unofficial users (30), registered agents (48) and casual workers (36), as well as 14 informal actors intervening in the supply of electricity. This last group are, in the majority of cases, youth of the various neighbourhoods commonly known as "engi- neers" (*ingenieurs*), who intervene on the networks each time there is a power cut, without having either the credentials or an official title. Note that the term "users" designates both the registered subscribers and the unregistered users of electricity provided by SNEL. Through interviews, documentary exploration, and observations of and inter- actions with these actors, it shows to what extent the actors of these arenas – on the basis of existing regulations and their strategies – negotiate the supply of and access to electricity. Such a perspective is at some remove from those which oppose the formal and the informal, the actor and the system, rational choice and conformism in considering that "the social is both constraining and enabling" (Giddens, 1987, p. 74). It postulates, following Pierre Bourdieu, that "within the universe par excellence of rules and regulations, playing with the rule is part and parcel of the rule of the game" (1990, p. 89). In other words, for this study "the norms are not considered as constraints which are imposed on the actors, but as a repertoire of available guides to action, in limited number, amongst which they manoeuvre, which serve as reference points for them, and which permit certain forms of anticipation and predictability" (Olivier de Sardan, 2013, p. 16). They constitute 'the limits and reference points delimiting a field of manoeuvre within which the strategies of social actors can be deployed' (De Herdt & Olivier de Sardan, 2015).

To gain an understanding of the games of these actors and the entan- glement of logics in the provision of electricity, the study explores the concepts of public norms, social norms, practical norms and hybrid governance which makes sense of the behaviour of the actors observed on the ground. It then describes the public electricity service in the DCR, showing that the SNEL – which is responsible for its management – is an idol with feet of clay, given that this public company, despite its vast hydroelectric potential, does not manage to meet the demand for electricity in the city of Kinshasa. Finally, in exploring the interactions between agents and users, it unearths the practical norms which encase the supply of electricity, the principles and logics which underpin them, and the grounds for their acceptability.

Theoretical and conceptual framework

To speak of the regulation of public services in the DRC is to question the norms which anticipate, frame and orient the behaviour of the public agents in the performance of their duties. From the socio-anthropological perspective adopted in this study, a complete understanding of the forms of regulation involves – apart from the exploration of legal or regulatory texts – the analysis of the daily interactions between agents and users. It is thus in the domain of the real delivery of collective goods and services where the effective regulations of public institutions within the DRC clearly appear (De Herdt & Poncelet, 2011).

In light of our observations regarding the SNEL agencies, the public electricity service appears as a site of normative pluralism in which public and practical norms intersect (Olivier de Sardan, 2008, p. 8). The first are state based or professional in origin. Concretely, they are the laws, regulations, collective agreements or other procedural rules which are designed to organize the functioning of services, to structure the behaviour of agents and to define their duties and rights (Olivier de Sardan, 2008, p. 8). They correspond, as far as this study is concerned, to the group of regulatory provisions issued by the SNEL to govern connections to its electrical network, the payment of bills, or the handling of outages.

The second are practical norms which result from the interactions between actors in a concrete situation. Within the framework of the functioning of public services, they are the result of the professional practices of the public actors in their relationships with the users and attest to the capability of social agents (public actors and users) to self-regulate in a concrete situation.

By practical norms, Jean-Pierre Olivier de Sardan means the "various informal regulations, de facto, tacit or latent which underlie the practices of the actors which have a gap between public norms and social norms" (2013, p. 1). For this author, these norms are derived from a permanent and incremental process of adjustment and innovation, which is carried out by the recycling and progressive displacing of the norms in place, through innumerable iterative processes. These norms are implicit, informal, and they are neither formulated nor codified as such. They take concrete form in the informal arrangements which the agents of public services embark on with the users. They are localized to the extent that they are produced and reproduced above all on a local or reticular basis, within services over the course of interactions and routines. They are plural, by which is meant that can have very different and, by nature, very varied forms, and "they cover the large gap between explicit norms and practices" (De Herdt & Olivier de Sardan, 2015). Some can be adaptive, pragmatic or palliative, and make up for the shortfalls of professional and social norms, whilst others can be transgressive or rebellious and violent, contravening public and indeed social norms. They can also be resources or constraints for the agents, and can bring them into conflict with each other.

Products of the interactions between actors (agents and users), or of institutional "bricolage" (Cleaver, 2012), practical norms pertain to the modalities of putting into practice public norms and social norms. There exist dialectical relationships between these two types of norm, in other words, ones of complementarity and tension. Legal norms at times serve as a frame of reference for development strategies and the implementation of social norms or practices. The latter make the former more flexible and enable them to be put into effect. However, the relationships between these three types of norm are also marked by tensions. The legitimization of certain practical norms can also work in the other direction as a de-legitimization of certain official professional norms which are at variance with the excesses of these same norms (Olivier de Sardan, 2013). As we see in the following discussion, legitimacy and illegitimacy of public and practical norms hold to the perceptions that actors have of them with regards to the constraints of their environment (Baaz, Olsson & Verweijen., 2018).

Public and practical norms) and informal (i.e. practical) norms are raised, in the sense used by Gauthier de Villers (2002) and Sylvie Ayimpan (2014, p. 25–35). Professional norms proceed from the formal, given that they are both institutional, recognized, and based on the rational-legal model that characterizes modern bureaucratic organizations. Practical norms engage the informal, understood here in its broadest sense, integrating all practices, not only those which do not conform to written rules, but also those which escape recognized and instituted forms in bureaucratic rest on logics of action. That is to say, they rest on the reasons to act or the rationalities that give meaning to the behaviour of actors (cited in Bréchet & Schieb-Bienfait, 2009, p. 2). Logics of action themselves obey an ethic – understood as a system of values which orient the behaviour of actors – and, in the case in question, mark the symbolic boundaries between the professional world (SNEL) and the world of actors (agents and users). If the public norms of the SNEL refer to the ethic of public services that takes the form of values such as common interest, loyalty, accountability, impartiality, responsibility and so on, by contrast the practical norms refer to the ethic of survival, whose values are pragmatism, opportunism and so on. Yet as we shall explore further, this symbolic boundary is porous, and actors oscillate between the two worlds according to the constraints and stakes which are present. In so doing, they accentuate a blurring between public and private, a fundamental characteristic of neo-patrimonialism (Médard, 1990) or decentralized patrimonialism (Willame, 1972).

In another paradigm, formal (i.e. professional organizations. These informal practices combine in reinterpreting the traits which are borrowed as much from traditions and local values as from models inherited from the West.

In this space, practical and social norms are articulated around public norms. In the same way, the former, due to their deep-rootedness and their visibility, can don the status of the latter. Thus, the governance of public services in the DRC is on the intersection of the regulation of legal oversight (represented by public norms), and autonomous regulation (characterized by social and practical norms). As we stated earlier, one might say that this governance pertains to "joint regulation", to use Jean-Daniel Reynaud's phrase, a "semi-autonomous field" according to Sally Falk Moore, or to "hybrid governance" (Malukisa Nkuku, 2017b). The notion of hybridity here comes fully into its own, insofar as it incites us to consider the two types of norm described above in the context of their entanglement in the functioning of Congolese public services. Hybridity, according to Jean-Pierre Olivier de Sardan (2008, p. 7), intuitively connotes coexistence between official norms and the practices which distance themselves from them. It here takes on a meaning of individual arrangements between public agents and users, who, in the delivery of collective goods and services, mobilize – depending on the case – social norms, public norms and practical norms in their negotiations.

It is in this light that the interactions around the distribution of electricity in Kinshasa are analysed in this study.

Jean-Daniel Reynaud holds that a "theory of social rules which refrains from treating them as exogenous to the social relationship itself or as an overall social balance must look into their sources and the situations in which they are formed" (2003, p. 103). From this perspective, practical norms – to speak as the ethno-methodologists do – are indexical, matching up to the elements of the context or situation which generates them. An understanding of the context is vital to grasp the modes by which the norms which regulate the interactions between actors are generated, such as the situation which prevails over the SNEL agencies analysed in this study.

The public electricity service in Kinshasa

SNEL: National company, enemy of electricity?

Electricity is one of the sectors considered to be strategic the world over. In the DRC, the government considers electricity as the motor of the DRC's economic and social development, and has made it one of the five major components of the programme known as the "revolution of modernity" (*révolution de la modernité*, formerly *cinq chantiers*, the "five building sites"). The management of this strategic energy has been entrusted to the SNEL. This public enterprise was transformed into a commercial company by limited responsibility shares in 2009. Although the electricity sector was liberalized in 2014, the SNEL has remained until today the major operator, if not the sole provider, of electricity in the city of Kinshasa.

The SNEL has at its disposal a powerful hydroelectric network (fourth largest in the world with 600 billion KWH) and thermal power stations to ensure the servicing of electrical energy. There is estimated to be 774,000 GWh per year of technically exploitable hydropower, corresponding to 100,000 MW of power (UNDP, 2013, p. 14). Despite this hydroelectric potential, only 2.5% of it is used (or 2,566 MW) (UNDP, 2013, p. 14). As a result, access to electricity is provided to only 1% of the population in rural areas, 35% in urban areas, with a national average of between 9% and 16%, compared with an average in sub-Saharan Africa of 31% (World Bank, 2017, p. 2–3). A large proportion of this production is geared towards exportation, thus leaving local demand unsatisfied.

The city of Kinshasa is supplied through the Inga and Zongo hydroelectric power stations, situated in the province of Kongo

Central. The level of electricity supply – 37% over the whole of the city (World Bank, 2017, p. 3) – is highly unequal, leaving many so-called "dark pockets" in peri-urban and slum areas. This bears witness to discrimination in the provision of electricity between the planned city of colonial origin and the postcolonial self-build estates, where periods of selective power shortages are increasing, and where households often find themselves in darkness due to power failures of long duration.

For the most part, Kinshasa is experiencing acute electricity supply precarity. The public electricity service is failing in this respect. In every district within this city, it is rare that electricity is maintained for 24 hours. It is often interspersed with untimely interruptions, due either to selective power shortages initiated by the SNEL in order to allow transformers to rest, or to power failures which plunge whole neighbourhoods into darkness for a year or even more. To this irregularity in supply is added the poor quality of the current (low intensity, voltage instability), which is at the root of the damage sustained by household electrical appliances, and which often results from tinkering by certain SNEL agents who, instead of activating the three phases which the electrical cabinets are fitted with, only acti-vate one or two. In the majority of neighbourhoods in Kinshasa, the inhabitants complain that electricity has become a "husband of the night" (a demon). It is supplied when the households cannot make use of it (from midnight to 4am) and interrupted when they have most need of it (between 5am and 11pm). In addition, within the framework of selective power shortages employed by the company to avoid its electrical installations overloading, the agents seem to be prompt when interrupting the electricity supply, but slow when it comes to restoring it, leaving users without current for several hours. Everything happens as if the SNEL agents are uncomfortable with the idea of seeing households regularly illuminated. It is for that reason, and to ridicule it, that the SNEL has been renamed by the Congolese as the "national company, enemy of electricity".

From self-justification to scapegoat theory

The deterioration of the electricity supply in Kinshasa is contin-gent on a multiplicity of factors which are different in nature. The explanations provided by both the SNEL managers and agents and subscribers demonstrate that they proceed from self-justification, and borrow from the scapegoat theory. Each party exonerates itself and attributes the responsibility to others. The SNEL managers and agents evoke technical-civic factors and place the responsibility on the state and the users, whilst the latter point the finger at politico-managerial factors and blame both the SNEL and the Congolese state.

For the SNEL managers and agents, the company's poor performances are explained by the shortfall in the production of energy due to the dilapidation of the installations, and the low level of equipment distribution due to systematic non-investment and the insolvency of the state over two decades. Not only does the state not invest sufficiently in the sector, but it does not honour its debts to the company. As has been pointed out to us by those taking part in the investigation, a number of politicians do not pay electricity consumption fees. The same is true for the economic operators they sponsor, as well as military camps and public buildings. This lack of investment is at the root of the machine stoppages and the bottlenecking of energy thoroughfares through the saturation of transmission and distribution lines. From this situation arizes the mismatch between the supply and demand for electricity, which is the source, amongst other things, of the alternating supply of electricity between neighbourhoods.

According to the SNEL's General Managing Director (GMD), this mismatch is escalating with the creation of new estates in the city and small-scale industries in residential areas (mills, machine and soldering workshops, etc.), which bring about damage to MV and LV cables in certain places. Moreover, the distribution network, according to the GMD (SNEL GMD, 2014), is subject to collateral damage linked to road improvement work, anarchical construction, the unremitting occupation of rights of way, the use of materials of doubtful quality or non-standard materials in privately owned installations, etc. To this are added interventions by some who lack civic-mindedness (repeated assaults on the network), fraudulent connections and the overconsumption of the current by subscribers who, encouraged by flat-rate pricing, leave light bulbs on during the day and in unoccupied rooms during the night, or simultaneously use several household electrical appliances (television, radio, portable stove, iron, fridge, etc.). If the GMD (2014) is to be believed, these assaults carried out on the distribution networks, principally on low voltage, contribute to the premature deterioration of equipment, which is subjected to excessive loads. This principally concerns distribution transformers, electrical cables, electromechanical appliances, etc.

For their part, the users attribute the SNEL's poor performance to inadequate management of the company following the political recruitment of administrators, and the withdrawals made by them from the company's revenues to the benefit of political masters. The most-cited example is the disappearance of $30 million paid by the Republic of the Congo to the SNEL, attributed to a former director of the head of state's cabinet. These misappropriations of funds prevent the company from renewing its facilities and extending its distribution network. According to this viewpoint – in part shared by the SNEL's agents and lower-management personnel – appointments to the leadership and to other positions within the company are political. They do not have the aim of improving services, but rather the withdrawing of the company's revenues to the benefit of political masters. Public companies and services in the DRC in many respects function according to a feudal logic. The political authorities (lords) place at their head managers (vassals) who, through rising special concessions, must supply them with resources of every kind. Furthermore, the deterioration of electricity provision in their neighbourhoods bears witness to how little interest the political authorities have in the population's socio-economic conditions, and also to their political strategy of keeping the population in ignorance by preventing their becoming informed via the radio and television, having deprived them of electricity. Finally, for the interviewees, the behaviour of certain agents who bring about power cuts so as to be bribed by the subscribers is not unrelated to the failure of the servicing of electricity in Kinshasa. In the Kasa-Vubu and N'djili districts, the bar managers have installed televisions or large screens and negotiate interruptions to the electricity supply on the occasion of football matches, so as to oblige those keen on the sport to go to these spaces, where buying a drink is a condition of gaining admittance.

Uncertain alternatives

To overcome this energy crisis, multiple actions and projects have been undertaken, but do not seem to offer appropriate solutions. These initiatives aim either at the rehabilitation of what is already in place, or the construction of new production, transmission and distribution equipment.

Concerning the production and the transmission of electricity, the SNEL is trying to keep operational the Inga facilities, which regularly break down due to their dilapidation. Furthermore, the Congolese state has implemented the construction of the second Inga–Kinshasa line, designed to supply the capital exclusively. Moreover, the Congolese government, in partnership with South Africa, has implemented the ambitious Inga 3 project, which aims to make the site the largest hydroelectric complex worldwide, producing 4,800 MW.

Regarding this project, François Misser (2015) has drawn attention to several challenges which risk compromizing its completion. There are geological, hydrological, technological and financial challenges; a multiplicity of actors involved, which renders coordination more complex; and political motivations. In addition, even if it reached completion, this project – requiring the mobilization of close to $14 billion (Misser, 2015, p. 237), funds which are difficult to raise – is essentially outwardly directed and will not solve the DRC's energy crisis, because it places the needs of the South African company EKSOM and the Katanga mining industry above those of the rest of the Congo. Indeed, the project's clauses provide for 52% of production, or 2,500 MW, for South Africa (Misser, 2015, p. 246), 27%, or 1,300 MW, for Katangan industry (Misser, 2015, p. 247), and 21%, or 1,000 MW, for the SNEL, of which only 600 MW are locked in, with the provision of the remaining 400 MW dependent on the flow rate of the Congo river. In these conditions, Inga 3 will merely give birth to a mouse, only producing for the national network between 56% and 33% of the current capacity of Inga 1 and 2. Finally, and this amounts to another challenge, the project's launch risks bringing about the shutting down of the Inga 1 and 2 turbines throughout the whole duration of the works being carried out, due to the reduction of water they will bring about (Misser, 2015, p. 248). This will exacerbate an already precarious situation.

Whilst waiting for the completion of this ambitious project, the SNEL is initiating ad hoc projects, notably the "Electricity for All" project funded by the African Development Bank (AfDB), the objective of which is to increase the level of electricity servicing in Kinshasa's peripheral districts (Masina, Kimbaseke and Mont-Ngafula). This project consists of installing new electrical cabinets, poles, and of laying in cables and street lights in the districts. Apart from the system of alternating selective power cuts to avoid overloading its facilities, the SNEL has undertaken the installation of prepayment meters to rationalize consumption and the commercialization of electricity, and to foster transparency in the management of revenue. Finally, the company regularly organizes radio and television awareness-raising campaigns when sports events are broadcast, asking subscribers to consume electricity rationally by, in particular, using energy-saving light bulbs and regularly settling their bills.

These initiatives are nonetheless far from resolving the thorny question of the irregular electricity supply. The persistence of the energy crisis in the DRC demonstrates the limits of the SNEL and the Congolese governments' policies, which focus their actions primarily on hydropower and the Inga site, forgetting other energy sources such as wind turbines, solar power and methane gas, which are nonetheless available in the DRC. The SNEL service being deficient to a large extent, the population resorts to other sources of energy, in particular the consumption of wood fuel and charcoal (92% of energy consumption), which has grown exponentially since the 1990s and currently safeguards households' energy and nutritional survival (Trefon et al., 2011, p. 39). In certain households with a relatively high standard of living, we can today observe the recourse to small, private electricity generators which make up for the shortcomings of the SNEL, but which give rise to various forms of pollution.

Apart from several attempts at collective mobilization – notably through the *pelisamwinda* (light the lamp) operation, initiated by national parliament member Clément Kanku Tshibwabwa in order to urge the SNEL to improve its servicing of electricity in Kinshasa – the population, in accordance with its means and constraints, resigns itself to individual efforts, such as the installation of single busbar systems (that is, a specific line drawn from the cabinet, supplying only one household), the purchasing of generating units, fraudulent connections, illicit transmissions, the corruption of the agents, and so on.

Public norms and practical regulation of electricity

Faced with the failure of the SNEL, and in the absence of a credible and reassuring alternative, it can be observed that, on the one hand, the population resorts to other practices which, it is true, 'evade the forms instituted by the law, customs and the institutions' (De Villers, 2002, p. 20), but enable access to electricity. On the other hand, faced with the failure of their company, the agents trade public-service ethics (which oblige them to respect public regulations) for the ethics of survival (which push them to act pragmatically).

The supplying of electricity in Kinshasa, as elsewhere for that matter, is subject to the regulation of the SNEL, through which legal oversight is carried out. This regulation presides over the relationship between the company and the subscribers in determining the rights and obligations of each party. In particular, it sets out the conditions of access to electricity, payment methods for the consumption of electrical energy, and the management of the facilities.

The allocation of an electrical power connection to an applicant is notably subject to the latter submitting a request to be connected to the agency within their jurisdiction, presenting proof of residential ownership, the validation by SNEL agents of the quality of the electrical installations at home, and the payment of administrative costs. These fees include: fees for the approval of the circuit plan, setting up fees, fees for the receipt of facilities, subscription policy fees, connection estimate fees, the studies department's approval fees, technical and analysis visas, and VAT fees. The applicant who complies with these obligations is connected to the electricity network, becomes a subscriber, and each month pays his bills within five days after receiving them, beyond which the company is within its rights to interrupt the supply without notice. Objections concerning the amount to be paid, if there are any, must be addressed to the same agency within the same time limit, at the end of which they are no longer accepted. In these transactions, the SNEL strictly forbids subscribers from paying the sum of the bills to agents at home, and from intervening in the networks in the case of a power cut.

In every case, subscribers are asked to present themselves at the appropriate SNEL counter and technical services of their jurisdiction. According to regulations, no subscriber may have two lines (overhead and underground) from the same busbar system, nor transmit electricity to their neighbours, no matter what the reason might be. Nor can they object to agents having access to the meter without incurring penalties, notably flat-rate billing or disconnection without notice.

All these regulatory provisions are, in reality, an institutional tree which hides the forest of informal practices. Neither the agents nor the subscribers scrupulously observe them. They are readjusted, got around, transgressed or even deployed from a strategic point of view by the agents and the subscribers.

Apart from the planned districts of Limete and Kasa-Vubu – heirs to the infrastructure of colonial origin and the first years of post-colonialism – access to electricity in the districts and neighbourhoods of Kisenso, Masina and N'djili generally operates within the shadow of SNEL regulations. It is carried out on the principle: "let's get connected first and sort the rest out later". In the three self-build districts, the majority of connections to the SNEL network have been undertaken by the users themselves without the company having any knowledge of it, either with the collusion of agents, or by the company but with no verification either of the residential ownership deeds or the quality of the electrical installations. These fraudulent connections are subsequently made official by the agents who, benefiting from the "corporatist accountability" (Blundo, 2012)[5] of the managers of the subscribers, slip the names of the illegal users into the company's registers so that they receive bills in the same way as legitimate subscribers. They can also remain clandestine to the benefit of the accomplice agents, who receive money from the free-riders.

For the SNEL agents every service must be subject to the "fee-for-service" norm, even for tasks which come under their standard job specifications (Olivier de Sardan, 2011, p. 517). Whether the interventions are lawful or illegal, they ask the users for incentive fees, as well as electrical equipment handling and transportation fees, which are nevertheless included in the administrative costs paid by the applicants.

This permanent quest for informal supplementary earnings opens up a space of play governed by the principle "everything is negotiable". It should be noted that in all the transactions around the provision of electricity – be they a connection, the payment of a bill or the repairing of equipment – the magic formula remains *tokosololakaka* (we will negotiate) or *tobomana te, kobanga te, tokoyokanakaka* (let's not kill each other, don't be afraid, we will come to an understanding between ourselves).

This is the case for the settling of bills. In the five districts investigated, bills are generally paid with a delay exceeding the five days fixed by the SNEL. Contrary to the instruction stated on all invoices stipulating that "the bills are to be paid within five days of being presented; if this time limit is exceeded suspension of our electricity supply will be carried out without notice", the agencies send a power cut-off notification, which opens the way to all kinds of negotiations between agents and users. Even if in certain cases the cutting-off of the electricity supply occurs after this deadline, in the majority of cases the households which are late in paying their bills arrange the situation with the SNEL agents according to four modalities. The agents may understand the subscriber's situation and grant them an additional deadline whilst urging them to settle this obligation at the earliest opportunity; they can also ask the subscriber to "get rid of them" (*tindikabiso, longolabiso* or *libérez biso*) by offering them a tip, just as they may threaten to interrupt the supply as stated in the contract in order to get the subscriber to negotiate, and, finally, the subscriber, on his own initiative, may offer the agents a tip whilst promising to settle the bill.

It can happen that certain subscribers who are late in paying their bills resort to "intercession" to avoid the interruption in the electricity supply. These subscribers, on the strength of their social capital, call upon "intercessors" or "umbrellas",[6] who are recruited from the SNEL's managerial structure, or political or military structures, so as to delay or prevent the disconnection. The more tenacious amongst them systematically close the doorways to their plots of land to prevent the SNEL agents gaining access to the meters, whilst others negotiate with the agents a document called a *"prise-en-charge"*, which exempts them from paying the bills.

The non-payment of bills by certain subscribers cannot solely be interpreted as the inability, due to their poverty, to honour the commitment vis-à-vis the SNEL. It is also an expression of protest against the irregularity of the electricity supply and against the flat-rate fee. The majority of subscribers consider themselves the victims of "fraud" on the part of the SNEL and the public authorities, who make them pay for a service which they typically have not consumed, such as the public lighting tax, included in the SNEL bill on behalf of the municipal administration authorities despite nearly all the main roads in a city being in darkness.

Moreover, the irregularity of the electricity supply has led to the emergence of another practical norm: the diversification of feed points. This consists of, for the user, increasing the possibilities of accessing electricity, in particular through the exclusive use of an electricity line, dividing connections into two, or through clandestine transmissions. At Limete and Kasa-Vubu, in particular, certain subscribers, in order to solve the problems of untimely interruptions in the electricity supply, demand from the SNEL a single busbar system. This strategy of exclusive use has been adopted in its collective version in the districts of Masina and N'djili, where the inhabitants have had a whip-round in order to obtain a single busbar system exclusively for their streets. In these districts, some subscribers split the connection by plugging into two or three lines from the same electrical cabinet, or from different cabinets, contravening the provisions which forbid it. Elsewhere, particularly in the districts of Kisenso, Masina and N'djili, transmissions of current between neighbourhoods, avenues and plots of land are the rule in order to manage the untimely outages and the selective power cuts decreed by the company, with the deprived or cut-off entities getting connected by using electrical leads – which are generally not fit for purpose – plugged into the line of entities served with electricity. These transmissions are sometimes carried out for no charge, at other times for a fee or in a participatory manner, in the sense that the beneficiaries are called upon to contribute to the settling of the bill.

The ban on subscribers intervening in the electrical networks is breached, in particular through the prevarications of SNEL agents, by the practical norm of self-support (*auto-prise-en-charge*). Generally speaking, in the five districts covered by the investigation, power failures which are considered minor are repaired by the members of the household themselves or by informal repairmen, recruited from amongst the youth who pass themselves off as electricians, but have neither the qualifications nor the position. Despite the risks they represent, these unlawful interventions are seen in a positive light by those interviewed, for whom "if it is necessary to count solely on the SNEL, we can't have any current".

Logics of action of the actors in the electricity service

The effective governance of electricity in the local arenas (SNEL agencies scattered throughout the city Kinshasa) as it has been analysed earlier is significantly marked by practical norms. These norms, which underpin the arrangements, negotiations, manoeuvres and cooperation between agents and users, adjust, relax, bypass or transgress the company's public norms. They contribute to the daily regulation of electricity provision in Kinshasa and attest to the skills the actors concerned have in reconciling the prescribed (public norms) and the unprecedented (practical norms), thus positioning the public electricity service between legal oversight and the autonomy of the actors – or, to put it better, within hybrid governance. It would be well worth taking the wager, following Pierre Bourdieu (1990, p. 94), that without these spontaneous regulations, corrections, adjustments and accommodations carried out in the relationships between the actors of the local bodies, the SNEL would – in light of the precarity in which its agents work and in which its subscribers live – be condemned to powerlessness by the rigidity of its professional norms.

The resilience of these practical norms can be found in the logics that drive the actors and in the forms of acceptability they assume. The arrangements, negotiations, stratagems, tactics, cooperation and so on which underpin the effective delivery of electricity, even though they are illegal or irrational from an institutional perspective, nonetheless are not lacking rationalities. The rationalities of these irrationalities, in the words of Maurice Godelier (1966), serve as an axiological foundation for the informal practices of the SNEL agents and users, which we consider in terms of logics of action. We have discerned seven of them, namely:

- *Logic of the gift*, which relates to subscribers who supply electricity free of charge to households which are not registered, or which have been disconnected from the SNEL network due to insolvency. This increases the consumption of electricity, yet without raising the price to subscribers, due to flat-rate billing as a result of the absence of meters.
- *Logic of reciprocity*, which characterizes the users reciprocally lending each other electricity each time the SNEL interrupts the electricity from one neighbourhood to another.
- *Logic of partnership*, through which certain subscribers agree to supply electricity to their neighbours in return for sharing financial charges (bills).
- *Mercantilist logic*, which pushes certain users to turn their neighbours into their own subscribers, demanding that they pay the fees each time they provide them with electricity.
- *Corporatist logic*, which occurs between agents who protect each other and mutually help each other out.
- *Logic of survival*, which drives both the agents and the users: the former looking for informal extra income to make ends meet, whilst the latter must find a way of meeting their energy needs.
- *Logic of decentralized patrimonialism*, which incentivizes agents of different levels to systematically corrupt the public electricity service to the detriment of collective objectives. This transforms their functions and legal prerogatives into mechanisms of underground, individual revenue capture.

These logics of action are not exclusive in relation to the others – they can become entangled in the practices of one and the same actor and be activated differently depending on the circumstances.

Foundations of the acceptability of practical norms

The interactions between the SNEL agents and subscribers, as demonstrated in this study, are constructed within the shadows of the norms enacted by the company in the form of practical norms. The latter enjoy a certain acceptability in the eyes of the actors, and even the company itself. Through them "local authorities enter ... into complex negotiations and exchanges which moreover enable the norms to be adapted to the situation" (Bourdieu, 1990, p. 85). They are, in this respect, less the expression of a certain anomie or of a culture of the informal, than the result of adapting to the context in which they unfold. In our opinion, three factors may explain this acceptability, even if implicit, of the conduct of the agents and users.

First, these practical norms become legitimized owing to their practical character, offsetting the administrative burden which takes on another dimension in the public services of the DRC. They shorten and make more flexible the formal procedures which cost the users time, energy and money. The users seem to prefer them to the public norms, which render access to the public electricity service complex.

Second, the acceptability of the practical norms is also related to the failure of the SNEL, which does not meet the exceptions either of its own agents or those of its subscribers. Indeed, in lacking the means needed to carry out their duties, the SNEL places its agents in such a make-do-and-mend situation that they themselves have to find solutions to the problems inherent to their services. That is why agency heads are obliged to use temporary staff for certain daily tasks, given these practices are prohibited by the company. Likewise, in providing subscribers with electricity irregularly, the SNEL predisposes them to develop alternative electricity access mechanisms.

Third, and finally, practical norms become legitimized through their conformity with the social norms of solidarity, reciprocity and trust which create social ties (Ayimpam, 2014, pp. 245–8). Unlawful connections and transmissions of electric current between neighbourhoods, avenues, plots of land and households – whilst at a certain level integrating a market rationality – respond more to the imperative to fashion social ties and create a safety net in a society in crisis such as the DRC.

Electricity supply and joint regulation in Kinshasa

In view of the above, it appears that the field and distribution of electricity is a plural space in which there exists a plurality of toolkits guiding the conduct of the actors. It is thus presided over by a "joint regulation". Through it, the practical norms of the actors (agents and users) enter into negotiation with the state's control regulations in order to ensure a balance between the normative ideal and contextual contingencies.

Joint regulation, in the SNEL's local arenas, filters through the coexistence of public norms and practical norms, public logics and private logics, monopolistic modes and competitive modes, the ethics of public service and the ethics of survival.

Between legal oversight and autonomy

The effective delivery of electricity wavers between the professional norms enacted by the SNEL and those which result from the professional practices of the agents in their interactions with the users. The SNEL's norms prescribe the conduct of both the agents and the subscribers, in terms of connection, the payment of bills and the management of electricity provision equipment, whilst the agents and the users adjust or circumvent them through arrangements, negotiations, stratagems, schemes, manoeuvres, tactics and opportunism. This conduct on the part of the users hybridize with the SNEL's professional norms, and with the social norms which impose solidarity, reciprocity and trust. Finally, the local electricity distribution agencies present themselves as worlds in which official norms and practical norms are stacked on top of each other.

In that respect, the agents mobilize the company's formal regulations as bargaining chips in their negotiations with users, the same time taking into account the implicit regulations described above which render these negotiations possible. Consequently, the company's control regulation, rather than being coercive, appears adjustable depending on the contexts. The official norms, as one respondent pointed out, "are difficult for low-income workers". Their strict application would leave little opportunity for the households of the city of Kinshasa to gain access to electricity. That is why, in practice, they do not always assume a restrictive character, but serve as a framework for negotiations and arrangements between the agents and the users.

Between public and private

Another element which emerges from observing the real functioning of the SNEL is that the company assumes a double status: public and private. It is public because officially this company belongs to the Congolese state, which determines its status, endows it with resources – no matter how negligible they may be – and appoints its officials. Yet, it is also private insofar as the agents within the agencies exploit their statutory positions for personal gain, in accordance with norms they themselves establish.

In this implicit process of privatizing the SNEL's electricity network (Mpiana Tshitenge, 2015), the agents, as public actors, turn their bureaucratic positions into genuine production units of informal income. They privatize the powers and prerogatives attached to their functions of legal oversight to ensure their survival. Through negotiations and arrangements, they permit subscribers to continue to receive electricity and, for their part, pocket money for themselves and to the benefit of those who appoint them; to the detriment, naturally, of the company.

Between public service ethics and the ethics of survival

The interactions between the SNEL agents and the users, on closer inspection, show that their behaviour is torn between public service ethics based on the rational-legal mode, and the ethics of survival founded on pragmatism. They are torn between the obligation to observe the regulations of their company and ensuring their own survival. The practical norms analysed in this study thus enable them to resolve this dilemma. In their arrangements, both the agents and the users resort to the public norms of the company to settle the questions linked to their own survival. They "apply or have respected the regulation insofar as ... the interest of applying it or having it respected outweighs the interest of closing one's eyes or making an exception" (Bourdieu, 1990, p. 87), and "stop complying with it when they are affected by a change or a situation which does not permit all of them to adhere to the logic imposed by the state" (Malukisa Nkuku, 2017b, p. 55).

Thus inscribed in the local actors' logic of survival, the practical norms which encase these interactions guarantee the population access to electricity at lower costs and minimize the erosion of their meagre incomes by resorting to other energy sources in a context of "quasi-(de)electrification" (Trefon et al., 2011, p. 44). For the SNEL agents, they constitute a mechanism for harnessing income to supplement the meagre salaries paid by the company. In other words, the entanglement of public norms and practical regulations must not be seen simply as a culture of the illegal, but a real response to the failures of the SNEL and the precarity of the Kinshasa population, for which the public authorities do not provide satisfactory solutions.

Conclusions

The delivery of electricity in Kinshasa, as analysed in this study, brings to light the hybrid governance applicable to the ensemble of public services in the DRC. This governance wavers between legal oversight (in other words, the norms enacted by the SNEL), and the autonomy expressed by the implicit norms which result from the interactions between agents and users. It has been largely demonstrated in this study that these implicit norms highlight the self-regulating capacity of the actors in the local arenas of electricity distribution which are the SNEL agencies. But this power to produce norms finds itself framed by the public norms of the company, as well as the social norms of the social world, which are integrated into its dynamic. Finally, these SNEL agencies, as semi-autonomous spaces, become worlds of stacking up norms and practices which – whilst being marginal – enjoy a certain acceptability in the eyes of the actors who take account of their ability to meet expectations, to which the SNEL does not manage to offer credible and reassuring alternatives.

Without being specific to the SNEL, this mode of delivering the public electricity service borrows from the overall dynamic of the society which, owing to the failure of the state, becomes increasingly distant from public norms. Following Sylvie Ayimpam (2014), it is this dynamic which results in thousands of Kinshasa's residents being left to their own devices to live, integrating them into social networks which generate other forms of sociability. The practical norms analysed in this study cannot be reduced to dysfunction. In the context of the decay of its state and of its company, the SNEL, they enable the agents to make ends meet at the end of the month thanks to the extra income they procure, and enable users to gain access to electricity. They thus contribute to maintenance of electricity provision in Kinshasa.

Even though these alternative mechanisms contribute to the maintenance of electricity provision, it should be noted that this is done neither to the satisfaction of the subscribers nor to that of the company which supplies it – even less so to that of the Congolese state, the guarantor of collective wellbeing. Accusations are increasingly thrown on all sides, expressing the disenchantment between the company and its clientele, who are just waiting to make the divorce official. More and more, the subscribers are informing SNEL managers of their intention to disaffiliate from its network as soon as another service provider establishes itself in the DRC. This thus raises the question of the survival of the SNEL in this new competitive space opened up by the liberalization of the energy market, given the discredit that has turned it into the "national company, enemy of electricity". Will it not suffer the same fate as the Congolese Post and Telecommunication Office, which declined under the blows of private cellular telephony companies? Perhaps being exposed to competition will force the SNEL to improve its services, to rise up to meet the expectations of its clientele, and perhaps to stay operational.

Notes

1 We thank the Académie de recherche et d'enseignement supérieur de Belgique, which funded the study, and the researchers Eder Kitapandi, Franck Ngandu, Junior Kongolo, Génerose Meta, Alain Shemisi, Nene Ndogala, Joël Kabasele and Vicky Nkuasa for their participation in the various stages of research. The comparatist aims of the socio-anthropological approach have determined the choice of the five districts in order to grasp the effect of the difference in their standing on the heterogeneity of the practices, representations and logics in the interactions between the SNEL agents and the users as regards the provision of electricity. On this subject, it is necessary to point out that the districts of Kisenso, Masina and N'djili (in the section investigated) are self-build districts arising from the postcolonial breakdown of the state and its economy, whilst the Kasa-Vubu and Limete districts, in its residential area, are of colonial origin, benefiting from relatively suitable electrical installations.

2 The term "users" in the framework of this study designates both the subscribers as well as the free-riders who consume the electricity supplied by the SNEL, whereas the term "subscribers" is exclusively reserved for the people or households who are officially connected to the SNEL's distribution network.

3 Interview. Agent of a Kasa-Vubu agency. Kinshasa (August 2016).

4 Enquête collective rapide d'identification de conflits et des groupes stratégiques. For more information on the framework of data production, see Bierschenk & Olivier de Sardan, 1998; Olivier de Sardan, 2003.

5 By corporatist accountability, Blundo means the different

pressures placed on them by other work colleagues or the corporation who share their same activity space.

6 A common term for patrons or protectors.

References

Ayimpam, S. (2014) Économie de la débrouille à Kinshasa: *Informalité, commerce et réseaux sociaux.* Paris: Karthala.

Baaz M. E., Olsson, O. and Verweijen, J. (2018) Navigating "taxation" on the Congo River: The interplay of legitimation and officialisation. *Review of African Political Economy.* DOI: 10.1080/03056244.2018.1451317.

Bierschenk, T. and Olivier de Sardan, J.-P. (1998) ECRIS: Enquête collective rapide d'identification des conflits et des groupes stratégiques. In: Bierschenk, T. and Olivier de Sardan, J.-P (eds.) *Les pouvoirs au village: Le Benin rural entre démocratisation et décentralisation.* Paris: Karthala, pp. 253–72.

Blundo, G. (2012) Le roi n'est pas un parent: Les multiples redevabilités au sein de l'État postcolonial en Afrique. In: Haag, P. and Lémieux, C. (eds) *Faire des sciences sociales.* Paris: EHESS, pp. 59–86.

Bourdieu, P. (1990) Droit et passe-droit. *Actes de la recherche en sciences sociales.* 81-82: 86–96.

Bréchet, J.-P. and Schieb-Bienfait, N. (2009) Logique d'action et projet dans l'action collective: Réflexions théoriques comparés. LEMNA working paper 2009/15.

Cleaver, F. (2012) *Development through Bricolage: RethinkingInstitutions for Natural Resource Management.* New York, NY: Routledge.

De Herdt, T. and Poncelet, M. (2011) La reconstruction entre l'État et la société. In: De Herdt,

T. (ed.) À la recherche de l'État en R-D Congo. Acteurs et enjeux d'*une reconstruction post-conflit*. Paris: L'Harmattan, pp. 7–38.

De Herdt, T. and Olivier de Sardan, J.-P. (2015) Introduction: The game of the rules. In: De Herdt, T. and Olivier de Sardan, J.-P. (eds) *Real Governance and Pratical Norms in Sub-Saharan Africa: The Game of the Rules*. London: Routledge, pp. 1–16.

De Villers, G. (2002) Introduction. In: De Villers, G., Jewsiewicki, B. and Monnier, L. (eds) *Manières de vivre: Economie de la 'débrouille 'dans les villes du Congo/ Zaïre*. Tervuren/Paris: Institut Aficain-CEDAF/L'Harmattan, pp. 12–31.

Giddens, A. (1987) *La constitution de la société*. Paris: PUF.

Godelier M. (1966) *Rationalité et irrationalité en économie*. Paris: Maspero.

Kaufmann, J.-C. (1996) *L'entretien compréhensif*. Paris: Nathan.

Malukisa Nkuku, A. (2017a) Gouvernance hybride des parkings publics à Lubumbashi: Quand la fiscalité informelle supporte la fiscalité formelle. *Canadian Journal of African Studies/Revue canadienne des études africaines* 51 (2): 275–91.

Malukisa Nkuku, A. (2017b) La « gouvernance réelle » du transport en commun à Kinshasa, La prééminence des « normes pratiques » sur les normes officielles. PhD Dissertation: Institute of Development Policy and Management, University of Antwerp.

Médard, J.-F. (1990) Etat patrimonialisé. *Politique africaine* 39: 25–36.

Misser, F. (2015) Inga: Ambition nécessaire mais projet à mûrir. In: Marysse, S. and Omasombo Tshonda, J. (eds) *Conjonctures congolaises 87: Entre incertitudes politiques et transformation économique*. Paris: L'Harmattan, pp. 230–54.

Moore, S. F. (2000) Law and social change: The semi-autonomous social field as an appropriate subject of study. In: Moore, S. F. (ed.) *Law as Process: An Anthropological Approach*. 2nd ed. London: Routledge and Kegan Paul Books, pp. 54–81.

Mpiana Tshitenge, J.-P. (2015) Privatisation par le biais du réseau électrique de la SNEL dans la périphérie de la ville de Kinshasa. In: Bogaert, J. and Halleux, J.-M. (eds) *Territoires périurbains:* Développement, enjeux et perspectives dans les pays du sud. Gembloux: Presses agronomiques de Gembloux, pp. 205–19.

Olivier de Sardan, J.-P. (1995) *Anthropologie et développement: Essaie en socio-anthropologie du changement social*. Marseille/Paris: APAD/Karthala.

Olivier de Sardan, J.-P. (2003) *L'enquête socio-anthropologique de terrain: Synthèse méthodologique et recommandations à l'usage des étudiants*. Niamey: Lasdel.

Olivier de Sardan, J.-P. (2007) De la nouvelle anthropologie du développement à la socioanthropologie des espaces publics africains. *Revue Tiers Monde* 191 (3): 43–552.

Olivier de Sardan, J.-P. (2008) À la recherche des normes pratiques de la gouvernance réelle en Afrique. Afrique: Pouvoir et politique. Discussion Paper 5.

Olivier de Sardan, J.-P. (2011) Promouvoir la recherche face à la consultance: Autour de l'expérience du LASDEL (Niger-Benin). *Cahiers d'*études africaines 202-203: 511–28.

Olivier de Sardan J.-P. (2013) Les normes pratiques: Pluralisme et agencéité. Inverses [Online]. Available from: www.inverses. org/wp-content/uploads/2013/03/ OlivierDeSardan_Normes-pratiques-article-2.pdf [Accessed 23 November 2018].

Poncelet, M., André, G. and De
Herdt, T. (2010) La survie
de l'école congolaise (RDC):
Héritage colonial, hybridité et
resilience. *Autrepart* 54 (2): 23–41.
Reynaud, J.-D. (2003) Régulation
de contrôle, régulation autonome,
régulation conjointe. In: De
Terssac, G. (ed.) *La théorie de la
régulation sociale de Jean-Daniel
Reynaud.* Paris: La Découverte,
pp. 103–13.
SNEL General Managing Director
(GMD) (2014) Réponses du
Directeur General de la Société
Nationale d'Electricité aux
préoccupations soulevées par les
honorables députés nationaux
suite à la question orale avec débat
posée par l'honorable Clément
Kanku Bukasa. Available from:
www.snel.cd/dl/Reponses_DG_
Parlement.pdf [Accessed 17
November 2017].
Trefon, T., Hendriks, T., Kabuyaya,
N. and Ngoy, B. (2011)

L'économie politique de la
filière de bois à Kinshasa et à
Lubumbashi. In: De Herdt, T.
(ed.) À la recherche de l'État en
R-D *Congo: Acteurs et enjeux d'une
reconstruction post-conflit.* Paris:
L'Harmattan, pp. 39–71.
UNDP (United Nations
Development Programme)
(2013) République Démocratique
du Congo: Rapport National
« Energie durable pour tous à
l'horizon 2030 ». National plan
and strategy report.
Willame, J.-C. (1972) *Patrimonialism
and Political Change in the Congo.*
Stanford, CA: Stanford University
Press.
World Bank (2017) Project appraisal
document on a proposed grant
to the democratic republic of
congo for an electricity access
and services expansion project.
World Bank and International
Development Association. Report
no. Pad2055.

6
Police at Work in Bukavu: Negotiating Revenue-generation in Urban Pirate Markets

Michel Thill

Introduction[1]

A few years ago, at a very busy road-intersection in front of Nyawera market in central Bukavu, capital of South Kivu province in the Democratic Republic of the Congo (DRC), the Congolese police established a police post. Initially, it was a white tent, then, after that was blown away by a heavy storm in late 2016, it was replaced by a windowless, blue-iron shipping container, which in turn was substituted with a larger, solar-panel powered container in late 2017. The police container houses around a dozen police officers. Their main duty is to keep in check the sprawling pirate markets where the mamans *(market women) sell goods on the sides of the roads without formal permission. This is a task much easier said than done. Several times a day, the police move out of their post to chase away the* mamans. *The* mamans *tend to scatter in several directions, only to reclaim their place as soon as the police have withdrawn to their post. This back and forth may proceed calmly, almost like the performance of a ritual, or it can turn into an explosive spectacle, which leads to heated and occasionally violent confrontations that draw in dozens of bystanders and paralyse road traffic.* [2]

* * *

Following De Herdt's and Titeca's call to "zoom in on the practical dilemmas faced by public servants" (this volume), this chapter explores the everyday work of the *Police Nationale Congolaise* (PNC, Congolese National Police) through their practices and encounters with the public in Bukavu's markets, in order to explore what they can tell us about the functioning of public services in urban DRC.

I argue, first, that existing police practices aimed at generating revenue are a response to, and are shaped by, practical norms, which have emerged from, and thus reflect, the underlying and sometimes conflicting *raisons d'être* of the police institution. Second, while police officers have developed a diverse set of such revenue-generating practices, various state and non-state market animators fiercely negotiate and contest them on a daily basis. Their negotiated nature points towards their highly contextual and relational makeup, revealing the challenges of and limits to police work. Finally, an analysis of these encounters and negotiations also contributes to larger discussions on the production of statehood in post-conflict urban settings.

The chapter draws on a concept developed by Olivier de Sardan "that [is] likely to prove the most supple and empirically productive for approaching reality 'as it is'" (2008, p. 4), namely practical norms. As De Herdt and Olivier de Sardan (2015) highlight, in practice the actions of many state officials, including the police, are not solely guided by the many official, social and professional laws, codes, rules and regulations in place, but also by so-called practical norms, which are born out of a complex interplay between these various repertoires and local contextual exigencies. This chapter's analysis of police practices in and around market sites will draw on the exploratory concept of practical norms to help explain their negotiated production, as well as their ever-changing contextual and relational nature.

The chapter is divided into seven sections. The next section will situate the analysis in the existing academic literature. A third section gives an overview of the practical norms guiding the PNC. After contextualizing market sites in Bukavu in a fourth section, the following two offer case studies of how revenue-generating practices unfold and are fiercely negotiated on an everyday basis in such public spaces, shaping police-community relations and, ultimately, (ideas of) the state. A final section summarizes the key findings and presents concluding thoughts for further research on the state.

The chapter is part of fieldwork conducted in Bukavu between August and December 2016, and follow-up research in April and May 2017, during which a total of 111 interviews on police–community relations were conducted. It relies on two additional sources: general observations from when I lived opposite a city market in Bukavu, and a one-month ethnographic study of markets. This study produced around a dozen field reports and included semi-formal individual and group interviews with 22 market actors and informants, including salespersons, trade union associates, administrative authorities, police officers and journalists.

The literature on public services, real governance and practical norms

Over the last twenty years, driven by the difficulties of studying (African) states, scholarship has begun to look more closely at the production of statehood and public authority, and their meaning in conflict-affected regions (Abrams, 1977; Lund, 2007; Mitchell, 1991). This work posits that, in order to gain a better understanding of statehood in countries such as the Congo, the salient question to ask is not how a state should govern, but how supposedly weak or failed states do, in fact, govern. This research has shown that order and public authority are fluid notions, arising from a variety of sources and are constantly negotiated between state and non-state actors (Bierschenk, 2010; Hansen & Stepputat, 2001). Various concepts have been proposed to capture and make sense of this process, including "twilight institutions" (Lund, 2007), "governance without government" (Raeymaekers, Menkhaus & Vlassenroot, 2008), "hybrid political orders" (Boege, Brown, Clements & Nolan, 2008), "states at work" (Bierschenk, 2010) and "negotiating statehood" (Hagmann & Péclard, 2011).

In order to investigate these processes of state-making and unmaking, this research calls for an empirical enquiry into what Olivier de Sardan (2008) has called "real governance", in order "to uncover the concrete interactions and practices that produce public authority" (Hoffmann & Kirk, 2013, p. 36). Public services such as education, health, security and justice have become prime fields of investigation for this bottom-up, empirical research, which shows the often glaring disparity between what is codified and what is implemented, between official norms and actual practice, or practical norms (Olivier de Sardan, 2008). Instead of focusing on what ought to be or on what is not, this concept is born out of a desire to better understand how public services are actually governed on a daily basis, and what everyday micro-level practices of various public service providers look like. Without such an understanding of the actual rules governing a given public service, effective "promotion of institutional change" (De Herdt & Titeca, this volume) will remain elusive.

One key result emerging out of this empirical research is that, while certainly not unique to the African continent, "the characteristic feature of African bureaucracies is their enormous heterogeneity". Their fragmented appearance as "never-finishing building sites" (Bierschenk, 2010, p. 11) reflects the fact that plurality in actors as well as norms abounds in such sectors. Simone (2005, p. 3), for example, mentions that an estimated 75% of all basic needs in urban Africa are supplied informally. Titeca and De Herdt (2011) showcase such dynamics in the education sector in the DRC, whose formal characteristic of being a public service provided by the state is largely kept up through parents' monetary contributions. Moreover, such "motivation fees" (*frais de motivation*), amongst other fees, have turned schools into valuable sources of revenue generation for the state administration: "Whereas in normal times schools were subsidized by the state, this flow of finance has been largely reversed as schools have been turned into what one could call points of taxation" (De Herdt & Titeca, 2016, p. 475). In the security and justice sector, Baker (2010, p. 597) writes that an estimated 80–90% of the people in the so-called "Global South" live in a context in which they depend on non-state providers of such services. The abundance of actors involved in security is thus a key feature of this sector. And so are these actors' practices. In the DRC, recent research has highlighted taxation as a key instrument through which armed actors not only aim to generate revenue, but also try to govern (Hoffmann & Verweijen, 2018; Hoffmann & Vlassenroot, 2014; Hoffmann, Vlassenroot & Marchais, 2016; Sánchez de la Sierra, 2015; Schouten, 2016; Titeca, 2011).

Plurality also characterizes bureaucracies' normative landscape. In so-called fragile states, there is no lack of regulation, but, if anything, an over-abundance of rules and norms. Official, social and practical norms exist side-by-side, forcing public servants to carefully navigate and negotiate these tension-ripe arenas. Some norms can dominate over others, obfuscating what is legal, what is legitimate, and what is not. Illegal trade and smuggling across the north-western borders of Uganda, for example, is perceived as a licit and legitimate business not only by traders, but also by border communities. This trade has thus become a widely accepted practical norm, whereas the state's official norms and its tax claims on cross-border trade are perceived as illegitimate (De Herdt & Titeca, 2010).

Non-codified norms such as social and practical ones are not only produced outside of the state bureaucracy. "Instead, the informal norms are produced, in part at least, within the apparatuses themselves" (Bierschenk, 2010, p. 15), showing that official and practical norms can influence each other and be deeply intertwined (De Herdt & Titeca, this volume). Again, the DRC's education sector is a prime example. While the existence of negotiated parents' fees reflects the lack of state funding, these same fees also throw a lifeline to employees of the education sector, who are thus able to uphold their professional norms and continue work as public administrators. Moreover, teachers' and school managers' bending of the official rules allows them to "govern with empty pockets", and ultimately serve to reproduce state authority, if not always its legitimacy (De Herdt & Titeca, 2016).

In the DRC, Baaz, Olsson and Verweijen's (2018) research on taxation practices by state authorities on the Congo river emphasizes that traders active on the river assess the legitimacy of the wide range of taxes raised by a multitude of state actors according to their degree of "officialisation". Even illegal taxes can be perceived as legitimate depending on who raises them, in what manner, for what purpose, and with what and for whose benefit. That such revenue-generating strategies by state actors are officially illegal is thus of little relevance in practice. Indeed, as Verweijen writes, the payable interventions of the Congolese army in civilian affairs often occurs as a response to popular demand and thus "may have some – albeit tenuous – legitimacy" (2013, p. 69). While some civilians do perceive some such interventions as illegitimate, Baaz and Verweijen (2014) argue that the army's practice of arbitrating civilian disputes has become normalized as a result of its continued occurrence in the militarized context of the eastern DRC. In the case of the Congolese traffic police, for example, drivers know what amount of *massage* ("massage", i.e. sum of money) to pay to whom at which road intersection (Baaz & Olsson, 2011; Sánchez de la Sierra & Titeca, forthcoming). Other such fees, however, are negotiated on an everyday basis. The nature and result of these negotiations have a direct impact on the degree of their perceived legitimacy, which can thus change over time and, indeed, from one day to the next (Baaz, Verweijen & Olsson, 2018; Titeca & De Herdt, 2010).

Despite a recent upsurge in research on African police services (Beek et al., 2017), scholarly work on the micro-practices of public and security services in the DRC's urban society remains in its infancy. Notable exceptions are the Congolese traffic police (Baaz & Olsson, 2011; Malukisa Nkuku, 2017; Sánchez de la Sierra & Titeca, forthcoming) and an anti-gang unit in Kinshasa (Thurman, 2017). But these articles are limited to special police units, with specific tasks, and thus do not necessarily encompass the work of the Congolese police as a whole. The police institution is a worthwhile research subject for exploring real governance. It sits at the intersection between state and society, and is thus "intimately concerned with the day-to-day operation of state power and constantly encountering the public" (Hills, 2000, p. 2). In Bukavu, as shown in the introductory depiction, daily negotiations between the police and urban dwellers are all too visible, most commonly around one or another form of revenue-generating practice. Such encounters can therefore serve as windows into daily experiences of police at work. In what follows, this chapter will explore the police's negotiated and contested attempts to generate revenue in a specific public space: urban (pirate) markets. Before delving into concrete examples, however, it is important to first explain why the police engage in revenue-generation in the first place.

Practical norms and revenue-generating practices within the PNC

From the days of the Congo Free State, state security forces have had a troubled relationship with the Congo's population, marked by violent oppression, abuse and theft.[3] The roots of this difficult relationship are first and foremost to be found in the oppressive nature of government from King Léopold II to Mobutu (Callaghy, 1984; Kakudji Mbavu, 2001; Schatzberg, 1988; Young & Turner, 1985). A second reason lies in the impact of the Congo's socio-economic decline on the functioning of state institutions since the mid-1970s. This acute downward spiral ultimately led to the rise of a large informal economy, to Mobutu calling on his security forces to live off the population and to the mantra of Article 15: *débrouillez-vous* ("fend for yourselves") (Baaz & Olsson, 2011; MacGaffey, 1991; Raeymaekers, 2007). And yet, public services, including the police, continue to function. Trefon (2009) notes that in fragile states marked by widespread scarcity, public services persist for three reasons. First, they are instrumentalized by the political elite for its own survival and enrichment; second, they ensure the survival of public administrators themselves; and, third, there remains a high popular demand for their services. This is no different for the PNC, where all three of these reasons have led to the emergence of a practical norm at the heart of which lies the need for revenue-generation. This norm, made up and simultaneously produced by a set of diverse revenue-generating practices, has in turn come to shape actual police work.

Instrumentalization has given birth to a practice commonly known as *rapportage* ("reporting").[4] It requires police officers to pay a certain amount of money to their superiors, usually on a weekly basis, who in turn pass it up the hierarchy. A police officer working for the *Inspection Générale Provinciale* (IG, Provincial General Inspection) – the body in charge of ensuring that the police force adheres to their professional norms – explained *rapportage* as follows: "The commander expects a report. Now this report happens to be money. Where do they [the policemen and women] find it? By harassing." For a police officer, he said, "working is harassing".[5] Those who do not comply with this principle can be rotated to less lucrative posts, thrown into jail and/or dismissed from service.

While *rapportage* is less practiced by the police deployed across police stations, for specialized police units, whose work consists of regulating particularly lucrative spaces – be this the *Police de Circulation Routière* (PCR, traffic police), the *Police des Frontières* (border police), the *Police des Mines* (mining police) or the *Groupe Mobile d'Intervention* (GMI, Mobile Intervention Group) – it has become the dominant practical norm, overriding any others. Exposed to its pressures, these units have also become the most known for engaging in violent revenue-generating mechanisms. The population naturally condemns these practices, which lay heavily on them as their major victims,[6] and so do most police officers. Indeed, the aforementioned police inspector regularly receives written complaints from rank-and-file policepersons objecting to the practical norm.[7] Regardless of their disapproval, however, the hierarchical nature of the police, the severe punishment against non-compliance of orders, and the personal search for means to make a living gives police officers in these units little room for manoeuvre. As De Herdt and Olivier de Sardan point out:

> Many practices are *not* consensual; they often evoke pragmatic logics and routines that would question, contest or redefine those [other, such as professional] constitutive rules. Moreover, sometimes, practices do not so much play with or around the rules of the game but play with or around (or against) their *enforcement*. (2015, p. 3, emphasis in original)

Precise *rapportage* figures are hard to come by. Numbers largely remain estimates based on personal accounts, which vary from study to study.[8] During their 2010/11 research, Baaz and Olsson (2011, pp. 228–9) reported such fees as ranging between $20 and $50 per traffic police post per day in Bukavu, and a total of between $500 and $800 moving up the ranks on a daily basis. A local NGO found in 2013 that police officers at the Nyawera and Beach Muhanzi police posts in Bukavu, both relevant to this chapter's research sites, each have to "report" $100 per week (SAJECEK/Forces Vivces, 2013). A police officer interviewed in 2016 mentioned that a traffic policeman stationed at a busy road-intersection in Bukavu has to pay $120 per week and claimed that, in PNC circles, it was rumoured that a former provincial police commissioner made around $30,000 each month, much of which originating from the *rapportage* system. Local administrators claimed that *rapportage* across Bukavu generates $1,500 per day, which adds up to around $45,000 per month. A civil society activist said that a traffic police officer paid $10 per day to his superior of which the officer could keep $3.[9] This latter case raises the question of the distribution of *rapportage* between hierarchy and street-level police. Baaz and Olsson (2011) indicate that anything collected above a pre-agreed sum can be retained by the police officer himself. The extra income through *rapportage* may thus considerably inflate a regular police officer's monthly salary, which stands at between $60 and $100.

Moving on, personal and institutional survival has led to the development of often less violent and more negotiated revenue-generating mechanisms. At police stations, for example, police regularly demand fees for civilians to open, close or withdraw a case. They charge for writing a report and demand subsidies for pre-paid telephone units, transport and basic office stationery such as paper and pens. While negotiable, most civilians have nevertheless come to grudgingly accept, and expect, this practice when entering a police station.[10] Another, non-violent way for any police officer to make ends meet is to solicit financial help from their social network, including colleagues, family and friends, or to set up mutual solidarity funds known as *Likilimba*. These funds unite groups of police officers, who each contribute a part of their monthly salary. Each month, on a rotational basis, the fund is allocated to one of the group's members, allowing the recipient to afford larger one-off expenses such as school tuition fees, large amounts of staple food such as cassava or rice, or modest investments in side-businesses (Njangala, Thill & Musamba, 2018; Thill, Musamba & Njangala, 2017; Thill, Njangala & Musamba, 2018).

Finally, popular demand for police services has led to direct financing from the population at large. Police officers thus mentioned that civilians sometimes voluntarily give financial encouragement to the police when they think they have done a good job, in order to support them in their difficult socio-economic position. Analysing the education sector, De Herdt and Titeca (2016) argue that the public service is not merely kept up because there is a popular demand for it, but also because it provides an opportunity for end-users to rene-gotiate their terms of inclusion in the sector's regulatory framework, thus simultaneously accepting and reproducing the authority of the state as a regulator. At the same time, teachers bend the "rules of the game" in order to increase their meagre salaries. Similar dynamics can be observed in the case of the police institution: civilians, for example, pay senior police officers to settle private matters such as land disputes or debts in their favour, a practice commonly known as *traffic d'influence* ("influence peddling"), thus accepting the police's state authority and legitimizing its role in civilian disputes, but making it work to their advantage (Baaz & Verweijen, 2014; Titeca, 2016; Verweijen, 2013).

In sum, the reasons for the persistence of the police service have given rise to a practical norm occupied with the imperative of reve-nue-generation. Made up of a set of diverse revenue-generating practices, it has come to reshape police work. The diversity of these practices, ranging from violent harassment and charging for police services via reliance on social networks and (invited) interference in civilian affairs to voluntary contributions, reflect their highly contex-tual and relational nature. Ultimately, these micro-level practices play an important part in the reproduction of the state and state-hood in the DRC. This can best be captured through encounters between police and community, during which they are negotiated and contested. Urban markets are a prime setting of such encounters.

The micro-cosmoi of urban markets

If the school is the "taxation point" for the education sector, at which teachers and school managers ask for fees to provide a service, there are several such "taxation points" for the police service: the police station, the road intersection, border posts, ports and markets. Markets are spaces crucial for trade, social interaction and public life in any village, town or city in the DRC. As such, they can provide a glimpse into the social order of a given area. Catherine Newbury's research in South Kivu in the 1980s showed what taxation practices at a market in Buloho can tell us about state–society relations, in this case the frustrations of market women who felt exploited by local government officials and their excessive taxes (1984, pp. 40–41). More recent research on markets in rural areas in the DRC similarly shows how such public spaces, due to their potential to yield revenue for a variety of actors, can reflect the local power balance and provide hints towards the larger governance structures prevailing in a given area. In rural areas, the army, armed groups and customary chiefs are important players in extracting cash and in-kind resources from such markets (Hoffmann, Vlassenroot, & Marchais, 2016; Verweijen, 2015). While the above examples are set in rural areas, markets can be considered as windows into social order in urban areas as well. In an urban context characterized by high unemployment, inequality and widespread poverty, a wide variety of people flock to markets each and every day, hoping to make a living in their hustle and bustle. Urban markets thus provide economic opportunities to hundreds of families and thousands of people. Its central animators are the *mamans du marché* ("market women"), who are the engines of the socio-economic space around which public life at markets unfolds.[11] Amongst the *mamans*, there are those who sell in formal markets – often in open, roofed structures – and those who sell on so-called *marchés pirates* ("pirate markets"). The latter are informal market sites at which *mamans* sell goods without an official licence, commonly along roads leading to the main market. The local specificity of each market means that the social make-up of its actors differs from market to market. The actors' diversity and plurality leads to a wide range of interactions and negotiations amongst and between them, making each market a truly unique socio-economic micro-cosmos.

The geographical focus of this chapter largely lies on three market sites in Bukavu: the Nyawera market located in the neighbourhood (*quartier*, lower administrative entity) of Ndendre, part of the district (*commune*, higher administrative entity) of Ibanda; and Beach Muhanzi and Brasserie markets, both situated on the shores of Lake Kivu, the former in the neighbourhood of Nkafu, district of Kadutu, the latter in the neighbourhood of Cikonyi, district of Bagira. These three markets are particularly busy due to their location on important roads and their proximity to residential areas. Besides the police, they also feature an interesting mix of other coercive actors such as marines, intelligence agents and street kids. Moreover, at all three, pirate markets flourish. The goods of the *mamans* selling here, which are laid out on the ground, reduce the space available to the countless pedestrians and vehicles, causing endless altercations between and amongst these groups as well as with the police. Because these informal markets block traffic, cause risks of a hygienic nature and escape formal taxation by municipal authorities, Bukavu's mayor banned them from operating in 2012, and again in 2014 (DRC, 2012, 2014).[12] The 2014 ban threatened that all goods sold on pirate markets were to be confiscated and incinerated by the PNC.

As "every inch of town is negotiable", this has opened up a fierce negotiation over space, in which the police find themselves at the frontline. The result is "a somewhat awkward but fruitful complicity between the governing and the governed, each party simultaneously trying to enlarge its sphere of influence and power" (Geenen, 2009, p. 347). The following two sections aim to capture some of these moments of negotiation between the PNC and the *mamans*.

Negotiating revenue-generating practices: From violence to collaboration

Some of the police officers deployed in the police containers present at Nyawera and Brasserie are part of the GMI, a unit well known for its aggressive manner of operation. Their popular nickname, *Ebola*, gives away their reputation. In moments when the police move out, *Hange na Ebola* ("Watch out for the police") can be heard as *mamans* announce their imminent arrival. The *mamans*, whose livelihoods depend on selling goods at these pirate markets, return after each chase. As the police have no means of effectively and permanently keeping away the *mamans* occupying the public space in question – and thus failing official and professional norms – they seek alternative arrangements, which also allow them to satisfy their own revenue-generating needs and obligations. These interactions, then, provide a useful insight into how practical norms and their associated practices unfold on an everyday basis.

The most established revenue-generating practice observable across Bukavu's pirate markets consists of the police demanding a daily tax of the *mamans*, commonly 200 Congolese francs (equalling the district's tax paid by *mamans* in official markets), for their right to remain in the contested space and sell their goods in peace. Such a regular tax is frequently the result of a negotiated, and sometimes violent, process. In late October 2016, for example, a GMI unit was deployed at Brasserie with the explicit task of evacuating the pirate markets, which obstruct traffic on the principal road. In the first days, this unit harassed and coerced the *mamans*, which led to much resistance on their part. After a while, however, both parties established a modus operandi: each *maman* paid 200 francs a day in exchange for selling her goods in peace. Those who did not pay were harassed and left unprotected from attacks and theft by the many *maibobos* ("street kids") present at the market, particularly in the late hours of the day.[13] Similarly, at Beach Muhanzi, police try to uphold and reinforce this practical norm with violence. In an instance in which a *maman* was not able to pay the agreed daily tax of 200 francs, the police patrol crushed her tomatoes, causing the *maman* to complain that: "Each day, you come and ask us to pay a tax and we pay. Today, you come and trample our vegetables. Where will we find the money to continue paying you?"[14] Those police officers who resist this revenue-generating practice are side-lined. At Brasserie, a local police commander, for example, attempted to adhere by his professional norms and put an end to these taxes. Before long, however, he was rotated out of his position, showing the power of practical norms once they gain a foothold in a public service and become institutionalized.[15]

By definition, however, practical norms are context-dependent and can therefore change. At Nyawera, a market in which many of the *mamans* are soldiers' wives, known to be fierce and less intimidated by the police, this practice of routine payments to the police seems less common. When a new police unit set up in the Nyawera police post in early November 2016, it tried to impose a regular tax of 200 francs a day. After initial reluctance by the *mamans*, they eventually acquiesced to the fee. Despite this negotiated agreement, however, the police came to chase them away. This violation of the unwritten contract caused a public confrontation between *mamans* and police on a very busy street-intersection, drawing in dozens of bystanders, which brought much of the circulation at Nyawera to a halt. In this confrontation, at least a dozen fish were crushed by the police, who had to eventually call in reinforcements from the provincial police headquarter. Here, then, violence resulted from the police not following their own negotiated practice, which, ultimately, left no winners – the police did not generate any revenue, and the *mamans* lost some of their goods.

The practice of imposing taxes coexists with other police mechanisms of revenue-generation. A more violent and direct practice common across all three observed markets is confiscation. Confiscated goods are taken to the police post and either appropriated by the police officers or sold back to the *mamans* for an inflated, if negotiable, fee. In one case, the wife of a police officer at Nyawera told a journalist that she had cooked fish every day for a whole month, which her husband had confiscated from the market.[16] At the pirate markets of Beach Muhanzi, a *maman* complained that the police confiscated 10 kg of her flour because she was not able to pay the 200 francs tax the previous day. To recover her goods, she would have had to pay 5,000 francs to the police, more than a *maman* can hope to earn in a day.

Another practice consists of police officers requesting in-kind contributions from the *mamans* to support their work and livelihood. As such, this practice can be compared to the *efforts de guerre* ("war effort") contributions solicited by the army or armed groups in rural areas (Verweijen, 2013, 2015). If *mamans* refuse to make such a contribution, police officers may well revert to more violent mechanisms such as the above-described practice of confiscation.

The multitude of actors present at markets provides ample opportunities to become collaborative and commission help in the search for revenue. At Nyawera, the police have contracted support in chasing the *mamans* from a group of civilians, so called *Barasta*,[17] who spend their time at the market helping to carry heavy loads of goods for a small fee. In general, the *Barasta* are less violent in their methods than the police, but nevertheless do chase the *mamans* away on a regular basis. At the same market, some police elements also collaborate with an agent working for the *Agence Nationale de Renseignement* (ANR, National Intelligence Agency). This woman is present at the market to spot fraudulent or stolen goods being sold, an activity which itself lies outside ANR professional norms. If she does identify such merchandise and encounters resistance by their owners, she calls the police to help her out. In such cases, the police elements and ANR agent split the confiscated goods and/or the fines to be paid by the owner.[18] At Beach Muhanzi, some police elements occasionally work directly with *maibobos*. One strategy is for the latter to accuse market visitors of theft or to involve them into brawls. Once the police show up, the victims of these cons are threatened with arrest and detention, which can be avoided by paying a fine on the spot.[19] Such cooperation practices, informally known as *coop*, the French abbreviation for cooperation, further underline the contextual and relational nature of revenue-generating practices, while also blurring the lines of state and non-state policing work by drawing in non-state actors.

In sum, the diverse revenue-generating practices deployed by the police reflect their struggle to bridge often contradicting practical, official and professional norms: to follow the demands of *rapportage* (practical norm), to uphold the mayor's decrees on pirate markets (official and professional norms), and to ensure their own survival. That they are negotiated between, and indeed produced by, different state and non-state actors, shows their fluctuating and volatile nature, and explains to some extent why public services may appear as "never-finishing building sites" (Bierschenk, 2010, p. 11). In this vein, the next section will look more closely at existing rivalries between the police and the multitude of other state and non-state actors at markets.

Facing competition: The police and their rivals in revenue-generation

To further complicate the picture, there are actors directly competing with the police and their allies in the generation of revenue at market places. At Beach Muhanzi and Brasserie, the police have to compete with *maibobos* and *marins* ("marines" who are part of the naval force), who have posts on the shores of Lake Kivu, close to both markets. Both groups engage in similar, if often more violent, revenue-generating practices as the police themselves, thus competing over the same resources. For the police to go about their work in such a contentious environment therefore becomes much more challenging.

Several *maibobos* are active at Beach Muhanzi and Brasserie. Some *maibobos* groups are organized in gangs and can be rather violent. Indeed, the police tend to have difficulties managing them. At Bukavu's central market, called Nyamugo, for example, two *mamans* said that the police are careful of tackling the *maibobos* too brazenly "because they are afraid of the many *maibobos* there" who may overwhelm them.[20] At Beach Muhanzi, despite the occasional *coop*, the situation is similar. One *maman* complained that "[the police] is powerless against them [the *maibobos*]. They are too many, muscular and dangerous".[21] Indeed, a police officer described Beach Muhanzi as "a focal point for bandits"[22] and an observer commented that "from 6:30pm onwards, it is them [the *maibobos*] who make the law".[23]

The *maibobos* harass the *mamans* on a daily basis, from stealing their goods or belongings to physical abuse. One *maibobo* practice, common across Bukavu markets, is a phenomenon called *lance-pierre* ("stone throwing") – some *maibobos* throw small stones from a safe distance into the market areas until the *mamans* run for cover. Once the *mamans* have fled, they steal their unguarded goods. More specific to Beach Muhanzi is another strategy. On rainy days, the ground and unpaved roads leading to the market turn into mud, making access difficult. Well knowing that the rain will slow down police interventions, the street kids consequently increase their activities.[24]

The most infamous *maibobos* gangs at Beach Muhanzi have become so powerful that they use similar revenue-generating practices than the police and establish mafia-like protection rackets in return for freedom from harassment. The tax amounts vary widely, some *mamans* saying that they are forced to pay 200–500 francs a day, others claiming that the *maibobos* collect 200 francs each week. This variance points to the aggressiveness of the street kids. As one *maman* put it: "If they [the *maibobos*] see that we have more [to give], they ask for more".[25] The sheer numbers of street kids and their readiness to use violence coupled with the limited effectiveness of the police considerably limits the PNC's competitiveness in the hunt for resources on Beach Muhanzi's pirate markets.

At the main market at Beach Muhanzi, it is the marines who seem to be the dominant actor in revenue-generating practices. One *maman* stated that "the marines are active on the shores of the lake, the police only on the road".[26] Another said that "when the police intervene at the shores of the lake or at the port [just next to the market], the marines pretend to leave the affair to them, but they are not happy". This points to the competitive nature of police–marine relations, each trying to carve out their own space to generate revenue. Furthermore, similar to some elements of the police, the marines use the *maibobos* to engage in *coop*. The street kids steal food or other goods on the marines' behalf for them to then sell back to the *mamans*. One *maman* said that the marines have thus established their own indirect taxation system, in which the street kids collect in-kind or cash taxes from the *mamans*, part of which they hand over to the marines each evening.[27]

At Beach Muhanzi and Brasserie, then, the presence of other coercive actors engaging in similar revenue-generating practices complicates the police's own work. The *mamans*, on the other hand, find themselves facing street kids little inclined to negotiate and ready to use violence to get their way. This limits the *mamans'* ability to resist and negotiate, and in turn increases their vulnerability. That the police are struggling to impose their own order is reflected in their lack of authority at Beach Muhanzi. Here, several *mamans* said that they rarely call on the police to intervene in cases of harassment or theft. According to them, the police are not reliable, their post too remote, and they anyway release the street kids only for the latter to return and take revenge. As an alternative, the market committee has enrolled its own policing unit, largely made up of youngsters who help keep away the *maibobos*. They, however, also ask the *maman*s for a daily tax of 200 francs.[28] At Beach Muhanzi and Brasserie, then, marines and street kids undermine the police's practices and authority, and increase uncertainty around the *mamans'* work place. Cynically, the *mamans* may be better off at Nyawera after all, where the police hold the upper hand in revenue-generating practices, thus guaranteeing a modicum of certainty and stability.

Conclusion

This chapter explored everyday police work in Bukavu's markets and pirate markets in order to shed light on the real governance of the police institution. It argued that the police are governed by practical norms, whose purpose is to generate revenue, and which have in turn come to shape police action. Revenue-generating police practices, however, are the subject of fierce and sometimes violent negotiations and contestations amongst the many state and non-state market animators. Their negotiability and diversity reflects their highly contextual and relational nature, while also showcasing the limits of police authority in a Congolese city.

Practical norms allow us to showcase everyday state practices and thus capture moments of statehood. In the DRC – a country in a constant state of uncertainty – negotiation is central to, and indeed possibly the purpose of, political life (Englebert & Tull, 2013). The revenue-generating practices underlying police–community encounters, which give all market animators a role to play in "doing the state" (Migdal & Schlichte, 2005, p. 14–15), are similarly negotiated, shaping how the Congolese state is perceived and imagined. In sum, if the state is both a set of practices and an idea, then the negotiated nature of revenue-generating practices very much reflects the image of the "negotiated state", which these practices help produce – forever pluralist, fluid and changing (Hagman & Péclard, 2011).

The chapter also hinted at the fact that, where the police can more or less impose and enforce their own practical norms, relative certainty in relations between them and the *mamans* ensues. Where the police compete with other coercive actors over revenue-generation, practices may turn more violent and produce more uncertainty. In the current renaissance of the "local turn" in international relations and peacebuilding studies (Autesserre, 2010; Leonardsson & Rudd, 2015; MacGinty & Richmond, 2013), this should give us pause for thought. By definition, state actors are invested in the "language of stateness" (Hansen & Stepputat, 2001), which carries with it a degree of authority lacking in other non-state groups, even as they simulate this language with varying degrees of success (Hoffman & Verweijen, 2018). Dismissing the value of a state police service due to its supposedly harmful practical norms neglects appreciating "security governance systematically as a social space within which actors vie to establish authority over resources and people. This social space is not defined by scale (i.e. the local vs. non-local), but by social relations between different actors and networks connecting them"

(Hoffmann, Vlassenroot & Büscher, 2018, p. 12). Disregarding the contextual and relational character of police work in fragile states may therefore risk giving too much attention to non-state actors, regardless of their actual legitimacy (since being local is no substitute for legitimacy) or ambitions for the general welfare of people (Meagher, 2012). While this is a call for caution in formulating policy considerations, it should simultaneously be understood as an encouragement to conduct more and much-needed research on the actual everyday functioning of the police and other public services in fragile and conflict-affected states.

Notes

1 The author would like to thank Gentil Kulimushi and Julien Namegabe, without whose local knowledge of and research assistance in Bukavu markets, this chapter would not have been possible. Parts of this paper were presented at a UCB conference in Bukavu on 8 December 2016, and the ISA conference in Baltimore on 23 February 2017, and benefited from constructive feedback by Tom De Herdt and Kristof Titeca, as well as Pierre Englebert and Oliver Jütersonke, to whom the author would like to express his gratitude. This chapter is part of a PhD project supported by Luxembourg's National Research Fund from 2015 to 2018. The project has received funding from the The Hague-based Knowledge Platform Security and Rule of Law (KPSRL) and the New York-based Social Science Research Council (SSRC). For the exclusion of any doubt, it shall be noted that the author is solely responsible for this chapter, its arguments and flaws.

2 Authors own words, following: Interview. Police officer. Mukukwe, Ndendere (9 November 2016); Interview. Police officer. Nyawera, Ndendere (9 November 2016). All interviews were held in French and translated into English by the author.

3 For overviews of colonial and post-independence policing, see Henriet, 2017; Lauro, 2011, 2016; Nlandu Mayamba, 2012.

4 While this seems to be the most common name used for this system in Bukavu, other names do exist as well (See for example Baaz & Olsson, 2011, p. 228).

5 Interview. Police inspector. La Botte, Ndendere. (29 November 2016).

6 There are regular interventions about the practice on local radio stations and in newspapers and civil society briefings (See for example Le Souverain Libre, 2016; Kalondji, 2015).

7 Interview. Police inspector. La Botte, Ndendere (29 November 2016).

8 A recent multi-year study on rapportage in the Kinshasa traffic police, conducted by Kristof Titeca, Albert Malukisa Nkuku and Raul Sánchez de la Sierra, aims to quantify such figures. Publications are forthcoming.

9 Interview. Police officer. Place du 24, Ndendere (3 December 2016); Interviews. Members of civil society and local administration. Nyakavogo and Ndendere (14 & 18 October 2016).

10 Interview. City administrators. Cimpunda (6 October 2016); Interview. Police officer. Kasali. (11 October 2016); Interview. Police officer (11 May 2017); Fieldwork observations during

internship at police station. Panzi (May 2017).

[11] While there are also men selling at markets, by far the majority of salespersons in Bukavu are women. This is likely related to historical patterns of division of labour at the household level (See for example: Newbury, 1984, pp. 38–39).

[12] Interview. Former member of Urban Security Council. Nyawera, Ndendere (12 November 2016). See also Kalondji (2015) and Le Souverain Libre (2016).

[13] Report from research assistant (1 November 2016).

[14] Report from research assistant (16 November 2016).

[15] Report from research assistant (13 May 2017).

[16] Interview. Maman. Nyawera, Ndendere (24 November 2016); Interview. Journalist. Hippodrôme, Ndendere (16 November 2016).

[17] Commonly referred to as *Barastas* because some of them have a Rasta haircut, they wear orange or yellow vests on usually blue clothes, and sit in front of the main market. They used to be a handy workforce for the mayor, but have become idle and now seek other preoccupations to make a living. Interview. Two Barastas. Nyawera, Ndendere (23 November 2016); Interview. Police officer. Mukukwe, Ndendere (9 November 2017). The *Barasta* are also said to function as the eyes and ears of the police, for example by informing them of the presence of thieves in the area.

[18] Reports from research assistants (8 & 23 November 2016).

[19] Interviews. Various market animators. Beach Muhanzi, Nkafu (22 November 2016).

[20] Interview. Mamans. Beach Muhanzi, Nkafu (22 November 2016).

[21] Interview. Mamans. Beach Muhanzi, Nkafu (22 November 2016).

[22] Interview. Police officer. Beach Muhanzi, Nkafu (11 November 2016).

[23] Report from research assistant (6 November 2016).

[24] Interview. Public administrators. Ciriri (19 October 2017); Interview. Two market trade union associates. Beach Muhanzi, Nkafu (22 November 2016).

[25] Interview. Mamans. Beach Muhanzi, Nkafu (22 November 2016).

[26] Ibid.

[27] Interview. Mamans. Beach Muhanzi, Nkafu (22 November 2016); Interview. Civil society activist. Ndendere. (13 May 2017).

[28] Interview. Mamans. Beach Muhanzi, Nkafu (22 November 2016); Interview. Two policing unit members. Beach Muhanzi, Nkafu. (22 November 2016).

References

Abrams, P. (1977) Notes on the difficulty of studying the state. *Journal of Historical Sociology* 1 (1): 58–89.

Autesserre, S. (2010) *The Trouble with the Congo: Local Violence and the Failure of International Peacebuilding*. Cambridge: Cambridge University Press.

Baaz, M. E. and Olsson, O. (2011) Feeding the horse: Unofficial economic activities within the police force in the Democratic Republic of Congo. *African Security* 4 (4): 223–41.

Baaz, M. E. and Verweijen, J. (2014) Arbiters with guns: The ambiguity of military involvement in civilian disputes in the DR Congo. *Third World Quarterly* 35 (5): 803–20.

Baaz, M. E., Verweijen, J. and Olsson, O. (2018) Navigating "taxation" on the Congo River: The interplay of legitimation and "officialisation". *Review of African Political Economy* 45 (156): 250–66.

Baker, B. (2010) Linking state and non-state security and justice.

Development Policy Review 28 (5): 597–616.

Beek, J., Göpfert, M., Owen, O. and Steinberg, J. (eds) (2017) *Police in Africa: The Street-Level View.* London: Hurst & Company.

Bierschenk, T. (2010) States at work in West Africa: Sedimentation, fragmentation and normative double-binds. University of Mainz, Department of Anthropology and African Studies. Working Paper 113.

Boege, V., Brown, A., Clements, K. and Nolan, A. (2008) On Hybrid Political Orders and Emerging States: State Formation in the Context of "Fragility". Berghof Research Center for Constructive Conflict Management. Berghof Handbook Dialogue 8.

Callaghy, T. M. (1984) *The State–Society Struggle: Zaire in Comparative Perspective.* New York, NY: Columbia University Press.

De Herdt, T. and Olivier de Sardan, J.-P. (2015) Introduction: The game of the rules. In: De Herdt, T. and Olivier de Sardan, J.-P. (eds) *Real Governance and Pratical Norms in Sub-Saharan Africa: The Game of the Rules.* London: Routledge, pp. 1–16.

De Herdt, T. and Titeca, K. (2016) Governance with empty pockets: The education sector in the Democratic Republic of Congo. *Development and Change* 47 (3): 472–94.

DRC (Democratic Republic of Congo) (2012) Arrêté 401/BUR/M.BKV 008/2012 portant interdiction des marchés pirates sur toute l'étendue de la ville de Bukavu (24 May).

DRC (Democratic Republic of Congo) (2014) Arrêté 401/BUR/M.BKV 006/2014 portant interdiction des marchés pirates dans la ville de Bukavu (29 May).

Englebert, P. and Tull, D. (2013) Conestation, négociation et résistance: L'Etat congolais au quotidien. *Politique africaine* 129 (1): 5–22.

Geenen, K. (2009) "Sleep occupies no space": The use of public space by street gangs in Kinshasa. *Africa* 79 (3): 347–68.

Hagmann, T. and Péclard, D. (2011) Negotiating statehood: Dynamics of power and domination in Africa. In: Hagmann, T. and Péclard, D. (eds) *Negotiating Statehood: Dynamics of Power and Domination in Africa.* Oxford: Wiley-Blackwell, pp. 1–23.

Hansen, T. B. and Stepputat, F. (eds) (2001) *States of Imagination: Ethnographic Explorations of the Postcolonial State.* Durham, NC: Duke University Press.

Henriet, B. (2017) Ordering the wetlands: Policing and legitimate violence in the Leverville Concession (Belgian Congo, 1911–1920). In: Blanchard, E., Bloembergen, M. and Lauro, A. (eds) *Policing in Colonial Empires: Cases, Connections, Boundaries (ca. 1850–1970).* Oxford: Peter Lang, pp. 41–61.

Hills, A. (2000) *Policing Africa: Internal Security and the Limits of Liberalization.* London: Lynne Rienner.

Hoffmann, K. and Kirk, T. (2013) Public authority and the provision of public goods in conflict-affected and transitioning regions. JSRP: Justice and Security Research Programme Working Paper 7.

Hoffmann, K. and Verweijen, J. (2018) Rebel rule: A governmentality perspective. *African Affairs* [online pre-print version]. Available from: doi.com/10.1093/afraf/ady039

Hoffmann, K. and Vlassenroot, K. (2014) Armed groups and the exercise of public authority: The cases of the Mayi-Mayi and Raya Mutomboki in Kalehe, South Kivu. *Peacebuilding* 2 (2): 202–20.

Hoffmann, K., Vlassenroot, K. and Büscher, K. (2018) Competition, patronage and fragmentation: The limits of bottom-up approaches to security governance in Ituri.

Stability: International Journal of Security & Development 7 (1): 1–17.

Hoffmann, K., Vlassenroot, K. and Marchais, G. (2016) Taxation, stateness and armed groups: Public authority and resource extraction in Eastern Congo. Development and Change 47 (6): 1434–56.

Kakudji Mbavu, E. (2001) La Police et le Maintien de l'Ordre Public Au Congo-Kinshasa (1965–1997). Master's Thesis. Ottawa: Ottawa University.

Kalondji, E. (2015) Des policiers brutalisent des vendeurs des « marchés pirates » [Web blog post]. Available from: speakjhr.com/2015/09/des-policiers-brutalisent-des-vendeurs-des-marches-pirates [Accessed on November 21, 2018].

Lauro, A. (2011) Maintenir l'ordre dans la colonie-modèle: Notes sur les désordres urbains et la Police des Frontières Raciales au Congo Belge. Crime, Histoire & Sociétés 15 (2): 97–121.

Lauro, A. (2016) Suspect cities and the (re)making of colonial order: Urbanization, secuirty anxieties and police reforms in postwar Congo (1945–1960). In: Campion, J. and Rousseaux, X. (eds) Policing New Risks in Modern European History. Basingstoke: Palgrave Macmillan, pp. 57–85.

Le Souverain Libre (2016) Cauchemar pour les vendeuses à la sauvette. Le Souverain Libre 91.

Leonardsson, H. and Rudd, G. (2015) The "local turn" in peacebuilding: A literature review of effective and emancipatory local peacebuilding. Third World Quarterly 36 (5): 825–39.

Lund, C. (2007) Twilight institutions: An introduction. In: Lund, C. (ed.) Twilight Institutions: Public Authority and Local Development in Africa. Oxford: Blackwell, pp. 1–12.

MacGaffey, J. (1991) The Real Economy of Zaire: The Contribution

of Smuggling and Other Unofficial Activities to National Wealth. Philadelphia, PA: University of Pennsylvania Press.

MacGinty, R. and Richmond, O. P. (2013) The local turn in peace building: A critical agenda for peace. Third World Quarterly 34 (5): 763–83.

Malukisa Nkuku, A. (2017) «Courtoisie routière» à Kinshasa et à Lubumbashi: Un instrument politique pour le maintien de l'ordre public. Revue internationale des études du développement 3 (231): 9–31.

Meagher, K. (2012) The strength of weak states? Non-state security forces and hybrid governance in Africa. Development and Change 43 (5): 1073–101.

Migdal, J. S. and Schlichte, K. (2005) Rethinking the state. In: Schlichte, K. (ed.) The Dynamics of States: The Formation and Crises of State Domination. Farnham: Ashgate, pp. 1–40.

Mitchell, T. (1991) The limits of the state: Beyond statist approaches and their critics. The American Political Science Review 85 (1): 77–96.

Newbury, C. (1984) Ebutumwa Bw'Emiogo: The tyranny of cassava. A women's tax revolt in Eastern Zaire. Canadian Journal of African Studies/Revue canadienne des etudes africaines 18 (1): 35–54.

Njangala, R., Thill, M. and Musamba, J. (2018). Kuishi kama mbwa ama nguruwe (Living like dogs and pigs): A Bukavu policeman's lot is not a happy one [Web blog post]. Polisi Siku Kwa Siku. Available from: www.kpsrl.org/blog/kuishi-kama-mbwa-ama-nguruwe-living-like-dogs-and-pigs-a-bukavu-policemans-lot-is-not-a-happy-one [Accessed on November 21, 2018].

Nlandu Mayamba, T. (2012) Mapping police services in the Democratic Republic of Congo: Institutional interactions at central, provincial and local levels. Institute of Development Studies. Research Report 71.

Olivier de Sardan, J.-P. (2008) Researching the practical norms of real governance in Africa. Africa: Power and Politics. Discussion Paper 5.

Raeymaekers, T. (2007) The power of protection: Governance and transborder trade on the Congo-Uganda frontier. PhD dissertation. Ghent: Ghent University.

Raeymaekers, T., Menkhaus, K. and Vlassenroot, K. (2008) State and non-state regulation in African protracted crises: Governance without government? *Africa Focus* 21 (2): 7–21.

SAJECEK/Forces Vivces. (2013) Une Corruption à ciel ouvert s'observe à tous les postes de Police de Circulation Routière au Sud Kivu: Les agents de PCR contraints à se faire corrompre au prix de 500Fc, Ya "massage". Bulletin Surprise 31. Bukavu: SAJECEK/Forces Vives.

Sánchez de la Sierra, R. (2015) On the origins of states: Stationary bandits and taxation in Eastern Congo. Households in Conflict Network Working Paper 194.

Sánchez de la Sierra, R. and Titeca, K. (forthcoming) Corrupt Hierarchies.

Schatzberg, M. G. (1988) *The Dialectics of Oppression in Zaire.* Bloomington, IL: Indiana University Press.

Schouten, P. (2016) Extractive orders: A political geography of public authority in Ituri, DR Congo. JSRP: Justice and Security Research Programme. Working Paper 30.

Simone, A. (2005) Introduction: Urban processes and change. In: Simone, A, and Abouhani, A. (eds) *Urban Africa: Changing Contours of Survival in the City.* London: Zed Books, pp. 1–26.

Thill, M., Musamba, J. and Njangala, R. (2017) Kukufa mu gratuité (to die for nothing): Making a living in Bukavu's police. [Web blog post]. Polisi Siku Kwa Siku. Available from: www.kpsrl. org/blog/kukufa-mu-gratuite-to-die-for-nothing-making-a-living-in-bukavus-police [Accessed on November 21, 2018].

Thill, M., Njangala, R. and Musamba, J. (2018) Putting everyday police life at the centre of reform in Bukavu. Briefing Paper (March). London: Rift Valley Institute.

Thurmann, L. (2017) Somewhere between green and blue: A special police unit in the Democratic Republic of the Congo. In: Beek, J., Göpfert, M., Owen, O. and Steinberg, J. (eds) *Police in Africa: The Street-level View* London: Hurst & Company, pp. 121–33.

Titeca, K. (2011) Access to resources and predictability in armed rebellion: The FAPC's short-lived "Monaco" in Eastern Congo. *Africa Spectrum* 2: 43–70.

Titeca, K. (2016) Informal revenue collection mechanisms among the Congolese traffic police. Presented at the OCAF: Oxford Central Africa Forum.

Titeca, K. and De Herdt, T. (2010) Regulation, cross-border trade and practical norms in West Nile, North-Western Uganda. *Africa* 80: 573–94.

Titeca, K. and De Herdt, T. (2011) Real governance beyond the "failed state": Negotiating education in the Democratic Republic of Congo. *African Affairs* 110 (439): 213–31.

Trefon, T. (2009) Public service provision in a failed state: Looking beyond predation in the Democratic Republic of Congo. *Review of African Political Economy* 36 (119): 9–21.

Verweijen, J. (2013) Military business and the business of the military in the Kivus. *Review of African Political Economy* 40 (135): 67–82.

Verweijen, J. (2015) The ambiguity of militarization: The complex interaction between the Congolese armed forces and civilians in the Kivu provinces, Eastern DR Congo. PhD dissertation. Utrecht: Utrecht University.

Young, C. and Turner, T. (1985) *The Rise and Decline of the Zairian State*. Madison, WI: University of Wisconsin Press.

7
The Public Transport Sector in Kinshasa: The Battle Around the "Spirit of Death"

Albert Malukisa Nkuku and Kristof Titeca

Introduction

State-provided public transport is largely absent in Kinshasa. Instead, an endless stream of private minibuses transports the citizens of Congo's capital, and hence provide a public transport organized from the ground up. This does not mean that the situation is rosy. Many of these minibuses are in a bad state, being very old and having a wide range of mechanical and other problems. As a result, accidents are common. Moreover, reports from the drivers' trade union argue that 50% of transport conductors do not know the traffic rules (Radio Okapi, 2013b). Similar problems are encountered for cars in general: technical controls are rare, and contribute to the difficulties of Kinshasa's traffic.

The Mercedes 207 minibus has become a symbol for this situation. The blue and yellow painted minibuses are omnipresent in the Kinshasa landscape, and are the main means of transport. They are a symbol of the "fend for yourself" (*débrouillez-vous*) attitude of the Congolese population – in the absence of the state-provided public transport, Congolese have invented their own form of public transport in an attempt to get themselves around the city as cheaply as possible. These vans were originally manufactured to transport goods rather than people, and consequently they do not have windows or seats in the passengers' section. As a result, windows are cut into the sides of the van, while wooden benches are put inside, allowing as many passengers as possible to be crammed into the vehicle. The reason for their popularity is straightforward – they constitute the cheapest possible vehicle (and are bought second-hand from overseas).

At the same time, these minibuses are controversial, as they are notorious for causing accidents, which is why they are commonly called "*esprit de mort*" (spirit of death). Reasons for this reputation included overcrowding, reckless driving, and the vehicle being in a bad state of repair. These vehicles are bought in an already problematic state, being on average between fifteen and twenty years old, making them among the oldest in sub-Saharan Africa (Kumar & Barrett, 2008). Their state of repair has become much worse through the difficult conditions in which they operate, and the various replacement parts, mostly chosen for their cheap price rather than whether they are appropriate (Inkwayi Tungila & Ebamba Boboto, 2013, p. 126). In the words of the representative of the minibus drivers' trade union (Association des chauffeurs du Congo, or ACCO),[1] "the vehicles we are currently using, when we send them to the technical control, it's only to sign their death certificate" (Radio Okapi, 2014c). This statement is very much shared by the administrators of the technical control centres: although many cars in Kinshasa suffer from technical problems (which is why many avoid these controls), this appears to be particularly the case for the "spirit of death" minibuses.

After the 2011 elections, the government announced a plan to modernize the sector, and make Kinshasa's traffic safer. Concretely, it announced two measures. First, it wanted to enforce the technical control on vehicles, by introducing a one-stop shop for technical control, allowing all necessary documents to be bought at once. Second (and related with the previous point), the government wanted to outlaw the "spirit of death" minibuses, given their notorious insecurity. The questions this chapter addresses relate to the extent to which the state is able to intervene in a sector which has largely been functioning without, or even despite, the state. Specifically, how is the state able to regulate a sector which is crucial for the everyday life of many people, and in which it has played almost no role?

In order to answer this question, this chapter takes the following approach. First, it introduces the relevant literature on this issue, in which we primarily rely on the literature of the (Congolese) state, as well as the literature on informality. Second, the chapter introduces the transport sector of Kinshasa, and how technical controls operate (or rather, how they should operate, as in reality they are rarely properly implemented). Third, it shows how the government has been trying to outlaw the "spirit of death" minibuses, but has so far failed to do so, as the minibuses are an important source of political support. Finally, it analyses how a range of recent reforms (the so-called "revolution of modernity") have tried to improve road safety by introducing a one-stop shop technical control, and (again) outlawing the "spirit of death" minibuses. In doing so, this chapter shows the ways in which political elites use the transport sector as a political support base, with attempts to regulate the sector allowing political elites to act as "protectors" and "saviours", particularly in regard to the "spirit of death" minibuses.

This chapter relies on extensive field research between 2012 and 2015. Over 200 interviews were conducted with a broad range of actors within the wider transport sector, such as government officials involved at various levels, trade union representatives, drivers and so on. Research took place in the technical control centres where the one-stop shop takes place, the offices of the various government agencies involved in this measure, and the police stations where arrested cars were taken to. Moreover, the first author used participant observation as a key methodology – not only was he a passenger of these minibuses, he also became a mini-bus owner himself, through which many of the dynamics were experienced first-hand.

Fending for oneself ... and for political support

In her seminal work on the second economy in DRC, Janet MacGaffey (1987) showed how the population was left to "fend for itself" (*se débrouiller*). In the absence of state-provided development, public services are provided and organized by non-state actors, and in particular the "spirit of death" minibuses.

Yet, in the DRC, it is not only non-state actors who are left to fend for themselves – state actors are left to do so too. It has been widely demonstrated how, over the last decades, the state budget has imploded, resulting in civil servants' salaries being woefully insufficient to live on, let alone provide public services. Historically, this can be traced back to the Zairianization policy under the Mobutu regime, which in 1973 expropriated enterprises owned by foreigners, described by Young and Turner as "the most sweeping and comprehensive set of nationalizing measures yet undertaken in independent Africa" (1985, p. 361). This, however, had extremely negative consequences. In the words of Emizet, the consequences of "nationalization was a social and economic disaster, because most of the enterprises were handed to politicians and their relatives who had no managerial experience" (1998, p. 104).

The consequences were also dire for the civil service. Gould described the situation of civil servants in the 1970s as "abject impoverishment ... Negligence of their social needs leaves them to their own devices" (1980, p. 69). From the perspective of the civil servants, this "fending for itself" was manifest in various ways. On a micro-level, this meant that civil servants looked for ways to extract informal revenue from citizens. In his speech of 20 May 1976, President Mobutu famously encouraged his civil servants to "steal cleverly". In Mobutu's words, "If you want to steal, steal a little cleverly, in a nice way. Only if you steal so much as to become rich overnight, you will be caught" (Gould, 1980, p. xiii). In doing so, public services became de facto privatized, with civil servants becoming part of a system in which there is little choice but to engage in these practices, both for the purposes of survival and for self-enrichment. In the words of Rene Lemarchand, what happened was a privatization of state positions, or the drawing of "personal benefits ... from the appropriation of public office" (1988, p. 153). The state continued to hire civil servants, but assumed that they would "steal cleverly" (De Herdt, Titeca & Wagemakers, 2012). Although the state budget eventually increased over the years – specifically through the renewed engagement of donors throughout the 2000s (De Herdt, Titeca & Wagemakers, 2012) – these practices remained, termed by Pierre Englebert the "capacity of legal command", or "the capacity to control, dominate, extract or dictate through the law" (2009, p. 114).

In other words, although the resource base of the state has fluctuated wildly, the power associated with the state has not, and it is used to extract revenue from the wider population. Generally, civil servants continue to work not for the salary itself, but for the "income-earning opportunities linked to one's professional position" (Baaz & Olsen, 2011, p. 227). Concretely, this has meant that state uniforms have been used to extract bribes from citizens (De Herdt & Titeca, 2016).

On a meso- and macro-level, and as highlighted in the introduction, this signified a profound informalization of the state administration (Bierschenk, 2010). State administrations are transformed into pockets of power, in which various actors look for ways to extend their power, and for ways of generating informal revenue. This manifests itself in various ways. For example, it means that there can be competition between various state services for the extraction of informal revenue. It also means that, on an individual level, civil servants need to pay to gain access to these pockets of power, bureaucratic clientelism having become a defining characteristic of the Congolese bureaucracy. Concretely, it has been shown how traffic police need to provide a regular informal payment in order to keep their position (Baaz & Olsen, 2011). The "capacity of legal command" (Englebert, 2009) not only manifests itself in the relations between civil servants and citizens, but also within state administrations – state actors will use the formal administrative power they have to dominate other state actors. In other words, superiors use the power they have to demand an extra contribution from their subordinates, or even put these in competition against each other, in order to achieve the highest income possible.

In these circumstances, not adhering to official regulations, and infractions (such as traffic violations) do not necessarily constitute a problem for state actors, but an opportunity, allowing them to achieve various forms of gain, both financial and political.

First, this situation of illegality allows civil servants the opportunity to profit financially. Selling the official paperwork in order to legalize a situation, or giving an official fine to a citizen, is one option, but (from a "fending for yourself" perspective) is not very interesting, as this revenue ends up in the public treasury. It is financially much more interesting to threaten to give a high official fine, but instead extract a bribe that ends up in the civil servant's pockets. In doing so, the citizen buys themself short-term protection, but not in a legal way. Moreover, for many civil servants, knowledge of the official regulations is secondary to opportunities for extraction. For example, during our research, both analysts and actors within the police administrations kept emphasizing the lack of knowledge traffic police had of the traffic code. In the words of one analyst: "The traffic police are insufficiently aware of the traffic code. There is very little knowledge of the traffic rules!"[2] They are, however, notorious for extracting revenue from drivers (Malukisa Nkuku, 2017).

On the other hand, many actors do not comply with the official regulations, often because they lack the necessary official papers. This is particularly the case in the traffic sector. For example, previous research has shown how most drivers in Kinshasa lack the necessary documents to operate legally (Emizet, 1998, p. 117), while the cars themselves often do not meet basic technical requirements. As a minibus driver summarized:

> What's the problem between the police agents and us in reality? If we have to be honest, we have to acknowledge that our vehicles are generally in bad shape, and that we also lack transport documents. And even when we have these, they are false documents.[3]

As the quote above shows, this widespread failure to meet official state regulations further facilitates extraction by civil servants. This situation not only affects the street-level situation, but also impacts on a broader political level, allowing politicians to come in and "rescue" the population (such as drivers) from harassment. These dynamics have been described in detail in the literature on informal economy. On the one hand, the concept of "informality" has been criticized as being obsolete in countries such as the DRC – given the absence of a functional formal economic sector, the informal sector has also ceased to exist. As Klein explains: "As a paired negotiation each marker depends on the integrity of the opposing term. But with criminalization, the key referent of formality has defected across the binary divide, and become absorbed by informality. The rest is simple: no formal sector, no informal sector" (1999, p. 568). As the founding father of the "informal economy" concept, Keith Hart concludes "state collapse has attained such proportions that it seems almost pointless to clarify that the informal economy is the dominant sector" (1995, p. 122; see also: Hart, 2001). Moreover, which regulations count as "formal" or "informal" fluctuate. For example, informal practices become regularized, and as a result it becomes unclear which regulations count as formal or informal. For this reason, a number of authors prefer the terms "unofficial" and "official", to "informal" and "formal" (Baaz, Olsson & Verweijen, 2018; Roitman, 2004). Yet, on the other hand, there is a range of literature which – although it agrees with the profound intertwining of formality and informality – highlights the specific political dynamics at stake regarding informality. In particular, the works of Kate Meagher (2006, 2008, 2010) have been influential in this regard, arguing "however much formal and informal forms of organization interpenetrate ... the intertwining of formal and informal forms of organization does not eliminate the power differences between them" (2008, p. 1). Concretely, this means that "informality blocks more acceptable forms of political access, as well as increasing the vulnerability of informal actors to the machinations of more powerful social groups" (Meagher, 2008, p. 4). In other words, through a lack of formal protection, and the lack of possibility in creating formal linkages with the state, informal traders have a tendency to "form links with the state through incorporation into cliental networks with local government and state-level officials" (Meagher, 2006, p. 576). By doing so, the traders receive protection from regulatory measures. Yet the result of this is that officials "make use of these links to serve their own personal and political agendas, rather than to address the occupational interests of informal manufacturers" (Meagher, 2006, p. 576). Judith Tendler (2002) calls this relation the "devil's deal" – politicians offer protection to informal traders from regulatory measures (such as tax, environmental or other measures) in return for political support. Tendler calls it this because, in this context, informality becomes more attractive, and formalization less so, making it difficult for both sides to exit the deal. While attractive in the short-term for the parties directly involved, its long-term advantages are unclear. Similar to Meagher, Tendler shows how informal traders' protection largely depends on individual links with patrons, rather than on a guaranteed framework. This kind of protection is crucial in the building up of political support bases for politicians – something which has been shown in a variety of contexts (Goodfellow & Titeca, 2016; Titeca, 2006, 2014). These linkages therefore primarily focus on nourishing political support and creating political rent, rather than on sustained employment-enhancing local development, which places the wellbeing of the trader at its centre.

In the following sections, we aim to illustrate the above points, showing how a lack of adherence to official regulations ("informality", for lack of a better term), as well as attempts at regulating public minibuses, constitute sources of profit for state-actors, both financially and politically (in building political support bases). Before we do so, we will first explain Kinshasa's public transport, and the attempts at reforming the sector.

Kinshasa's public transport: The spirit of death?

Despite reportedly being a city of about 12 million inhabitants[4] and covering an area of around 10,000 km^2, Kinshasa does not have a public transport company worth speaking of. Historically, this has always been the case. In postcolonial Kinshasa, a whole range of public bus companies were created. In chronological order, these were the *Société des transports kinois* and the *Office de transport et communication du Zaïre* (1967 to late 1970s) (Pain, 1984), the *Société des transports zaïrois* (SOTRAZ) (1979 to late 1980s) (Mwanza wa Mwanza, 1998), the *Société des transports zaïro-marocains* (TRANSZAM) (1989 to early 1990s) (Lelo Nzuzi, 2011), and GESAC (1998–2000). All these bus companies suffered the same problems. Namely, they were woefully unable to respond to the demand for public transport, and had very limited means at their disposal. Although central government initially gave them some funding, these funds quickly dried up.

The latest public bus companies operating in Kinshasa have suffered from the same problems. Table 7.1 provides an overview of the most recent public bus companies introduced in the city. As this table shows, a plethora of bus companies have been established, but have not proved to be successful, either not lasting long, or losing most of their buses. In doing so, they are an illustration of what William (1986) described regarding Zaire as "white elephants", in which profits are realized at the moment of investment, not at the moment of implementation. The result is mismanagement common in public projects in Congo.

Table 7.1 – List of public bus companies in Kinshasa

Name of company	Year introduced	No. of buses and minibuses introduced	Regulatory authority
City Train	1989	60	Central government
Stuc	2006	250	Central government
Régie des transports de Kinshasa (Retranskin)	2008[5]	88 + 69 taxis	Provincial government
New Transkin	2013	70	Provincial government
Transports au Congo (Transco)[6]	2013	500	Central government

Source: Malukisa Nkuku (2017).

As a result of these "white elephants" in the public transport sector, the majority of public transport is not provided by these public operators, but by private minibuses. While the public bus companies have been coming and going, the private minibuses have remained a solid provider of transport. Although they might not be in the best state, they are often the only choice for Kinshasa's citizens.

As explained in the introduction, the Mercedes 207 minibus "spirit of death" is the most used, but also the most notorious of these minibuses. The "spirit of death" first appeared in Kinshasa around 2006 and ended up being the dominant mode of transport amid strong population growth and the failure of public transport companies (Inkwayi Tungila & Ebamba Boboto, 2013). The popularity of the minibuses can be explained by its ability to use roads which other modes of transport (such as full-sized buses) are not able to frequent, as well as their capacities – between 24 and 28 passengers fit in a minibus. Moreover, the minibus is considered cheap to buy, as well as being regarded as strong and easy to repair. As Inkwayi Tungila and Ebamba Boboto summarize:

> They assure, other than public transport, other services which are necessary for the daily life of the Kinois: moving services, transport of construction material from their sale points to the construction sites (*chantiers*), transport of fresh produce from their places of production or conservation towards their vending points and vice-versa, catering, and so on. (2013, p. 127)

It is also worth noting that the "spirit of death" drivers and trade unions contest the name "spirit of death", given the negative image it gives to their vehicles. Equally worth noting is that, in order to counter this image of death, certain drivers have the habit of putting religious stickers invoking God, Christ or saints on their minibus, such as "God is good", "100% Jesus", "God is almighty", or bible verses.

Quid vehicle inspection?

As indicated in the introduction, a major reason for the insecurity of the "spirit of death" minibuses and other vehicles is the fact that they are in a bad state. While a technical control for vehicles exists, it is hardly operational. In this section, we describe how technical control functions, and what the difficulties are with the agencies involved.

Technical control is something which has been profoundly under-regulated in the DRC. It was only in 1998 that the public authorities became interested in this question. A ministerial by-law concerning technical control was instituted (RDC, 1998) and again adapted in 2011 (RDC, 2011) which makes a technical control obligatory for cars, to be obtained every six months in an official control centre. This by-law is currently still in place, but not implemented on the ground. The three control centres currently in place hardly have any work to do, with one of the control centres doubling as a garage in order to earn some income through vehicle repairs.

In theory, technical control works in the following manner. A vehicle goes to one of the three control centres.[7] These centres then verify if the vehicle conforms with technical standards and issue a technical report. On the basis of this document, the car goes to the next agency: the Division Urbaine des Transports et Voies de Communication (DUTVC),[8] responsible for delivering the certificate of technical control, which is valid for 6 months. The DUTVC

THE PUBLIC TRANSPORT SECTOR IN KINSHASA   151

controllers can also be deployed in the streets to check if cars are in order.

Apart from this, car owners also have to deal with a range of other agencies, which are described in Table 7.2.

Table 7.2 – State actors and their role in the technical control of cars

Actors	Status	Role
Technical control centre	Private enterprise (SCCT and TRINITY 3) and one public enterprise (INPP)	Control vehicle, establish a PV which needs to be transmitted to DUTVC, and deliver vignette of technical control to the driver
DUTVC (Urban Division for Transport and Means of Communications)	Administration in charge of transport regulation	Deliver certificate of technical control, transport authorization, and so on
SONAS (National Insurance Association)	Public enterprise	Provide insurance
DGI (General Directorate for Taxes)	Financial service of central government	Provide pink card and number plate
DGRK (General Directorate of Earnings of revenues of Kinshasa)	Financial service of provincial government	Provide receipt for payment at bank, and vignette for taxes on motor vehicles
FiBank and RawBank	Commercial banks	Receive taxes and issue payment slip to user

Source: Malukisa Nkuku (2017).

DUTVC controllers periodically go to the streets to check if drivers have the necessary technical control papers. The official revenue generated through this is minimal. Instead, the main purpose of these missions is to extract unofficial revenue (bribes) from the drivers. Part of these proceeds end up in the controller's own pockets, and part of it is transferred to his superior, who asks for a portion of their income. If the controller does not perform as expected, they risk losing their job.

An important aspect of this situation is the fact that many state agents do not earn a salary. Similar to other sectors, such as education, these actors have been engaged officially in the expectation that they will, one day, receive an official state salary (Titeca & De

Herdt, 2011). As long as this is not the case, they "live off the land", extracting revenue from passengers. Table 7.3 gives an overview of DUTVC's staff, which shows that only 16% of staff earn a formal state salary (127 out of 795).

Table 7.3 – Personnel of DUTVC in June 2014, for the districts of Funa and Mont-Amba

		District					
		Funa		Mont-Amba		Totals	
	Salary status	No.	%	No.	%	No.	%
Statutory agents	Paid Civil servants	82	17	45	14	127	16
Urban agents	Agents employed by the city without salary	51	11	52	17	103	13
"New units"[9]	Agents employed by the state without salary	347	72	218	69	565	71
	Totals	480	100	315	100	795	100

Source: Declarative list of in-service staff. DUTVC offices of the districts Funa and Mont-Amba.

For the large majority of DUTVC agents – the ones who do not earn a salary – their control missions (checking the drivers' papers) constitute their only source of income. Their official mission serves principally as a pressure mechanism, involving threatening to send a car to the control centre, where the driver can potentially be refused a certificate and/or have to pay a large fine.

The same mechanism holds for other state agencies such as SONAS or DGRK. Here as well, state agents have little or no pay, their income coming mainly from extracting revenue from drivers. As a result, a rotation system is in place in which various administrations take turns to be present on the street – in theory to check the papers from the drivers, but in reality to collect bribes. This system is in place to avoid overburdening the drivers, and is organized at a political (provincial) level – the governor and/or provincial minister of transport first have to grant permission for these missions, i.e. for each of these agencies to operate on the streets. Often, when harassment by one of the agencies has proved too much (e.g. DUTVC), the presence of the next agency (e.g. DGRK) is no longer allowed, as the actions of the first have provoked too much contestation by the population and the drivers' trade union. Moreover, during times of political tensions, the political authorities do not allow for these document controls, as they exacerbate political discontent. Adding to this are tensions with the traffic police officers. In theory, DUTVC officers need to collaborate with the traffic police in order to perform their street-level controls – police agents need to accompany DUTVC controllers in order to stop cars. Yet, traffic police officers consider the streets of Kinshasa, and particularly its revenue-generating possibilities, as their territory. Other state agencies encroaching on this (such as the agencies mentioned above) are seen as competitors. In other words, the police agents need to be convinced to assist, which is done by paying them to perform this task. As one police officer argued: "The commander receives an envelope of $20 per day. For the agents which are guarding vehicles, each vehicle gives them $3, while the agent which assists the controllers to arrest the drivers gets $1 per vehicle."[10] An additional complicating factor is that a number of the "spirit of death" minibuses are owned by police officers, further demotivating them to assist the DUTVC controllers.

Lastly, another common method is that the DUTVC hire so-called "Masters" (*maîtres*). These are men active in fighting sports, such as judoka, boxers, catchers and so on. These "Masters" (also called "*batu ya makasi*" or "strong men") only not guarantee the security in popular neighbourhoods, but assist the DUTVC in their control missions. If minibuses owned by traffic policemen are arrested, this can lead to tensions.

In sum, this section has shown how state controllers, which are supposed to control and regulate the transport sector, instead use this opportunity to create an income for themselves. Much of the controllers – civil servants – do not receive a state salary, and use the missions as an opportunity to extract unofficial revenue.

At a meso-level, different kinds of power dynamics are at stake. First, in order to keep their position, state controllers have to pay their superior part of their informal revenue. Second, within the administration, this leads to competition between various actors. As shown above, in the worst-case scenario, this leads to tensions between the police and the controlling agencies (DUTVC and others). In the best-case scenario, this leads to an informal agreement between the various controlling agencies, whereby each agency is allowed to extract informal revenue.

However, to what extent is this situation static? In other words, to what extent are policy measures able to reform and control the public transport sector, and in particular address road safety? In answering this question, we show how the illegality of the sector not only allows for the collection of revenue for the relevant state actors, but also the construction of political support. Specifically, we look at three episodes of attempted reform; two seeking to abolish the "spirit of death", and a third introducing the one-stop shop.

A "single dose" for the (dis)order in the transport sector

The preceding sections have described how the regulation and control of the transport sector is extremely challenging, and leaves the sector operating largely outside of an official regulatory framework – technical controls are rare, and unofficial revenue plays an important role in the actions of civil servants. Yet, during the 2011 electoral campaign, President Kabila promised a "revolution of modernity", of which the transport sector was a central part, the program being a successor of the "Five building sites".[11]

A central part of this "revolution" was addressing road safety.[12] The lack of technical controls, and the cars' mechanical problems, were seen as a major cause of accidents in Kinshasa. This is particularly the case for the "spirit of death" minibuses. Often, deadly accidents[13] involving them occurred, after which the debate around technical control would re-emerge – a debate which boils down to the legality of these minibuses. As argued above, most – perhaps all – were and are in such a bad state that they would not pass a technical control. Over the years, an increasing number of actors advocated for them to be declared illegal. This never led to action, until the "revolution of modernity". Below, we describe the various attempts to address road safety and outlaw the "spirit of death" minibuses. Or, in the words of the general police commissioner, "to give them a single dose" (Kanyama, 2014) – i.e. to finish the "spirit of death" once and for all.

Death to the "spirit of death"?

In 2012, increasing measures were taken to control the "spirit of death". Throughout Kinshasa, central government started a campaign in support of technical control certification and insurance papers (Radio Okapi, 2012d). This resulted in an operation launched by the police to control minibuses' papers, and hence check their safety. During these operations, around 200 "spirit of death" minibuses were confiscated (Radio Okapi, 2012b).

The drivers, however, reacted swiftly. The drivers' trade union (l'Association des Chauffeurs du Congo, or ACCO) called a general strike on 21 and 22 May 2012. During these two days, no mini-buses operated in the city, and transport was limited to walking. Much of the city was paralysed, with markets and schools largely deserted (Radio Okapi, 2012c). The overall atmosphere was one of frustration, primarily with the government. Car tires were burned to block the roads for those who did not respect the strike, and clashes occurred (Radio Okapi, 2012a).

At an emergency meeting on the 22 May (between the President and the council of Ministers), it was decided to put an end to the police repression. The Minister of Transport summarized the central government's change of direction by stating:

> The government has not forbidden any vehicle to circulate, whether it is a taxi, or the minibus called 207. Drivers are saying they are being harassed by police officers, or by what we commonly call the 'robots', the anti-riot police. It is normal there's contestation on the side of the drivers, but we are telling them that we are ready to assist them. (Radio Okapi, 2012e)

Following this statement, the ACCO called upon its drivers to go back to work. Moreover, the government – and in particular the President – did everything it could to make sure the strike came to an end, and that the wishes of ACCO were honoured. According to a representative of ACCO:

> After the meeting with the Head of State, we went with the governor of the town to the minister of the interior, who gave us money to sensitize the drivers. We went on the most commonly watched radio and TV stations to announce an end to the strike. We also were at the residence of the governor to celebrate this victory against the irresponsible decision of the prime minister and his ministry of transport.[14]

In other words, the President personally made sure that the strike came to end.

The one-stop shop

The attempts at regulating the transport sector did not stop there. As explained above, in theory, car owners need to pass through a whole variety of state agencies in order to meet all formal-technical requirements for their cars. The multitude of agencies present at various locations makes this rather complicated to do so. Moreover, the way these agencies operate – largely centred around the extraction of unofficial revenue rather than issuing official papers – further contributes to the lack of actual technical control. As part of the "revolution of modernity", the state wanted to create a one-stop shop for the technical control of cars. This would mean that all the control agencies mentioned in table 7.2 would be centralized in the technical control centres. In other words, the one-stop shop measure would make the technical control more efficient and effective. In doing so, the state also wanted to reduce opportunities for corruption in the various state agencies.

In June 2013, an agreement was signed between the state and the private control centres for the installation of one-stop shops. The governor of Kinshasa, André Kimbuta, urged all drivers to go as soon as possible in order to avoid forced controls. In his words:

> We understood there are vehicles which are driving but which are not in a good state. There are conductors which even do not have a driving permit. Well, we are going to tackle this. We said: now, for a vehicle to drive in the city of Kinshasa, a certificate of technical control is needed. (Radio Okapi, 2013c)

How did the one-stop shops perform? First of all, from January to May 2014, the introduction of the one-stop shop measure brought a major increase in revenue for the technical control centres, as illustrated by figure 7.1 below.

Figure 7.1 – Evolution of the technical control statistics 2011–14

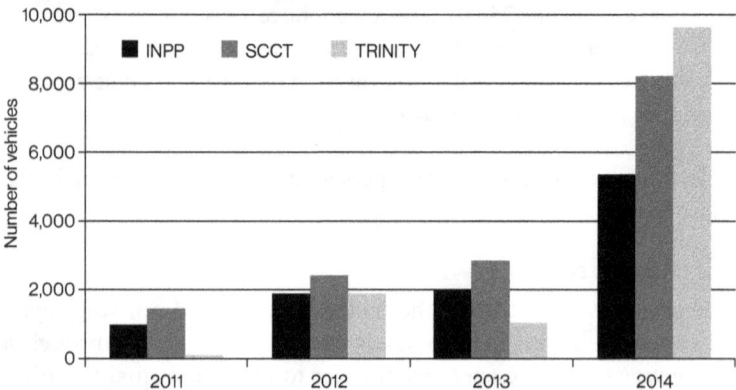

Source: Statistical data obtained from the direction of the control centers SCCT, TRINITY 3 and INPP.

In 2014, a total of 23,187 cars passed through the technical control centres, compared to 14,561 cars in the previous three years combined. In this situation, the agents of DUTVC and DGRK benefitted particularly, as they are able to extract a lot of revenue for themselves. As a DUTVC agent declared: "We will become unemployed tomorrow [i.e. this situation will not last very long], those who have not build up strategic reserves will lose out. I am planning to buy a three-wheeled motortaxi with this money".[15]

Why did DUTVC and DGRK in particular benefit? According to the one-stop shop measure, all state institutions of both the central government (SONAS and DGI) and the provincial government (DUTVC and DGRK) should be able to increase their revenue, as drivers are able to pay for their various requirements all at once. However, upon implementation, the provincial government unilaterally changed the rules of the game: Given the decentralization process which started in 2012, taxes were now managed by the provincial government (RDC, 2013). Using these powers, the provincial government gave an order to the agents of DUTVC and DGRK to only collect taxes for the provincial government. The central government agencies, DGI and SONAS, were no longer able to collect revenue and a number of them closed their offices in the technical control centres. In other words, immediately after the implementation of the measure, a power struggle emerged over monopolization of the revenue at the control centres, quickly won by the provincial government.

Moreover, the existence of the one-stop shop did not stop the activities of these institutions at street level. Particularly the central government agents DGI and SONAS (who were no longer able to operate in the control centres) instead shifted their extractive practices to the street level. Indeed, with the one-stop measure in order, their power had increased – they could now use this threat to force the drivers into higher payments. The following conversation between a controller and a driver is illustrative of this dynamic:

> You are telling me you don't have $20? I wanted to help you but you don't understand me. There you're going to the one-stop shop and you are going to regret bitterly. You know you have to start there by paying a fine of $100 to the bank? And if your vehicle has problems it is going to be seized? Even if it's good you still have to pay the transport authorisation. SONAS also waits for the insurance. So it is really as if you are entering in the mouth of the crocodile. It's up to you to decide. You will be

bombarded with an invoice you'll never be able to pay. You're
already arrested my brother, pay me $50 and I will liberate you.[16]

As the above shows, the one-stop shop is portrayed as the "mouth
of the crocodile", the ultimate punishment for the driver. This allows
for an easier unofficial revenue extraction process by the controllers.
According to our estimates, a driver had to pay between $10 and $40
to be released.

In other words, the introduction of the one-stop shop constituted
a major financial opportunity for civil servants, enabling increased
harassment of drivers. This not only created excitement (among
the civil servants), but also resentment – many of the drivers were
frustrated with this dynamic. As a result, the provincial government
intervened, with the Provincial Transport minister releasing a decree
stipulating that civil servants were only allowed to work on ten specified days in May (RDC, 2014a), and twelve days in August (RDC,
2014b), and not at all in June and July. Doing so allowed the minibuses without papers to drive on the other days and look for the
necessary papers in the meantime.

Yet, a few months later, the same minister admitted that the public
treasury had not sufficiently benefited from the one-stop measure
(Motemona Gibolum, 2014). In other words, although an increasing
number of cars had visited the control centres, the measure had not
brought in a corresponding increase in official income. Instead, the
unofficial income of the various controllers had increased exponen-

Figure 7.2 – Evolution of technical control in Kinshasa (January 2014 to
June 2015)

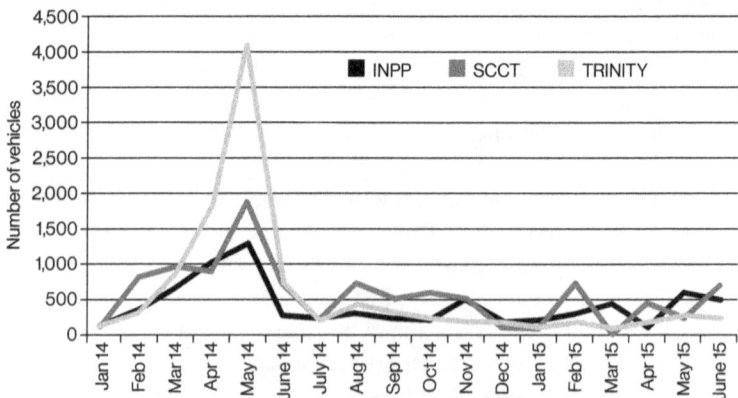

Source: Statistical data obtained from the control centres.

tially. Rather than reducing corrupt practices, the one-stop shop measure allowed predatory practices to continue, and even expand. The one-stop shop measure quickly disintegrated. This is clearly shown by the statistics of the technical control centres, shown in figure 7.2. From June onwards, the visits to these centres were decimated. This was the period when the police stopped their campaign of advocating for drivers to the control centres. From that time onwards, these centres returned to their original activities, such as vehicle repair.

The "single dose" for the "spirit of death"

The one-stop shop measure did not come alone. Upon implementation, it was accompanied by (again) strong actions against the "spirit of death" minibuses. On the 14 January 2014, the provincial police commissioner, general Célestin Kanyama, declared all "spirit of death" minibuses illegal. In a press conference, in which the representatives of the drivers' trade union were invited, he announced that:

> We tried different measures ... which turned out badly, they didn't work. But this time, after having identified the difficulties, we found a solution ... We bring you the single dose. If you don't heal from this single dose, you will never heal! There are things which should no more belong in Kinshasa. The 207 ["spirit of death" minibus] no longer belong in the commune of Gombe [centre of Kinshasa]! ... You have always known this, but this time you will see it! The authority of the state will be felt throughout the town and province of Kinshasa. (Kanyama, 2014)

In other words, in order to outlaw the "spirit of death" buses, the police were going to conduct severe operations – the "single dose". A one-week deadline was given by the provincial commissioner Kanyama.[17]

These measures were (again) strongly contested (Assogba, 2014). Although the population was complaining about the quality and safety of the "spirit of death" buses, these measures were not well received, because they did not include any alternatives. A similar opinion was voiced by the governor of Kinshasa, who had consistently argued that "before measures can be taken to stop the minibuses, a different option has to be presented" (Kimbuta, 2013).

Again, the drivers' trade union ACCO used its most effective weapon, calling a general strike on the 20th of January, one day before Kanyama's deadline (Radio Okapi, 2014a; RTBF, 2014).

An emergency meeting was called at the ministerial level, yielding a compromise – the measure against the minibuses was lifted (RDC, 2014c), and all cars were given 45 days to present themselves at the one-stop shop. However, this deadline was neglected (Africatime, 2014), as was a second deadline of another 45 days. As the carrot had failed, the stick then came in. In December 2014, the provincial police commander ordered all police units to impound these buses. In doing so, he again went directly against the Kinshasa governor, who had ordered "*courtoisie routiere*" (road courtesy), prohibiting the police from harassing or stopping any vehicle, including the "spirit of death". According to ACCO, over 200 minibuses were confiscated during this action.[18] This led to violent retaliation by the bus drivers – setting car tyres on fire, blocking traffic, attacking non-"spirit of death" buses and taxis (MediaCongo, 2014). In reaction to this eruption of violence, the government (again) ordered general Kanyama to stop his actions against the minibuses. A council of ministers at the provincial level ordered the "illegally confiscated" minibuses to be returned to their rightful owners.[19] This marked the end of the actions against the minibuses. Still today, they continue to be the most important form of public transport in Kinshasa – the "spirit of death" proved to be stronger than the "single dose".

The transport sector as a political support base

The various attempts at abolishing the "spirit of death" illustrate the political manoeuvring around this, but particularly the political importance of the sector. Various actors, in particular President Kabila, try to increase their legitimacy by giving favours to, and protecting, groups within the transport sector.

Central to these dynamics is the fact that President Kabila has little legitimacy in the capital. For much of the *Kinois*, he is considered an appointee of the international community, with little or no local popularity and accountability. Moreover, he is considered a foreigner – some claim he is Rwandan, others claim he is from Tanzania. In power since 2001, Kabila has never performed a speech in Lingala. As a result, he has always been defeated by opposition candidates in Kinshasa, often with slogans delegitimizing his nationality. He therefore needs to build legitimacy in Kinshasa, and intervening in favour of the "spirit of death" allows him to do so.[20]

The actions against the minibus 207 can be considered politically counter-productive. When the minibuses are confiscated, public transport is severely affected due to the lack of alternatives, which leads to major frustration by the general population, and retaliatory action by the trade unions. In a way, the informal sector is "too big to fail", or the formal sector too small to replace it. Attempts at formalizing the transport sector in this situation create opportunities for political elites, as the victims of these actions turn to the highest political level for protection. This is not only the case for President Kabila, but also for Governor André Kimbuta,[21] about whom the population argues "*a talela biso likambo oyo po pasi eleki*", or "come to our rescue, as this measure makes us suffer too much". At the moment when security agencies face contestation due to their harsh measures, the President and governor are able to act as the saviour of targeted groups, and gain in popularity through their intervention. In other words, for the President and the governor, it is a win–win situation – an attempt has been made to solve severe road safety problems, and a strong, yet short-lived, signal has been sent. At the same time, the President and the governor are able to position themselves as the protectors of the common man. The informal sector constitutes an important political constituency, and this is particularly the case for the transport sector, which is not only an important employment provider, but also provides a service to most of the *Kinois*. Concretely, by looking to protect them, political support is not only created among the vehicle drivers and owners, but among the wider population, which is able to enjoy its transport service again. By looking at the transport operators as a voting bloc, and by looking to protect them, the regime allows them to operate in illegality.

In line with what has been argued above, this situation can very much be considered a "devil's deal" (Tendler, 2002) – a continued situation of illegality allowing politicians to nourish clientelist forms of support. Actors operating illegally need protection from formal regulatory measures; intervention by the President and Governor gives them this. Yet, in the long term, it leaves them in a difficult situation, with citizens exposed to low-quality and dangerous public transport, and the bus operators vulnerable to the actions of other government agencies and exactions by civil servants. By bribing a DUTVC or other controller, a driver is able to buy short-term protection. However, given that he still does not have the official papers, he remains vulnerable to further harassment, a process which Meagher describes as "the fragmentation and demobilization of informal occupational interests in favour of the machinations of more powerful political forces" (2006, p. 579).

Conclusions

This chapter described the various attempts to regulate a transport sector which has been under-regulated by the state for a long time – car control centres are rarely frequented, and most cars circulating in Kinshasa would have difficulties passing the control tests. The state is also largely absent in the provision of public transport. The Mercedes 207 minibus, or "spirit of death", has become a symbol of this situation. It is technically deficient and often outright dangerous, yet also very efficient in providing public transport to Kinshasa's population. What happens when the state tries to regulate this sector, and particularly when it tries to outlaw the "spirit of death" minibuses?

Part of Kabila's "revolution of modernity" interventions in the transport sector, such as the technical control or the outlawing of the 207, are potentially beneficial. There are multiple reasons for this: increasing road safety, reducing air pollution, reducing traffic deaths, and creating more orderly traffic. Importantly, it also allows the state to take a public role and to convey an image of a "modernizing" state. Similar to the "5 *chantiers*" state programme, it shows a state which is in charge, bringing modernity and development through visible public services and a renewed transport sector. The "spirit of death" is very much the antithesis of this modernity – an old, almost broken vehicle, overcrowded with passengers and associated with dangerous accidents. Its interdiction therefore seems a logical step. The one-stop shop control – as an open and transparent control centre, uniting various state services – again fits very nicely into this idea of modernity. However, things did not turn out this way.

First, we have shown how the state administration does not function as a coherent body. Instead, it has been transformed into pockets of power, each trying to extract unofficial revenue. We particularly looked at how the "revolution of modernity" tried to modernize and facilitate the technical control of cars, and in doing so make the state administration more efficient. While initially successful, this quickly failed. Soon after its introduction, the one-stop shop not only reproduced the same predatory practices, it worsened them. By providing a stronger threat to extract revenue from drivers (the one-stop shop as the "mouth of the crocodile", in the words of an interlocutor) it actually increased harassment by controllers.

Second, the transport sector is a major site of political support, with various actors at different political levels using the transport sector as a vote bank. Faced with a situation of limited legitimacy in Kinshasa, the President is looking for various ways to increase his political legitimacy and support base. By nourishing the image of himself as the protector of the transport sector, and the "spirit of death" in particular, he is able to build clientelist legitimacy. Other actors are taking similar measures, such as the provincial governor, who similarly nurtures an image of himself as the protector of the informal transport sector. This situation makes it very difficult to abolish the "spirit of death", as it is politically more advantageous to protect the minibuses rather than get rid of them.

In analysing these processes, this chapter also contributes to the debate on formality and informality. On the one hand, the chapter shows the clear intertwining of both dynamics – informal revenue extraction practices have become institutionalized, and are fuelled, rather than stopped, by these reforms. The "informal" has become the dominant way of organizing the transport sector, with most of the minibuses operating in violation of the existing regulatory framework. On the other hand, the term "informality" still helps us to understand the wider political dynamics at stake. It highlights the major power differences at stake, with clientelist forms of interaction serving the political agendas of elite actors, rather than protecting the interest of the relevant actors and improving the overall conditions of the sector (Meagher, 2006, 2008, 2010), a process described by Tendler (2002) as the "devil's deal".

In this situation, reform of the transport sector remains very difficult – certainly given the lack of alternatives. While the battle for the regulation of Kinshasa's public transport will continue for a while, the "spirit of death" will remain an important mode of transport for considerable time to come.

Notes

1 ACCO is the trade union of drivers, the only legally registered one in DRC. It defends the interests of the drivers.
2 Interview. Analyst. Kinshasa (6 February 2015).
3 Interview. Minibus driver. Kinshasa (2 October 2013).
4 Taken from official statistics (RDC: INS, 2015, p. 71). Other estimates vary.
5 Retranskin went bankrupt after three months.
6 Many Transco buses and minibuses have difficulties getting

spare parts, and about 61 were damaged during the January 2015 demonstrations (Radio Okapi 2015).
7 SCCT (Société Congolaise de Contrôle Technique), the company Trinity 3 (a private company) and the CFCTA (Centre de Formation et de Contrôle Technique Automobile).
8 Urban Department of Transport and Means of Communication
9 Nouvelles Unités.
10 Interview. Chef d'antenne. Kinshasa (10 August 2015).

11 Cinque Chantiers.

12 Other central parts were addressing road infrastructure, in which significant investments were made. Another part of this program was the introduction (again)of new public buses. Two public bus companies were introduced (Transco and Retranskin). The government also aimed to modernize the sector of small-bus operators, and introduced the so-called "spirit of life" buses, a direct reference to the dangerous "spirit of death" minibuses. Announced in 2012, these buses were introduced in 2014 (Malukisa, 2017).

13 For example, an accident in 2013, in which 28 people were killed (Radio Okapi, 2013a).

14 Interview. Chairman of ACCO. Kinhsasa (7 August 2015).

15 Overheard conversation. Two DUTVC controllers. Kinshasa (12 May 2014).

16 Conversation overheard. Head of office and user. Kinhsasa (6 August 2014).

17 This message was repeated by the Commissioner General of the police, Charles Bisengimana, who argued on the radio that "the interdiction of vehicles which are not suited for circulation, among which the 207, commonly known here in Kinshasa as the spirit of death" (Radio Okapi, 2014b).

18 Interview. Provincial ACCO director. Kinshasa (April 2015).

19 This never materialized. Many of the minibuses are, at the time of writing, still at the police station.

20 It is also worth noting that a number of publications claim that Kabila himself is an ex-taxi driver (Blair, 2006).

21 André Kimbuta is not only the governor but also the also the member of parliament for Kinshasa, and prominent member of the ruling party PPRD. He is also able to act as the ultimate protector of the small-scale operators and citizens.

References

Africatime (2014) Un nouveau moratoire de 45 jours accordé aux "207". *Africatime*. Available from: fr.africatime.com/congo/articles/un-nouveau-moratoire-de-45-jours-accorde-aux-207 [Accessed 9 July 2017].

Assogba, D. (2014) RDC: les taxis-bus Mercedes 207 boudent le contrôle technique à Kinshasa. *Oeil d'Afrique*. Available from: archives.oeildafrique.com/rdc-les-taxis-bus-mercedes-207-boudent-le-controle-technique-kinshasa [Accessed 9 July 2017].

Baaz, M.E. and Olsson, O. (2011) Feeding the horse: Unofficial economic activities within the police force in the Democratic Republic of the Congo. *African Security* 4: 223–41.

Baaz, M. E., Verweijen, J. and Olsson, O. (2018) Navigating "taxation" on the Congo River: The interplay of legitimation and "officialisation". *Review of African Political Economy* 45 (156): 250–66.

Bierschenk, T. (2010) States at work in West Africa: Sedimentation, fragmentation and normative double-binds. University of Mainz, Department of Anthropology and African Studies. Working Paper 113.

Blair, D. (2006) Former taxi driver proves effective leader. *Daily Telegraph*. Available from: www.telegraph.co.uk/news/1525267/Former-taxi-driver-proves-effective-leader.html [Accessed 23 August 2017].

De Herdt, T., Titeca, K. and Wagemakers, I. (2012) Make schools, not war? Donors' rewriting of the social contract in the DRC. *Development Policy Review* 30 (6): 681–701.

De Herdt, T. and Titeca, K. (2016) Governance with empty pockets: The education sector in the

Democratic Republic of Congo. *Development and Change* 47 (3): 472–94.

Emizet, K. (1998) Confronting leaders at the apex of the state. *African Studies Review* 41 (1): 99–137.

Englebert, P. (2009) *Africa: Unity, Sovereignty, and Sorrow.* Boulder, CO: Lynne Reiner.

Goodfellow, T. and Titeca, K. (2012) Presidential intervention and the changing 'politics of survival' in Kampala's informal economy. *Cities* 29 (4): 264–70.

Gould, D. (1980) *Bureaucratic Corruption and Underdevelopment in the Third World: The Case of Zaire.* New York, NY: Pergamon.

Hart, K. (1995) L'entreprise africaine et l'économie informelle: Réflexions autobiographiques. In: S. Ellis and Y. A. Fauré (eds) *Entreprises et entrepreneurs africains.* Paris: Karthala/Orstrom.

Hart, K. (2001) *Money in an Unequal World.* New York, NY: Texere.

Kanyama, C. (2014) Public message broadcast on Congomikili (15 January 2014). Available from: www.youtube.com/watch?v=FoHL7ie_B6Q [Accessed 23 November 2018].

Kimbuta, A. (2013) Interview on Télé 50. No public transcript available (18 May 2013).

Klein, A. (1999) The barracuda's tale: Trawlers, the informal sector and a state of classificatory disorder off the Nigerian coast. *Africa* 69 (4): 555–74.

Kumar A. and Barrett F. (2008) Stuck in traffic: Urban transport in Africa. BIRD, Africa Infrastructure Country Diagnostic 44980.

Lelo Nzuzi, F. (2011) *Kinshasa: Planification & Aménagement.* Paris: L'Harmattan.

Lemarchand, R. (1988) The state, the parallel economy, and changing patronage systems. In: Rothchild, D. and Chazan, N. (eds) *The Precarious Balance: State and Society in Africa.* Boulder, CO: Westview, pp. 149–70.

Mwanza Wa Mwanza (1998) *Le transport urbain à Kinshasa, un Nœud gordien.* Paris: L'Harmattan.

MacGaffey, J. (ed.) (1987) *The Real Economy of Zaire: The Contribution of Smuggling and Other Unofficial Activities to National Wealth.* London: James Currey.

Malukisa Nkuku, A. (2017) La « gouvernance réelle » du transport en commun à Kinshsasa : La prééminence des « normes pratiques » sur les normes officielles. PhD Dissertation: Institute of Development Policy and Management, University of Antwerp.

Meagher, K. (2006) Social capital, social liabilities, and political capital: Social networks and informal manufacturing in Nigeria. *African Affairs* 105 (421): 553–82.

Meagher, K. (2008) Informality matters: Popular economic governance and institutional exclusion in Nigeria. Presentation at St Antony's College, Oxford.

Meagher, K. (2010) *Identity economics: Social Networks and the Informal Economy in Nigeria.* Suffolk: James Currey.

MediaCongo (2014) ACCO: Les chauffeurs des bus 207 s'en vont en grève! *MediaCongo.* Available from: www.mediacongo. net/article-actualite-996.html [Accessed 9 July 2017].

Motemona Gibolum, G. (2014) Provincial Minister of Transport. Letter no. SC/615/MTJSL/CAB-MIN/AND/AND/2014 (29 October 2014).

Inkwayi Tungila, A. and Ebamba Boboto, J. (2013) Faut-il interdire de circuler les « taxi-bus 207 », alias « esprit de mort » ? Pour les remplacer par quoi? *Congo-Afrique* 473: 119–33.

Pain M. (1984) *Kinshasa: La ville et la cité.* Paris: Editions de l'ORSTOM.

Radio Okapi (2012a) Les Kinois à l'heure de la grève des

transporteurs privés. Available from: www.radiookapi. net/actualite/2012/05/21/ les-kinois-lheure-de-la-greve-des-transporteurs-prives [Accessed 12 June 2017].

Radio Okapi (2012b) Paralysie du transport en commun à Kinshasa. Available from: www.radiookapi. net/emissions-2/dialogue-entre-congolais/2012/05/21/ ce-soir-paralysie-du-transport-en-commun-kinshasa [Accessed 12 June 2017].

Radio Okapi (2012c) Kinshasa: Les activités socioéconomiques paralysées par la grève des transporteurs privés. Available from: www.radiookapi. net/actualite/2012/05/21/ kinshasa-les-acticites-socioeconomiques-paralysees-par-la-greve-des-transporteurs-prives [Accessed 12 June 2017].

Radio Okapi (2012d) Sécurité routière: Importance du contrôle technique automobile. Available from: www.radiookapi. net/nationale/2012/05/22/ securite-routiere-importance-du-controle-technique-automobile#sthash.ottpe5RF.dpuf [Accessed 12 June 2017].

Radio Okapi (2012e) Radio interview with Justin Kalumba, Minister of Transport and Communication. No public transcript available (22 May 2012).

Radio Okapi (2013a) La problématique de la sécurité dans le transport en commun en RDC. Available from: www.radiookapi. net/emissions-2/dialogue-entre-congolais/2013/05/06/ ce-soir-la-problematique-de-la-securite-dans-le-transport-en-commun-en-rdc [Accessed 12 June 2016].

Radio Okapi (2013b) Kinshasa: 50% de conducteurs du transport en commun ne connaissent pas le code de la route. Available from: www.radiookapi.net/

actualite/2013/05/11/kinshasa-50-de-conducteurs-du-transport-en-commun-ne-connaissent-pas-le-code-de-la-route [Accessed 9 July 2017].

Radio Okapi (2013c) Kinshasa: Le gouvernement veut instituer le contrôle technique obligatoire des véhicules. Available from: www.radiookapi. net/actualite/2013/05/16/ kinshasa-le-gouvernement-veut-instituer-le-controle-technique-obligatoire-des-vehicules#sthash. wxRsf7dQ.dpuf [Accessed 11 June 2017].

Radio Okapi (2014a) Interdiction des 207: Le transport en commun déjà perturbé à Kinshasa. Available from www.radiookapi. net/actualite/2014/01/20/ interdiction-des-207-le-transport-en-commun-deja-perturbe-kinshasa [Accessed 12 June 2017].

Radio Okapi (2014b) Radio interview with Charles Bisengimana, Commissioner General of Police. No public transcript available (22 January 2014).

Radio Okapi (2014c) Radio interview with Henri Lisumbu, First Counselor of ACCO (17 March 2014).

Radio Okapi (2015) Kinshasa: 61 bus Transco endommagés dans les manifestations contre la loi électorale. Available from: www.radiookapi.net/ actualite/2015/01/23/kinshasa-61-bus-transco-endommages-dans-les-manifestations-contre-la-loi-electorale [Accessed 16 June 2017].

RDC (République Démocratique du Congo) (1998) By-law n° 409/CAB/MIN/TC/0002/1998. Minister of transport and communication routes.

RDC (République Démocratique du Congo) (2011) By-law n° 409/CAB/MIN/TVC/077/2011. Minister of transport and communication routes.

RDC (République Démocratique
du Congo) (2013) Decree-Law n°
13/001 of 23/02/2013, fixing the
nomenclature of the taxes, duties,
and royalties of the provinces
and the decentralized territorial
entities as well as their modalities
of distribution.

RDC (République Démocratique
du Congo) (2014a) Godard
Motemona Gibolum, mission
order n° 410.10/DUTVC/SGGP/
MTJSL/248/2014 (6 May 2014).

RDC (République Démocratique
du Congo) (2014b) Godard
Motemona Gibolum, mission
order n° 410.10/DUTVC/SGGP/
MTJSL/471/2014 (5 August 2014).

RDC (République Démocratique
du Congo) (2014c)
Announcement of Primature
(22 January). Available from:
fr.africatime.com/republique_
democratique_du_congo/articles/
matata-tranche-sursis-accorde-
aux-207-inpp-fikin-et-kingabwa-
ouverts-au-controle-technique
[Accessed 1 July 2017].

Roitman, J. L. (2004) Fiscal
Disobedience: An Anthropology of
Economic Regulation in Central
Africa. Princeton, NJ: Princeton
University Press.

RTBF (2014) L'interdiction
des minibus Mercedes 207
« esprit de mort » perturbe
les Kinois. Radio Télévision

Belge Francophone. Available
from www.rtbf.be/info/monde/
detail_l-interdiction-des-minibus-
mercedes-207-esprits-de-mort-
perturbe-les-kinois?id=8180810
[Accessed 9 July 2017].

Titeca, K. (2006) Les OPEC boys
en Ouganda, trafiquants de pétrole
et acteurs politiques. Politique
africaine, 103, pp. 143–59.

Titeca, K. (2014) The
commercialization of Uganda's
2011 election in the urban
informal economy: Money, boda-
bodas and market vendors. In:
Perrot, S., Makara, S., Lafargue, J.
and Fouéré, M. A. (eds) Elections
in a Hybrid Regime: Revisiting the
2011 Polls. Kampala: Fountain, pp.
178–207.

Titeca, K. and De Herdt, T.
(2011) Real governance beyond
the "failed state": Negotiating
education in the Democratic
Republic of Congo. African Affairs
10 (439): 213–31.

Tendler, J. (2002) Small firms, the
informal sector, and the devil's
deal. IDS Bulletin 33 (3): 1–15.

Young, C, and Turner, T. (1985)
The Rise and Decline of the Zairian
State. Madison, WI: University of
Wisconsin Press.

William, J.-C. (1986) Zaire, l'épopée
d'Inga: Chronique d'une predation
industrielle. Paris: L'Harmattan.

8
Garbage Collection in Bukavu: "The Political Class Does Not Take Care of Garbage Here"

Randi Solhjell

Urban waste management and sanitation are excellent themes through which to study the particularly tense everyday issue of governance functions. Simply stated, cities could quickly become dirty if no one cared about handling waste, which relates to how citizens and authorities interpret public spaces in urban settings. Simultaneously, citizens who wish to maintain a clean personal space need to have access to proper waste disposal. In other words, waste is a matter of public and private concern, and requires varied forms of governance.

This chapter focuses on the provincial capital Bukavu, in South Kivu. The empirical study is based on multiple research periods in the period 2012 to 2015 in Bukavu, DRC, combing participant observation, interviews and focus-group discussion with different citizens and authorities. Interview subjects were carefully selected on the basis of their role in service provision, while focus group members were selected based on their representing different socio-economic, gender, or age groups. Bukavu represents an interesting geopolitical site of contested access to and control of public goods, and serves as a space of intensified negotiations of statehood by having a high density of formal "stateness" (Hansen & Stepputat, 2001).

Urban waste management stands in contrast to a number of other public services discussed in this book. Namely, and though urban waste management is generally not considered a task for higher government officials, there is a lack of any "real" form of regulation, or financial or political support. In other words, waste problems represent a form of "politics of neglect" and a de facto governance of "not thinking about it" (van der Geest & Obirih-Opareh, 2009, p. 219). The exceptions to this are the politically significant areas for provincial, regime-affiliated elites (e.g. Place de l'Indépendance). However, these spaces are de facto political spaces rather than public spaces. This emphasis on keeping clean only politically significant places or neighbourhoods in which members of the public authorities reside, I argue, is a source of disconnection between the authorities (i.e. the state) and the populace. Citizens, represented through the two districts (*communes*) Kadutu and Ibanda, manage sanitation issues and waste in their private spaces. In between are the public spaces which are not strictly political or private, but are used, to varying degrees, as wasteland. The use of public space – such as rivers, broken pipes and the lake – as garbage disposal, is an unescapable concern for citizens regardless of their social status. This shows the day-to-day tension in state–society relations when it comes to waste management as an aspect of statehood; namely, negotiating territorial space.

It is important to note that what some see as waste, others see as opportunity. Therefore, waste can be defined as something "that ha[s] lost [its] value in the eyes of the first owner" (Cointreau, 1984, cited in Beall 1997, p. 953). Waste is here seen as precisely something that no longer has any value to the person who disposes of it. The main categories of waste that will be discussed are biodegradable waste and solid waste. Biodegradable waste – such as leftover food, plants and human bodily waste – is potentially recycled into compost for land fertilization. Solid waste – such as plastic, cans, paper and fabric – generally has a more technically demanding recycling process. Waste management thus becomes a matter of handling what gets discarded, which can be a private or public actors' duty and/or interest.

The chapter exemplifies how waste management becomes a place for urban state–society frictions between public authorities and citizens. Here, the daily governance of waste becomes the centre of disputes over what constitutes public space and public services. By daily governance, I mean what mechanisms are used, what institutions are in place, and how actors individually or collectively organize in order to tackle sanitation problems – in particular waste management – on a day-to-day basis (van Eeuwijk, 2009, p. 303). My observations reveal the tensions of belonging to a city with disputed ideas about what it means to be a citizen, and how to maintain public spaces and expectations of state-like authorities. I argue that despite the challenges of waste management services, the state can show remarkable resilience and dominance in the public sphere due to the high and unfilled expectations of citizens.

Here I see the state as something that is performed and enacted, not as a singular entity but rather as a series of experiences, with practical aspects of statehood and citizenship coming alive through the city (inspired by: Butler, 1988; Doty, 2003; Dunn, 2010; Migdal &

Schlichte, 2005; Weber, 1988). According to this line of thinking, the state is interpreted not as a pre-given entity, but rather as subjects in process (Migdal & Schlichte, 2005, p. 20). As Weber writes: "nation states are not pre-given subjects but subjects in process and that all subjects in process (be they individual or collective) are the ontological effects of practices which are performatively enacted" (1998, p. 78). This means, I argue, that political processes and negotiations over public goods occur continually, resulting in a dynamic de facto statehood that is never frozen in time but rather performed, created, transformed and reinvented. For instance, as Lund eloquently puts it, "the state did not rise like the sun at an appointed time. It was present at its own making" (2006, p. 675). In other words, citizens and the state do not hold natural or objective truths, but are constructed effects of various performances and processes in the making.

Moreover, it is precisely the engagement with lower-level bureaucrats and citizens that has inspired innovative perspectives on governance (e.g. Bierschenk & Olivier de Sardan, 2014; Hagmann & Péclard, 2010; Lund, 2006). In particular, this chapter will first discuss how a deprived district in Bukavu, namely Kadutu, deals with waste problems. Waste management is mainly conducted by the private citizens of Bukavu or through certain commercial industries. However, in the official documents for the city-hall authorities in Bukavu, it is stated that they are responsible for managing waste, especially in urban centres.[1] Thus, I will examine the administration, starting from the highest officials at the city level (in city hall) and then move down through the hierarchy of public servants in the three districts in which Bukavu is divided. As we will see, the main public outreach from the city-hall authorities seems to be sensitization campaigns, planting trees, and providing a few tricycles that require user fees.

Further, this chapter will discuss waste management perspectives from citizens in Kadutu, but also from a wealthier district, namely Ibanda. Kadutu and Ibanda are historically divided areas, the former being the African cité (peripheral zone) and the latter a European centre. These citizens are positioned as wanting to access waste services but, as revealed by the empirical data, they are also providers of waste services due to the politics of neglect. Ordinary citizens keep their daily problems of waste at bay by, for instance, throwing garbage in the lake, while public authorities tend to ignore any form of sanitary governance. At the same time, it is puzzling to see how people's private spaces, such as their homes or clothes, are kept exceptionally clean. Individuals' polished shoes, for instance, are remarkably spotless as citizens navigate their ways along the muddy trails of peripheral Bukavu. These forms of cleanliness demonstrate, as Bouju argues, "the will to reproduce the social relationship fostered with those who share this space" (2009, p. 146). In other words, the motivation to keep a place clean depends on a feeling of ownership and belonging. In sum, waste management can reveal a way of understanding the processes linked to ideas of what a state is, through performance and enactment, and what it means to be a citizen in areas of disputed authority.

Waste management from the providers' point of view

During the fieldwork, it was a challenge to identify the formal, administrative level of waste management in Bukavu. As the next section will reveal, there are indeed views on where the waste should be thrown (into rivers, sewage channels, the lake and so on), but identifying service providers in the public or private sector was more difficult. In this section, I will dissect the different levels of public administration when it comes to waste management. Administrative organization of Bukavu is structured as follows. At the top, the city hall (*Mairie*) has an appointed city mayor (*maire*) in charge of the city.[2] Within the city, there are three districts (*communes*) in Bukavu, namely Ibanda, Kadutu and Bagira. These districts each have a district mayor (*bourgmestre*) in charge who reports to the mayor. Further down the hierarchy in these territories, you have, in descending order, chiefs of neighbourhood (*quartier*), block (*cellule*), street (*avenue*) and finally those of "ten houses".[3] How important these arrangements are vary considerably across the city, whereas the more powerful individuals appear to be centred around central areas such as traffic junctions and/or markets.

This chapter starts with the city hall, following then the district level through Kadutu, where the district mayor is positioned, down to the level of neighbourhood chief in Kadutu. Finally, the last level will include the Kadutu market administration, together with the local waste workers. All levels are located within the city hall administration and demonstrate a high level of political neglect. This in turn results in frustration regarding waste management in the lower level administration. Finally, there will be a discussion on waste management for the elite through examination of a private company operating in the more affluent areas of Ibanda. In Ibanda, many private households rely on what the people in Kadutu are missing, namely space in their own gardens to either burn solid waste (e.g. plastic), or using leftover food and other biodegradable waste as fertilizers for the soil.

My first encounter regarding waste management at the city hall was particularly interesting. There was great confusion as to whom I should talk to in order to gain a better understanding of waste management in Bukavu. From the reception area, I was sent to the head of the urban planning department (*division urbaine*), who wrote a paragraph on my purpose, that I in turn was to give to another person at the secretariat of the city hall. This person, whom I would not meet in relation to this topic, was not per se in charge of waste management, but might know who to talk to. On the third day, when he was still not in the office and it was not known when he would return, I asked one of his colleagues if he knew of any state actors in charge of waste management in Bukavu. He replied with surprise, "Étatique?! Non."[4] Thus, waste management initially seemed to be an issue that was not perceived as formally supervized by any public institutions.

After several more attempts, I was eventually pointed to the service for the environment and conservation of nature (henceforth the environmental office), at the city hall.[5] I conducted two interviews with the head of the environmental office[6] in two separate years.[7] He claimed that his office coordinated all activities on waste management in the districts and that Congolese law gave the city hall authorities full responsibility for this issue. The most cross-cutting issue, however, was the aspect of a designated waste disposal area for citizens in Bukavu. I asked him several questions about this concern in both interviews. Even though he explained that the garbage disposal area called Irabati, next to Kabare – the closest chiefdom outside Bukavu, was not yet finished – it was being used to dump waste. He argued that the two main problems with waste management were that it was not prioritized by the authorities (politics of neglect) and that there was hardly any available urban space for that purpose. By placing himself as a passive subject – i.e. claiming that it was a lack of will among the "other" authorities – he enacted a state performance of neglect and resignation. The issue of waste had become a public bad – a negative effect on all citizens – but the level of responsibility was seen as a distant memory of the past, when the state performed by dominating space (as in the Mobutu era), in contrast to the current lack of governing the territory, namely the urban public space.

Moreover, it was interesting to note from our discussion his emphasis on the *outside* world's perception of the Congolese government when it came to controlling waste (i.e. the refugee crisis in

1994) rather than the population concerned, and thus placing the *image* of the state higher than the actual practice and performance of the state. The image, in this case, was seen through the issue of clearing waste from places that the outside world could see, and so giving the impression of a more organized state performance. He explained it in the following terms when I asked if the issue of waste was the least prioritized by the city hall:

> The city mayor's office is very concerned with the welfare of the population. We work on sensitizing them to avoid them throwing the waste into the channels and rivers and the lake. But at night, people throw their waste no matter what in the channels. Recycling costs money and we have not yet found a benefactor to help us. There are, for instance, local associations that collect waste, but they have difficulties because we ask the people to let their waste dry on sand so that it is not wet and ready for compost, but people neglect this. On the other hand, there is the problem of space for people; they don't have enough room for private recycling in their house.

I then noted that the issue of waste seemed to be a low priority of the city mayor despite the extent of the problem, and asked whether it had been forgotten completely. He responded:

> It hasn't been forgotten, but there is a lack of will among the authorities. The people are poor ... There are vehicles that can be used but the problem is the lack of space. During Mobutu, there were plots [of land], but these were sold. The good waste-disposal areas are so far away from the city. There used to be also the waste disposal by Ruzizi [river dividing Rwanda and the DRC], but this had to be removed when the refugees from Rwanda came [in 1994] because the problem of waste gave a very bad first impression when entering Bukavu. You know, the world's image of us. Now people use dangerous places for waste disposal where there are problems of landslides that can affect everything.

Yet, some city-hall investment in waste management does exist. This is largely in the form of tricycles – three-wheeled vehicles resembling motorcycles with room for carriage. The Head of the environmental office claimed that these vehicles had been provided directly by the city mayor himself to the three districts. Thus, I met with representatives of the Kadutu district to inquire further

about their work on waste management.[8] These district representatives, whose level is positioned hierarchically just below city hall
in the administration, expressed deep concern regarding the need
for more support from city hall and for the lack of means to deal
with problems of waste, especially with regard to the popular Kadutu
market. This district level did not have the right to collect taxes but
appeared closer to the population in a rapidly growing urban space.
By appearing closer to the local residents in Kadutu, these representatives distanced themselves from both the central urban and
government authorities, attempting to negotiate for the public's
well-being through their positions within the district and central
authorities. In doing so, they enacted a position as representatives
of the population, attempting to fulfil their duties to ensure a more
organized waste collection but at the same time calling for higher
levels of governance in providing rules and means. This exemplifies
the state as a process rather than an object frozen in time. The head
of administration explained it in the following way:

> We asked the central government in Kinshasa for help, as we have
> a big urban population in Kadutu. But we get no help from city
> hall. City hall collects a lot of taxes from companies but all is sent
> back to Kinshasa and not used in our district. Everything we get
> is from the central government.

The environmental supervisor, also present, then expanded:

> The problem is the mentality of people. We work now and then
> with students on sensitizing the people. But we lack means to
> educate people. But the lack of will from the government is also
> affecting people's mentality. They [people in Kadutu] cannot
> keep their waste in their house. They have to dump the waste in
> the river, people have no other choice.

Lower down the district hierarchy is the neighbourhood chief,
which is comprised of twenty representatives and an additional
twenty deputy positions dispersed among the three districts. I met
with one neighbourhood chief in Kasali, an area in central Kadutu,
who was willing to share with me some critical views on the aspect of
waste management. His perspective on the lack of space for public
waste is of particular interest. He expressed, as shown below, that
what used to be public is now privately owned, which in turn challenges any room for a public waste-disposal area. I argue that this

public-turned-private space in the city shows the contested living environment in Bukavu, which challenges one of the fundamental perceptions about what a state "should do", namely governing its territory. That is not to say that a so-called functioning state governs its territory in order to be called a state. Rather, the idea and practices of states attempting to control their territory, including land concessions and regulations, are essential to the dynamics of state-making. Land contestations are cross-cutting concerns in the eastern DRC and reflect statehood tensions, among other matters involving state and customary rule, identity and belonging, all of which show the dynamics of state-making processes (see e.g. Vlassenroot & Huggins, 2005). Thus, the issue of waste management serves as an example of these fundamental challenges, which will be returned to below. As the neighbourhood chief argued:

> When it comes to waste, we don't really have a public waste place. All waste places that used to be here have been sold ...
> The problem is all over the city, not just in this district. We repeat this again and again to the authorities. Instead, there are street children who work for 200 Congolese francs per bag of waste, collecting it on foot. [The problem] is not at the population level. I talk to the district mayor, who talks to the city mayor, but they say nothing to us. So we keep quiet with the population because we have nothing to say or give them.[9]

The common problems of waste in Kadutu are particularly elevated in the central market. Though this market is not directly positioned in the administrative hierarchy of the district, there is a direct link with the environmental office and the hygienic sanitation office at the Kadutu central market,[10] which are in charge of hygiene including waste management. Kadutu central market is owned by the city hall. The rent and income tax from the market seem to be important for the city hall, and thus the efforts of district waste services (such as tricycles) are directed to this area.

The head of the market's sanitation office was willing to explain some of his concerns regarding waste and how difficult it was to keep order with a large number of people visiting this popular market. Based on what he was telling me, there was a frustration with the lack of political will from the city-hall authorities. Of particular interest was how he described the lack of space for public waste, on the one hand, and the view that the state owns the land, on the other. The function of the state, from his perspective, would mean taking charge of its legal status as land owner and turning the land over into proper public usage. The *de jure* aspects of land ownership are certainly disputed, such as the 1973 general property law,[11] but it also demonstrates a considerable perception of state-like governance of public space. I argue that, in many ways, the 1973 general property law under Mobutu lives on by stating that "the soil is the exclusive and inalienable property of the State", where the public domain includes all the lands which are intended for public use or public services (DRC, 1973). The memory of a dominating, coherent state under Mobutu also affects present practices, and demonstrates the continued process of state-making. Imagining that land is owned by the state has major implications for de facto statehood, exemplified through disputes over governing waste. Regarding this, the head of office argued the following:

> There is a lack of means to get rid of the waste here. We have
> nothing. Transportation is a real problem. People from nearby
> villages come to Kadutu to sell or buy products and they just
> throw away the plastic, the banana leaves and manioc leftovers
> here. We at this office also have some technical issues. We have
> a small staff that collects garbage from the market but the only
> option then is to throw it in the river. There are no options other
> than using the river or the lake even though we know it pollutes.
> The city hall has never replied to our requests. There is no
> space to dispose of garbage here and the only option is far away
> [Irabati] ... The political class does not take care of garbage here.
> It is the city hall's responsibility. The land belongs to the state. If
> they really wanted, they could ask people to leave and use it for
> waste depots.[12]

After the interview, the head of office took me to the place where they disposed of waste, which was just across the street from the market, approachable through a trail between small wooden houses. The landfill area was in an area of numerous private houses and on a small hill leading down to the river Kahuha, which flows into Lake Kivu. The problem of waste mismanagement also affects public-health concerns and access to clean water. The citizens living in these surroundings find themselves, I argue, on the margin of the state. These waste sites create spatial relations for struggles of "a public that is yet to come" (Walters, 2008, pp. 203–204). By this I mean that there is a limited will to reproduce social relations between state-like authorities and citizens at the margins of the city, due to a lack of feelings of ownership and belonging within the public domain. On one hand, keeping the problem of waste at bay by throwing it into the river and lake is a solution to a neglected public problem for many citizens and local waste-workers. On the other, those in authority can blame the ignorance of ordinary people and then themselves neglect the problems of waste by living in leafier neighbourhoods and paying for a basic service to remove waste.

In order to demonstrate this, the group discussion with local waste-workers employed through the hygiene office at Kadutu market, illustrate these tensions. These are workers from the villages outside Bukavu with little or no education, and no knowledge of French. The income for each worker was stated to be around a few hundred Congolese Francs – around fifty US cents, per day. The following is an excerpt of the discussion:

Woman 1: We struggle in this work because we have no tools. We have to put the garbage bags on our heads and carry them to the dump. Sometimes the bags leak. We cannot carry them far in this way.

Interviewer: Do you get any assistance from the city hall?

[General assent that there is no help from the city hall]

Man 1: It is the responsibility of the city hall to help us with a place for waste, it is their duty. We expect help on this and they should provide us with transportation ... It is their duty; we still have hope. With the last city mayor we did get some funding for salaries. It is our right to expect this from the state.

Woman 2: We heard some time back that the city hall would help us remove the bags of garbage. We collected all the bags and took them to the place we were told to, but they never came to pick them up with their trucks. After some time, it began to smell and we had to get rid of it all. We lack encouragement ...

Woman 3: The government does not come to us, they only talk to the market owners. It is the market owners that pay our salaries ...

Man 2: The authorities have ill intentions. They take everything into their own pockets. Those who took over after the Belgians were brutal and their inheritance has continued in later generations.

Interviewer: If they are so useless, why are you afraid to speak up against their bad deeds?

Man 2: We cannot seem to shake them off [the state authorities].[13]

Elaborating on the point that it was impossible to "shake off" the state, the employees in further discussion explained that if they ever stopped working, the waste would pile up within two days. Then, the marketplace salespeople women would call up representatives at the city hall because the sellers paid taxes to them, and the city hall would send police to arrest the waste workers or, worse, the market owner, which, in turn, would mean serious repercussions for them and their families. At the same time, there are interesting aspects of these workers' expectations of the state. The high expectations of the state stand in contrast to the practice of city hall authorities, who, according to the workers, have continued to disappoint in the domain of waste management service provision. Their feelings of neglect and abandonment by the city hall, while still being under pressure to do their duty by the market owners, meant that these workers were only performing their public service at a minimum level – i.e. keeping the waste at bay by removing it out of sight of the market.

Finally, there are commercial actors involved in the waste business in more affluent areas. Travelling through the neighbourhood of Muhumba, where I lived during my stay, I discovered posters on the gates of restaurants and hotels advertizing Poubel Net, which can be interpreted as "Clean Waste",[14] and a picture of a modern waste-truck. I gained an interview with the chief secretary at Poubel Net in her office.[15] She explained that they were a part of a larger Canadian company named Groupe Ciel Ouvert[16] and that their focus was primarily on the disposal of household organic waste for paying clients. She also said that they had agreements with land owners in the area, whereby they would turn the biodegradable waste into compost for land fertilization. The cost of their service varied from one to twenty US dollars per month depending on who the clients were. She argued that, from her perspective, the local government was primarily a problem and it saw Poubel Net's service as a potential business opportunity rather than a source of waste-management relief. Here, private companies such as Poubel Net are calling for state practices and performances regarding regulation, management and finance of public goods provision. Meanwhile, state institutions are finding innovative forms of demanding taxes on private services that they are unable or unwilling to offer. The cost of the high-end services that Poubel Net offered were generally not an option for most citizens in Bukavu, however. As the chief secretary explained:

> Our clients are paying customers. Poorer people rely on youth organizations that can get rid of garbage at lower costs. But in order to operate, the Ministry of Environment demanded a lot of taxes from us. We pay six thousand [US] dollars per year in order to be allowed to operate. The lack of public waste disposal areas is a problem for the Government. The political authorities in la Botte [the provincial ministries' neighbourhood] use our services but they refuse to pay. They have a large debt to our company. The taxes they take from us and other companies are just pocketed. Sometimes when the bosses [in the public offices] are short on cash, they send lower ranking servants to demand payments from us on the basis of various taxation claims. It is fine to pay taxes, that is normal, but where the money goes is not okay ... We prefer clients like large humanitarian organizations, The Red Cross for instance, who have many ex-patriots and always pay at the end of the month ... People in the city are suffering as they cannot pay the money for this service. They have to throw their garbage on the streets and in gutter and sewage channels, blocking water and creating diseases. People send their kids to throw away garbage. It is a big problem for the city.

It is interesting to note how the chief secretary points to the lack of waste disposal areas as "a problem for the Government". This remark demonstrates a perception of expecting the state to deliver on certain services, while acknowledging the challenges of managing and accessing public space. Moreover, these ongoing negotiations between the public authorities and a private company when it comes to sanitation services and taxation also demonstrate the processual understanding of the state. That is, as a successive series of experiences between subjects attempting to access and manage sanitation services as an aspect of daily governance.

Waste management from the citizens' point of view

I conducted interviews and focus groups with adolescents, women and men in Ibanda and Kadutu, where we discussed, amongst other things, the issue of waste management. The men I interviewed in

Kadutu were not involved in waste management, as this was seen as a woman's and/or a youth's task.[17] The women I interviewed in Kadutu had very few material resources and lived in small houses with earthen floors and had on average eight children.[18] For them, human bodily waste problems (toilets) and the lack of space were particular concerns. From what they shared with me, these women were not in a position to pay for waste services. Instead, they were using water in the form of rain or streams to dispose of waste or, alternately, to burn it during the dry season. In addition, the women were extremely concerned with the issue of toilet facilities – a problem that was causing diseases and discomfort for them and their families.

The performative practices of waste management reduced these women to a marginal citizen position, where dealing with household waste was a matter of day-to-day survival. Their problems were connected to lack of space, but using the few public spaces – such as a water pump area or the river – to get rid of waste, in turn resulted in polluted drinking water. That these waste management practices led one of the women to consider their lives as similar to animals (see below) demonstrates the effect of these daily practices in making citizens feel rejected by the city hall authorities. In addition, one of the women expressed the fear of being arrested if they spoke up against the difficult situation they found themselves in. I argue that this is an example of the processual understanding of the state, namely of state-citizens' experiences of negotiating terms for delivering on waste and sanitation. The following is an excerpt of our discussion:

Woman 1: We don't have any place to get rid of the [toilet waste]. When the toilet is full, we wait for the rain to take it away. We don't have anywhere to dig for a new toilet; there is a lack of land …

Woman 2: We put our waste in bags and wait for the rain to take it away.

Woman 3: There is a waste place in Funu [one public water reservoir in Kadutu]. During the dry season we take it there to burn it or we take it to a stream. We also drink from the same streams. We live like some animals.

Interviewer: What can be done to improve your situation? Can you speak up against the situation?

Woman 2: If you want to speak up, they will arrest you!

Interviewer: What about organizing yourself so that you are more people together?

Woman 2: The leaders of the group will be hunted down and imprisoned.

In the preceding field visit, I had also conducted several interviews with women working at the central market in Kadutu.[19] Though a few said they paid small sums to youth groups who collected waste, they mainly relied on rivers, gutters and the colonial drainage systems.[20] During their attempts at disposal in the drainage system at Camp Saio – the main Congolese military camp in Bukavu – two of the women I interviewed reported that they had had several run-ins with local police officers, who would claim that garbage disposal was not allowed in what was considered to be public space. Rather than reporting the transgression to their chiefs or fining these women, the local police would usually negotiate for small sums of money. For the women that lived further away, it was easier to dispose of their waste without having to negotiate with the police, as the outskirts were subject to lax controls. The density of state-like actors in the urban space makes these relations and interactions between public authorities and citizens more frequent and harder to escape. The citizens in this case keep their waste problems at bay by throwing it in public areas (rivers, drainage, and lake). They thus, again, lack the incentive to maintain a clean, common city.

The youth in Kadutu expressed similar concerns about a lack of options when it comes to waste disposal and public toilets. During the discussion, these young people expressed frustration with the sanitation difficulties, but were at the same time joking, as well as suggesting business models for much-needed public toilets. In the conversation below, as well as in different encounters I had during focus-group discussions, it is interesting to note how certain institutions were talked about as both public and private in the same sentence. In discussion, public toilets were interpreted as places that were not in a private home, but in the popular Kadutu market that everyone could visit. At the same time, the young people considered these toilets as private because there was a user fee. Thus, there is an idea that for a toilet to be entirely public, there should be no cost associated with its usage. These perceptions of what public means, seen through the eyes of Kadutu youth, reveal a tension between the expectations citizens have of public services and what service providers consider proper use by citizens, such as taxes and sharing costs. I argue that these negotiations and expectations around public–private spheres reveal the constructed effects of various performances and processes in the making:

> *Girl 1:* We only have some public toilets in the market, but they are private. You have to pay the owners of the market to use them.

> *Boy 1:* There are no services for getting rid of waste here. We have to dump it in the river.

> *Boy 2:* I would like to start a business in public toilets. I would charge people and make money.

> *Girl 2:* Private toilets are a possibility. In people's houses … They are very dirty, but after you pay you can use it like you please. But the longer you stay, the more you pay, like with diarrhoea. [*Everyone laughs*]

> *Boy 3:* When the toilets are full, people wait for the rain. They release it into the gutters, the rivers and they pollute the entire neighbourhood.

> *Boy 1:* Like Salongo [community duties]. People collect the waste, but they have no place to put it …

> *Interviewer:* I just interviewed the city mayor and he claimed that the population is not educated and that they [the authorities] try to sensitize the population in behaving better. What is your reaction to this view?

> *Girl 1:* People are educated, but we don't have these services like garbage cans.

> *Boy 2:* It hurts to hear this. We are educated; we just don't have any options.

> *Interviewer:* Can you educate the government, like raise awareness so that they know what is going on?

> *Girl 1:* To raise awareness in the government is impossible

because they live in their beautiful houses. They never see this sad life.

Boy 1: We would like to do changes, but we lack the means to do that.[21]

The Kadutu youths' feeling of rejection from the government, due to the authorities living in their "beautiful houses" out of sight from the misery in Kadutu, was also a view shared by the Ibanda youth. The youth in Ibanda were living with a slightly more organized practice of waste disposal and had better access to WCs compared to their peers in Kadutu.[22] Nevertheless, as one argued: "The authorities are selfish. For them, they have enough. We have to change their minds to care about other people. The city is full of injustice. We are not satisfied."

Thus, and despite that these young people not needing to dispose of the waste themselves, they enacted the responsibility of the state in improving the situation of the communities. The problems of waste represented a state in process, where the youth saw the need to change attitudes and performances among authorities. Further, the organizations that collected waste in the youths' households were also dumping the waste into rivers, gutters and the lake. Thus, though they could maintain more sanitary private space without needing to deal with the waste themselves, the issue of waste in public spaces was inescapable even among more affluent citizens.

The women in Ibanda were also struggling with waste problems. However, these women, along with the aforementioned youth, may be considered lucky compared to their peers in Kadutu, who have to dispose of waste themselves. Yet, using sewage systems, gutters, public places (e.g. the playground) and the lake for garbage disposal is an inescapable concern for citizens across social status. Moreover, the different practices of waste management among the women, as exemplified below, demonstrate the plurality of state institutionalization in the everyday lives of these citizens. From renting services from the city hall to fear of imprisonment in case of unlawful garbage disposal, state performance is evident despite neglect and passivity in the public-waste management system. Below are some examples:

Woman 1: I keep the waste in bags and there's a car belonging to volunteers [Salongo] interested in cleaning the environment in Bukavu that collects the bags once a week. But it's not free of charge. Concerning waste from the toilet, I simply rent the vehicle from the city hall.

Woman 2: I live in an area where a car can't reach. To get rid of
the waste I pay some children who take the waste to an unknown
place. There is no public waste place in Bukavu! My toilet hasn't
been full yet. But in my quarter, my neighbours are used to filling
up the old toilets with the soil from digging a new toilet so that
the old is covered by earth.[23] Also, there are people, in my quarter,
who wait until it rains so that they can use water pipes to flush
their toilets and let it flow through the water channel. They do the
same with solid waste and everything flows down to the lake.

Woman 3: There was a large pit dug in Mukukwe by MONUSCO
[UN peace operation headquarters] where we used to throw the
waste. Since it was full, we had difficulty to get rid of the waste.
Nowadays we're throwing waste at the playground near the new
MONUSCO camp. With this, the problem is that the district
authorities are threatening with imprisonment in case they find us
throwing [waste] at this place. But the question is where do they
want us to be throwing the waste when there's nowhere for it?[24]

This tension between citizens and city hall and government authorities was further discussed with the men I interviewed in Ibanda.
These men were also experiencing difficulties with waste issues but
were relatively better off, in the sense that they were not as directly
affected, living in better neighbourhoods with WCs in their homes.[25]
Despite this, and being affluent than the women and young people in
Kadutu, these men expressed great concern with the waste situation.
On the one hand, they could see the potential resources in waste,
such as biogas (using organic matter to create energy), yet on the
other hand they saw the poverty of the city hall (who are responsible
for Bukavu) and recognized that the level of investment required to
harness these resources could not be placed on individual NGOs. In
addition, these men compared what they saw as neglect and passive
state performance in the DRC to the environment-friendly policies
of neighbouring Rwanda. Such comparisons show how another form
of state performance was possible and, I argue, exemplifies that the
process of state-making is not frozen in time:

Man 1: Waste should be managed by public services. In my area,
there is no designated place for garbage. People just wait for the
rain. It ruins the houses. Even during the dry season, we wait.
The waste is just outside the house. Rain water is the garbage
disposal. The population has no other option than to dump their

waste in the river or wait for the rain. The NGOs cannot finance
the waste issue for the entire city of Bukavu. Even myself, I own a
car, but there is no other place to dispose waste. The NGOs only
have limited project time and finance.

Man 2: There are some public places ...

Man 1: [*Interrupting*] Really? Define a public garbage place. Have
you ever been to Kinshasa? Things are even worse there. No, the
lake is our waste place. People lack opportunities and it affects
the lake. It will create serious pollution problems.

Man 2: But here are lots of initiatives, like local organizations.
People deal with waste using their own means and they recycle
into compost. Another initiative is to let the waste dry in sand and
then burn it. The problem is to finance the transport of waste and
to construct the place for turning waste into electricity, biogas and
so on. But also there is a need to change people's mentality.

Man 3: The city is dirty. The first method people use is to throw
waste in the river. People leave waste in the roads during the
night. Look at the government in Rwanda, where they focus on
biodegradable waste and where they have banned plastic bags.
This dirty city [Bukavu] is why we have cholera and mosquitos
causing malaria. You know, sometimes during the night, people
just leave their waste bags outside other people's houses. Or they
leave them in a pothole in the road before it is repaired. This
causes problems with flies and mosquitos. The plastic bags left
in the road are not biodegradable. The [Congolese] government
should invest in biodegradable products like in Rwanda. But the
government has given up in the DRC. It has given up in that
domain [waste]...

Man 3: But the government must also be sensitized, not only
the population. There is also the problem of applicability. You
see, there have been several studies done to find solutions to
non-biodegradable waste. But there are business interests in the
market of importing plastic bags and other goods from Dubai
and China. These people are afraid of losing their lucrative
businesses if there are bans on goods, like in Rwanda.

Conclusions

In this chapter, I argued that there are two interdependent spaces of concern when it comes to waste management – the city's private and public spaces. The study shows how private citizens keep the problem of waste at bay by using what I consider public space, namely rivers, the lake and drainage systems that are not privately owned. The city's public space is largely positioned under the responsibility of the city hall in Bukavu. The citizens, civil servants and district authorities all complained about the lack of a public waste-disposal system. This lack of proper waste-management was a problem causing pollution, public-health issues, and access to clean water.

As the study has revealed, there are considerable frictions in negotiating public space, and what "public" means in practice. As exemplified in the discussion with youth in Kadutu, a public place was assumed to be a place that was free of a user charge, and where anyone could spend time or speak freely without coming under surveillance. However, many participants in this study assumed that such a place did not really exist in Bukavu. Certain places – such as the central market in Kadutu, the stadium, two spaces used as football fields and playgrounds, the pubs and the churches – were discussed, but none of these really fitted with the concept of public space as perceived by the citizens. As one woman in Ibanda explained:

> No, there is no such place in Bukavu, even though the authorities tend to say that markets, football grounds and schools are public spaces. They aren't! What I know is that in other countries, there are places that people go to at any time for enjoyment or relaxation, public talk or for any discussion, and we don't have such things in Bukavu.[26]

What for outsiders can be interpreted as "public spaces", such as Place de L'Indépendence, a large, well-maintained roundabout centrally located with sculptures erected by President Joseph Kabila, was generally not perceived as a public space, but rather a political space, revealing a tension in negotiating statehood (Hagmann & Péclard, 2010).

In many ways, citizens from Ibanda and Kadutu expressed a perception of dismemberment from official public places. The fact that Place de L'Indépendence was a place kept spotless by a number of staff working for the district shows, unsurprisingly, how public authorities appreciate tidy "public spaces". However, this particular space was a demonstration of power by the central authorities, accompanied by district sanitation resources that could have been used for clearing waste from more crowded neighbourhoods. These are all examples of tensions that exist in the city when it comes to what is considered public, political or private spaces, what it means to be a citizen, and issues surrounding state-like authority. The daily governance issues in Bukavu also show how relations between citizens and authorities are performed and enacted through the process of managing waste. The police fining women, dumping garbage in the river, city hall and government representatives not prioritizing a waste depot, citizens expecting free services from the state, as well as many other practices, are all examples of the everyday governance issues that shape understandings of de facto statehood.

Notes

1 These official documents were made available through the office of Division de l'administration du Territoire, 1ere Bureau, Bukavu (September 2014).

2 The last local election was held in 2007 and the governor, city mayor and district mayor have since changed without elections, representing mainly the party of the presidential majority (PPRD).

3 Literally "*chefs de dix maisons*". In practice this number varies: there usually being no precise official records of housing arrangements.

4 "State actors?! No." Informal discussion. Bukavu city hall (15 September 2013).

5 L'Environnement et Conservation de la Nature. Though the district services are neglected, the Congolese government supports the preservation of nature, as evidenced by the largely functioning Institut Congolais pour la Conservation de la Nature.

6 Chef du Bureau, Service de l'Environnement et Conservation de la Nature.

7 Interviews. A. C. Rukomeza, Bukavu (19 September 2013 & 28 October 2014).

8 Interview. P. J-M. Koabashi, head of office and J. D. Tchalumba Olomwene, environmental

supervisor. Bukavu (22 October 2014).

9 Interview. M. Ramazani, Neighbourhood chief of Kasali. Kadutu (30 October 2014).

10 Assainissement Hygiénique, Marché Central de Kadutu.

11 Formally, the 1973 General Property Law (DRC, 1973) provides for state ownership of all land, subject to rights of use granted under state concessions in the DRC (see also Vlassenroot & Huggins, 2005). However, the law also permits customary law to grant use-rights to unallocated land in rural areas. This is a source of considerable legal tension concerning land tenure.

12 Interview. E. Mwomera, Head of office, hygienic sanitation office, Kadutu Central Market. Kadutu (24 September 2013).

13 Focus group. Waste collectors, Kadutu, Bukavu (September 25, 2013). Six women and four men, all senior citizens. Translated from Swahili and Mashi by Jonathan Magoma.

14 The word net is an abbreviation of the word nettoyage, to clean, in French.

15 Interview. Germaine. Bukavu (17 September 2013, Bukavu). Subject preferred to use her first name only.

16 Open Sky Group.

17 Focus group. Five men. Kadutu (9 October 2014).

18 Focus group. Nine women. Kadutu (4 October 2014). Translated from Swahili and Mashi by research assistant Jonathan Magoma.

19 Interviews and focus groups. Sixteen market women. Kadutu (25 & 26 September 2013). Conducted individually, in pairs, or in focus group meetings.

20 They especially depended on the Kahuha river which runs through the neighbourhood and out to Lake Kivu, as well as the streets or colonial drainage systems, for dumping their household waste.

21 Focus group. Eight youths. Kadutu (7 October 2014). Four girls and four boys, aged 15–18.

22 Focus group. Three students, Ibanda (9 October 2014). One girl and two boys, all students of ISP. Conducted in English.

23 This concerns traditional toilets. When a toilet is almost full, people start digging a new one next to the old one. The dirt from the digging is thus used to cover the old toilet.

24 Focus group. Four women. Ibanda (30 November 2014). Conducted and translated from Swahili and Mashi by research assistant Jonathan Magoma.

25 Focus groups. Five Ibanda men (14 & 21 October 2014). I had two sessions with them as there were many follow-up issues that I wanted to discuss further.

26 Focus group. Four women. Ibanda (30 November 2014).

References

Beall, J. (1997) Social capital in waste – a solid investment? *Journal of International Development* 9 (7): 951–61.

Bierschenk, T. and Olivier de Sardan, J.-P. (2014) *States at Work: Dynamics of African Bureaucracies.* Leiden: Brill.

Bouju, J. (2009) Urban dwellers, politicians and dirt: An anthropology of everyday governance in Dobo-Dioulasso (Burkina Faso). In: Blundo G. and Meur, P. Y. L. (eds) *The Governance of Daily Life in Africa: Ethnographic Explorations of Public and Collective Services.* Leiden: Brill, pp. 143–70.

Butler, J. (1988) Performative acts and gender constitution: An essay in phenomenology and feminist theory. *Theatre Journal* 40 (4): 519–31.

Doty, R. L. (2003) *Anti-immigrantism in Western Democracies: Statecraft, Desire and the Politics of Exclusion.* Abingdon: Routledge.

DRC (Democratic Republic of Congo) (1973) General Property Law. Law No. 73-021. Available from: www.wipo.int/edocs/lexdocs/laws/fr/cd/cd003fr.pdf [Accessed January 24, 2016].

Dunn, K. C. (2010) There is no such thing as the state: Discourse, effect and performativity. *Forum for Development Studies* 37 (1): 79–92.

van Eeuwijk, B. O. (2009) The daily governance of environmental health: Gender perspectives from Dar Es Salaam, Tanzania. In: Blundo, G. and Le Meur, P.-Y. (eds) *The Governance of Daily Life in Africa: Ethnographic Explorations of Public and Collective Services.* Leiden: Brill, pp. 301–15.

van der Geest, S. and Obirih-Opareh, N. (2009) Liquid waste managment in urban and rural Ghana? Privatisation as governance? In: Blundo, G. and Le Meur, P.-Y. (eds) *The Governance of Daily Life in Africa: Ethnographic Explorations of Public and Collective Services.* Leiden: Brill, pp. 205–22.

Hagmann, T. and Péclard, D. (2010) Negotiating statehood: Dynamics of power and domination in Africa. *Development and Change* 41: 539–62.

Hansen, T. B. and Stepputat, F. (2001) Introduction: States of imagination. In: Hansen, T. B.

and Stepputat, F. (eds) *States of Imagination: Ethnographic Explorations of the Postcolonial State*. Durham, NC: Duke University Press.

Lund, C. (2006) Twilight institutions: An introduction. *Development and Change* 37 (4): 673–84.

Migdal, J. S. and Schlichte, K. (2005) Rethinking the state. In: Schlichte, K. (ed.) *The Dynamics of States: The Formation and Crises of State Domination*. Farnham: Ashgate, pp. 1–39.

Vlassenroot, K. and Huggins, C. (2005) Land, immigration and conflict in Eastern DRC. In: Huggins, C. and Clover, J. (eds) *From the Ground Up: Land Rights, Conflict and Peace in Sub-Saharan Africa*. Pretoria: Institute for Security Studies, pp. 115–94.

Walters, W. (2008) Acts of demonstration: Mapping the territory of (non-)citizenship. In: Isin, E. F. and Nielsen, G. F. (eds) *Acts of Citizenship*. London: Zed Books, pp. 182–206.

Weber, C. (1998) Performative states. *Millennium: Journal of International Studies* 27 (1): 77–95.

9
Real Land Governance and the State: Local Pathways of Securing Land Tenure in Eastern DRC

Aymar Nyenyezi Bisoka and Klara Claessens

Introduction

In this chapter, we will analyse the different manifestations of the state in the domain of land governance in Eastern DRC, in order to improve our understanding of its modes of action in a so-called fragile state. Securing property rights, as well as the delivery and registration of land ownership and occupation rights, are roles that are classically associated with the state. However, the management of these rights and its related conflicts requires arbitration by a public authority, often outside of the state. In Eastern DRC, different non-governmental actors and local elites set up mechanisms to ensure this public role. Through the analysis of different cases studying the involvement of institutions and individuals that have no a priori links with the state (such as NGOs, customary authorities and economic actors) in the delivery of services in the domain of land governance, we will demonstrate how these actors are intrinsically linked with the state. This analysis will shed light on processes of state legitimization and state-building through these linkages.

Studying the delivery of public services in the domain of land management, and the role of state and non-state actors herein in the DRC, is particularly relevant given the country recently embarked on an ambitious land-reform process. After being re-elected in 2011, President Joseph Kabila highlighted the need for a land reform process to increase the well-being of both rural and urban populations, to limit the number of (land) conflicts, diminish the threat of large-scale land grabbing, to protect property rights more securely, and to facilitate access to credit:

> We will also improve the development and infrastructure of the national territory to achieve … a better living environment for our urban and rural populations. To this end, special attention will be given to land reform, with the aim of limiting the number

of conflicts, better protecting property holders and facilitating access to credit. (Kabila, 2011)

To kick-start the reform process, the Ministry of Land and the United Nations Human Settlement Programme (UN-Habitat) organized a nationwide dialogue. At a national seminar in 2012, the various actors drafted a document in which they agreed on the need for a thorough, inclusive, bottom-up revision of current land policies with respect to human rights and biodiversity (DRC: MAF, 2012).

The data in this chapter was collected by the two authors in the course of their respective PhD projects on land governance and access to natural resources in the Great Lakes Region between 2010 and 2016. Both research projects used an inductive, qualitative case-study approach, mainly through in-depth interviews and focus-group discussions with relevant stakeholders, such as small-scale farmers, concession holders, local elites, customary authorities, state authorities, and members of NGOs and civil-society organizations. What is presented in this chapter is only a small selection of relevant cases, analysed throughout these research projects.

In what follows, we will first unpack the most important theoretical concepts. Second, we will give an overview of land governance in the DRC, with particular attention given to the current land-reform process. Next, we will discuss three particular cases where non-governmental actors took up an active role in the delivery of public service in the land arena. We will show how the state is never far from these initiatives, either because it is called upon to grant them legitimacy or because its institutions and symbols are used or mimicked for the same purpose. These cases of land governance beyond the state not only take place in "informal" spaces or at the margins of the law. Referring to the state, or to its institutions and symbols, grants a certain degree of legitimacy to the state. This legitimation process gradually instils new rationalities, contributing to the strengthening of the idea of the state. Following De Herdt (2011), we then conclude that these rationalities constitute an historical "software", necessary for the functioning of the state under construction.

The state, public services and state formation

What makes the analysis of the state difficult is the fact that it is neither a nominalism – a neutral word serving as an instrument to label reality (Panaccio, 2012) – or simply a conceptualism; a reality endowed with an ontological existence (Marenbon, 1997). As political anthropology suggests, the state is what it announces itself to be as an idea, as well its everyday practice. Hence, to think of the state also implies demonstrating how practices of state legitimation and representation contribute to the process of its formation (Sharma & Gupta, 2006). This dual way of seeing the state is rooted in political sociology, where the state is seen as both a material and mental structure (Bourdieu, 2012).

However, state activities are not exclusively exercised by state institutions in the sense of Abrams and Bourdieu. Besides multiple and diverse manifestations of the state itself,

> ... there are also so-called traditional institutions vying for
> public authority, often bolstered by government recognition ...
> In such cases it is difficult to ascribe rationality to the "state"
> as a coherent institution; rather, public authority becomes the
> amalgamated result of the exercise of power by a variety of
> local institutions and the imposition of external institutions,
> conjugated with the *idea* of a state (Lund, 2006a, pp. 685–6).

Lund (2006a, 2006b) calls these institutions, which are not the state but which exercise public authority, twilight institutions.

A number of activities, negotiated between state and non-state institutions, contribute to the legitimization of the state. Here again, it is important to make the distinction between the state as a structure and the state as an idea. First, the structure of the state is shaped through its recognition by other forms of authority – including twilight institutions – participating in authorization processes, such as land-access negotiations. As Lund (2006b) demonstrates, the participation of the state in the process of recognizing an individual's access to resources reinforces the authority and legitimacy of the state, thus contributing to a process of state formation. According to him: "when an institution authorizes, sanctions or validates certain rights, the respect or observance of these rights by people, powerful in clout or numbers, simultaneously constitutes recognition of the authority of that particular institution" (Lund, 2006b, p. 675). Claims to access land, for example, grant authority to the part of the institution that authorizes access. The capacity of an institution to allow such access constitutes authority, and consequently contributes to the formation of the state.

In the context of this chapter, we start from the idea that the state can only be understood in relation to other political and social spaces that shape relations of domination between individuals and the groups to which they belong (Balandier, 1971). Legal pluralism is a valuable approach to look at this interaction between different co-existing social fields. "[It] draws attention to the possibility that within the same social order, or social or geographical space, more than one body of law, pertaining to more or less the same set of activities, may coexist" (von Benda-Beckmann & von Benda-Beckmann, 2006, p. 14). Each social field has different loci of authority that overlap and interact with other social fields. Because of this interaction and overlap, each field is semi-autonomous. This means that each social field generates internal rules and symbols, but is also sensitive to decisions and rules produced by surrounding social fields (Moore, 1978; Griffiths, 1986). The state, then, becomes a place of politics like so many other social spaces. This vision allows us to understand how state actors negotiate their power and authority with actors and institutions in other social and political spaces, and vice versa (Titeca & De Herdt, 2011).

The semi-autonomous quality of the different legal fields might raise questions about the use of state and non-state domains as analytically distinct categories. Indeed, if different social fields are permeable and mutually influencing, the strict dichotomy between state and non-state domains might be considered false. However, we choose to continue using both categories for the purposes of analytical clarity but also, more importantly, because we believe these are relevant categories in the everyday practices and imaginaries of involved actors.

Overview of land governance in the DRC

Below, we give a brief overview of land governance in the DRC, paying particular attention to the current land-reform process.

Historical overview

In general terms, a very broad amalgam of arrangements governs land access and land distribution in the DRC. Because several different ministries deal with land questions, they have overlapping and often conflicting interests and jurisdictions. Besides the state, there are other institutions that produce rules and norms governing land relations. These are often collectively framed under the simplified header of "customary", "communal" or "informal", but they actually include a broad range of arrangements that are historically informed and locally specific (Claessens, 2017).

Despite this reality, there have been several attempts to institutionalize or deny this normative and legal plurality. During the colonial period, a dual land-system was installed in which state law governed state land (*terres domaniales*), and customary law governed indigenous land (*terres indigènes*). This legal dichotomy created a normative duality in the social significance of land: "in the villages, land possession defined a social relation; on plantations, land possession ascribed alienable property rights" (Van Acker, 2005, p. 83). There was thus a de jure recognition of customary land tenure, but colonial interests always overruled local ones. In fact, "indigenous" rights were defined in a very restrictive manner, and the formalization of these flexible and complex customary systems often entailed reinventing those rights to suit the colonizer's political ends. The vast majority of the land was declared vacant, which led to the expropriation of most of the autochthone communities' land. In addition, the legislation transformed the value of land, allowing it to became a crucial source of monetary wealth with which to finance the colonial project (Clement, 2013; Nzongola-Ntalaja, 2002).

In 1973, Zairian President Mobutu introduced a process of nationalization or Zaireanization, which imposed 100% Congolese ownership on all agricultural, industrial and commercial enterprises.[1] For land exceeding 100 hectares, the political decision on land registration rested with the president or a competent minister. In practice, gaining access to large tracts of land, such as agricultural plantations or forest reserves, depended on being part of the inner-circle of the Mobutist state. Elites who acquired plantations during this time were locally known as *acquéreurs*,[2] or people with privileged political relations (Van Acker, 2005). This, combined with the introduction of the 1973 land law, "strengthened the state's control on the attribution of land rights. It was supposed to be an indirect instrument for the modernization of land institutions, as it allowed the privatization of land that was until then governed by customary arrangements" (Peemans, 2014, p. 19).

The 1973 land law declared all land to be state land. Before this, the colonial legal duality was still applied. From then on, public authorities that could issue registration certificates (*certificats d'enregistrement*) governed the land. Farmers or investors could apply for one of two kinds of certificate: a concession in perpetuity (*concession perpétuelle*), which is only available to Congolese citizens, or an ordinary concession (*concession ordinaire*), which is for 25 years but can be renewed (Mugangu Matabaro, 2008). The new land law made provisions for the management of land held under customary tenure.

Article 389 stipulated that land occupied by local communities could be held under customary arrangements through a presidential decree. However, even though the 1973 land law is still valid, this presidential decree has yet to be promulgated. Since 1973, the legal status of customary tenure has, to say the least, been highly ambiguous. There is considerable confusion over which authorities are responsible for governing them and over the rights of the users of the customary land (Mugangu Matabaro, 2008; Utshudi Ona & Ansoms, 2011).

Because of the introduction of the 1973 law, transactions based on customary law became illegal and local communities lost legitimate control over their land, at least on paper. In reality, however, because of the weak implementation capacity of the state and the legal ambiguity surrounding the management of the customary lands, the new law resulted in the de facto persistence of the colonial legal-duality between state and customary land (Vlassenroot & Huggins, 2005). This does not mean that land relations did not evolve. Vlassenroot and Huggins (2005) describe how the 1973 land law profoundly reshaped property structures and access rights. The role of customary authorities as guardians of the land was undermined, and they had to reposition themselves in the changing political landscape. As a result, traditional patron–client relationships gradually eroded, and were partly replaced by new patrimonial relations based on economic gain and wealth accumulation. More concretely, local customary chiefs tried to maintain the positions they had acquired under colonial rule by becoming gatekeepers during the transition from customary control to the introduction of the modern legal system (Vlassenroot & Huggins, 2005).

The current land reform process

The developments described above led to arbitrariness in land division and (re)distribution processes, tenure insecurity and the proliferation of land conflicts. The need for a thorough reform of the land legislation became imperative to addressing these problems. The DRC is one of the last African countries that have embarked on such a land-reform process. Initiated in 2012 and currently suspended, this reform attributes – at least on paper – great importance to local forms of tenure security, in line with the contemporary institutional and political framework about land governance on the African continent. This framework is relatively new and is part of a second generation of African land reforms.

Whereas the first generation of land reforms on the continent was inspired by the idea that customary land governance could not provide tenure security to boost investment and economic growth,[3] a second and more recent generation of reforms is influenced by research demonstrating the viability and negotiability of customary tenure, in combination with a more human-centred development discourse (Toulmin & Quan, 2000). The land reforms introduced in the immediate aftermath of independence in the 1960s and 1970s[4] proposed the state-led creation of private, individual property titles, whereas more recent reform programs focus on land decentralization through registration at the level of local governance structures (Delville, 2002). This should lead to the development of more flexible and lighter certification schemes, with the aim of securing land rights more quickly, and at a low cost, by relying on local communities when recognizing and validating rights (Colin, Le Meur & Léonard, 2009). The current land-reform process in the DRC should be situated within this second and more flexible wave of African land reforms (Nyenyezi Bisoka & Ansoms, 2015).

The leading land reform document, "Note De Politique Foncière Congolaise", puts forward several arguments when justifying the need for a thorough land reform (DRC: MAF, 2012). First, the obsolescence of previous land laws and their inadequacy in relation to new socio-economic dynamics linked to the requirements of fighting poverty and boosting development. Second, the inconsistencies in the current land administration, which are mostly due to the existence of different, co-existing norm and rule-making systems. This second argument, again according to the underlying logic of the land reform, potentially fuels conflict and impedes international investment (DRC: MAF, 2013). This discourse, stressing the importance of tenure security, is in line with the position of important donors such as the World Bank (Falloux & Rochegude, 1988). In its conceptualization of tenure security, the World Bank promotes the recognition and participation of local actors in the reform process, believing a direct link exists between land registration, private investment and poverty reduction. Furthermore, they establish a relationship between the informality of land rights and tenure insecurity (Lund, 2000).

The Congolese state thus proposes an approach based on participatory land governance, promoting land-tenure security in order to eradicate food insecurity and conflict, and to increase the viability of subsistence agriculture. This is supposed to pave the way for agricultural investment and increased productivity through the creation of a more open peasantry environment. Furthermore, this should eradicate, or at least reduce, the prevalence of land conflicts. Tenure security is then obtained through the clarification, recognition and formalization of local land rights, as well as more efficient and stream-lined land governance and administration (DRC: MAF, 2013). The proposed land reform thus assumes a direct and mechanical link between the proposed policies, the formalization of land rights, conflict prevention, increased investment and poverty eradication.

However, many actors have already cast doubts about the feasi-bility of such a policy in the context of the DRC (Claessens, 2017; Nyenyezi Bisoka & Ansoms, 2015). As proof, the process of land reform is completely blocked for the moment. On the one hand, political actors do not seem to make this reform a priority. On the other hand, chronic political instability does not provide for an oppor-tune moment for its implementation. Finally, the way in which this reform will really be implemented remains unclear, partly because of the significant social, political and economic differences between various Congolese regions. It is, for example, not clear whether or not the systematization and formalization of local transactions in writing will be effective (if at all possible) in the face of a customary oral tradition. Consequently, the Congolese state continues to rely on the outdated 1973 land law, and has great difficulty in providing quality services in land management and land dispute resolution.

In the meantime, local and international organizations, as well as individuals outside the state, have initiated mechanisms to manage and access the land, and to deal with the ever- increasing number of land conflicts. Often, as we will demonstrate below, they mirror, mimic and recycle the state's reference system, and as a consequence should not be analysed in isolation from the state. Furthermore, the state becomes a key player in the legitimization of these mechanisms of tenure security and conflict mediation.

The role of non-state actors and their relation to the state in land management

As was noted earlier, the Congolese state did not manage to reform the land code, and the state's capability to deliver public landed services – such as land-conflict mediation and the delivery of land titles – is dysfunctional. Consequently, a gap arises between the Congolese statutory land framework and actions and decisions in land management at the local level. In what follows, we will analyse three cases from the provinces of South and North Kivu in Eastern DRC, showing how non-state actors propose arrangements in order to position themselves in this framework. However, in order for these arrangements to work, they need the involvement of the state, both actively and discursively. The state manifests itself, formally or substantially, through the legitimization and implicit reinforcement of these arrangements originating outside the state.

Using pieces of paper to formalize local land rights in Kabare and Kalehe

Under the 1973 land law, only a few large landowners were able to register their land. The rest of the land remained governed by a broad variety of locally specific arrangements. In an attempt to secure property and access rights, "small papers" signed between the seller and the buyer of land are increasingly used in order to secure local land tenure (Mugangu Matabaro, 2008; Utshudi Ona & Ansoms, 2011). The purpose of these papers is not to cancel oral forms of land transfer, but rather to formalize these arrangements in the absence of an effective land law. However, they have sometimes increased confusion and created a proliferation of land conflicts because of the lack of uniformity and mechanisms to ensure authenticity and reliability. As a response, different non-state actors in South Kivu have initiated consultations with customary chiefs and local communities in an attempt to systematize these documents and to rationalize their content with the underlying idea to transform these papers into property documents, recognized by all relevant stakeholders including the state.

Yet, these documents are still very locally specific. In the territory of Kabare, they are referred to as "customary-type land contracts"[5] whereas in the territory of Kalehe they are known under the more general header of "occupation and exploitation of customary land" (Mushagalusa Mudinga & Nyenyezi Bisoka, 2014). For non-state actors, these pieces of paper are part of a process of securing land rights and preventing land conflicts. Furthermore, they serve to strengthen the position of local farmers by guaranteeing local tenure security and protecting them against any monopolization of customary chiefs, elites or powerful neighbours. Ideally, these documents could be used as a material basis for the land registry office in an attempt to apply for a registered title.

In Kalehe, different NGOs made efforts to formally introduce these certificates. First, individual consultations with the customary authorities were set up in order to convince them of the importance of written documents in avoiding property conflicts. Second, customary chiefs were invited to participate in a workshop to exchange ideas and draft different possible scenarios. Finally, a conference was organized with different relevant stakeholders. Besides customary authorities, representatives from the state apparatus – such as the local administrators and the local tribunals – participated, with the aim of harmonizing procedures for issuing certificates and giving them a legal status.

In Kabare, the process of establishing customary land contracts followed a similar trajectory. Here, the process began in 2009 with meetings initiated by civil society actors in order to raise awareness amongst local customary chiefs. During these sessions, the results of various research projects on land conflicts and their main causes were discussed. Next, bilateral meetings between a civil society organization and the customary authority of Kabare were set up in order to convince the latter of the importance of its involvement in the establishment of social peace through the provision of secure land access for its citizens. In 2012, this process resulted in the development of the customary-type land contracts.

Whereas the initiatives in Kabare and Kalehe originated outside of the state, they cannot be understood in isolation from the state. First, the move from an oral to a written tradition in transferring land rights is a way of imitating the state's instruments to recognize property, and hence can be seen as an attempt to attach a certain legitimacy to claims originating outside state arenas (Chimhowu & Woodhouse, 2006). Second, the spill-over of state instruments in non-state arenas is mostly accompanied by the presence of state actors. In both territories, attempts were made to include state authorities in the design and implementation phase. This can again be seen as a deliberate move to increase the legitimacy of local practices. Third, these initiatives have been supported by the European Union, the Swiss Cooperation and UN Habitat, institutions that are supporting the land reform process in line with the new land framework stressing the importance of local land security and decentralized land management. It is probably for this reason that clear elements of this framework are found in these initiatives. Finally, the objective seems to put in place certificates or contracts which would replace the "land contracts" provided for in the land reform – which is not yet in place. These NGOs thus seem to be taking the place of the state, which in principle should grant certificates to landowners in the spirit of the new land law.

Using pieces of papers to transfer property rights in Kalehe's plantations

The use of written papers to formalize arrangements originating outside of the statutory realm, to manage social relations and to prevent property conflicts, also occurs outside of the customary domain. On agricultural plantations obtained through an ordinary concession, for example, arrangements of land access and land distribution have been formalized through the use of written documents. This process grants public authority and political power to economic actors – the concession holders. In Eastern Congo, the word plantation refers to specific kinds of large agricultural concessions, most often outside the customary domain. Most of these concessions were established during the colonial period, when they used to produce tropical export crops. Today, after years of political unrest and decades of plunder, foreign colonial settlers have left, and export crops have been replaced by food crops for domestic consumption and sale in local markets. Local Big Men and leaders play a pivotal role in the distribution of land, labour and profits on the plantations. For this reason, the term plantation refers to a large extension of land, on which the management of production and labour derives from the disintegration of the colonial mode of production (Claessens, 2017).

In one particular plantation, Mukwidja, twenty hectares of the plantation have been divided into small residential plots by the concession holder, a local Big Man with connections in important elite circles. He is involved in different economic (e.g. as the president of a local mining cooperative), as well as political, activities. Additionally, as the paternal uncle of the *chef de groupement* (the local representative of the customary authority), he holds strong ties with the customary lineage.

The plantation is thus divided into an agricultural zone (the plantation) and a residential zone (the agglomeration), each with a different set of rules regulating access to the land. But in both zones, the most important gatekeepers are the concession holder and his manager. As in most plantations in the area, land access in the agricultural zone is managed through three land-access mechanisms: *métayage*, *salongo* (both implying labour in exchange for land access for seasonal production) and monetary rental contracts (Claessens, 2013, 2017).

In the residential zone, other rules with regard to land access apply. After having obtained the plantation in the early 1990s, the concession holder started dividing up the land in order to sell the

residential plots in the agglomeration. According to the concession holder, he divided 25 hectares into such plots in collaboration
with the land registry service, which issued him with a document
confirming the plantation's new legal position.[6] By the end of 2013,
twenty hectares were occupied by approximately 1,500 households.
People interested in obtaining a residential plot in the agglomeration
have to approach the plantation manager. Once the interested buyer
has transferred the money, or an arrangement for a credit sale has
been agreed upon, the plantation management prepares a "property
contract" in the form of a receipt. According to the concession holder,
these receipts transfer property rights to the buyer and, consequently
– once the transaction is completed – the land no longer belongs to
the plantation but to the "new owners of the land". The new owner
is now entitled to occupy, sell or install tenants on the plot. However,
according to the beneficiaries of these "property contracts", nobody
has yet been able to transform their receipt into a title at the land
registry office.

The property receipts are a very local and temporal attempt to
ensure tenure security, and to pursue the very personal agenda of
the concession holder. However, their legitimacy is confined to the
physical borders of the (former) plantation. The volatility of these
arrangements became clear in a neighbouring plantation where
similar land access arrangements were negotiated between the land
users and the plantation's management. However, when the management changed, they no longer recognized the written documents
issued under the governance of the previous management. These
developments worry Mukwidja's inhabitants. Local civil society
reacted by setting up a meeting with the concession holder. They
asked him to show documents from the land registry office proving
that the agglomeration had been officially parcelled out:

> To reassure the population, we asked [the concession holder]
> to show us the document of the land registry office proving that
> the creation of the agglomeration is legal. He said that he has
> the document, but he didn't show it to us. He also said that the
> receipt he gave us is sufficient and that we shouldn't panic. We
> accepted his words without being satisfied.[7]

Besides the practice of transferring property rights, the concession holder also refers to the state arena while legitimizing the local
land governance arrangements. He refers to the potential advantages
of the agglomeration's development in terms of economic prosperity,

security and stability. More concretely, he uses arguments related to the locality's economic and security situation, and states that its foundation contributes to a boost in local development. He calls it an "urbanization project" based on the model of Butembo, a city in the province of North Kivu, where he witnessed this little town develop into a regional trading hub. "When people keep on coming to Mukwidja, I prefer that it is an agglomeration instead of an agricultural plantation. Commerce is replacing concessions."[8] According to him, Mukwidja has some comparative advantages that will help develop the agglomeration into a commercial centre. The first is its strategic location between the region's two major towns of Goma and Bukavu, not to mention its advantageous position on the lakeside with access to the island of Idjwi and to Rwanda. In addition, he underlines the security advantage by stating that there has never been pillaging in Mukwidja; "every time armed groups and even the Congolese army were coming, I gave them something and every time they left without any problem." This is also confirmed by some inhabitants of the agglomeration:

> During this period of rebellion, our locality was very safe. After all, he is a man with good relations. He also developed good relationships with the leaders of the RCD,[9] military leaders and political leaders ... He was the only one that could talk to the rebels and he was the only one the rebels would listen to. He could tell them what to do and what not to do.[10]

This legitimizing discourse refers to the historical role of the colonial and the postcolonial state as the provider of security, development and the daily organization of the peasantry. Here it is important to distinguish again between the state as a system and the idea of the state (Abrams, 1977; Sharma & Gupta 2006). Indeed, since the implosion of the Congolese state in the 1990s, security and development are partly being organized outside of the state (Meagher, 2012). Despite these practices, claims with regard to the role of the state are to a large extent based on a collective memory of a strong and developmentalist state, mainly referring to the colonial period and the initial years of the one-party state, until the end of the 1970s. This imaginary of the state continues to influence claims being made with regard to the role of the state. In this sense, discursive references to strong leadership, development and security are important elements on which an ideal image of the state is constructed.

Formalizing local agreements in order to mediate land conflicts in Fizi and Uvira

For a final example of how local arrangements originating outside of the statutory realm are clearly linked with the state, and even with more international frameworks, we move southwards to the Ruzizi planes, where land-use and land-access conflicts between cattle holders and agriculturalists are prevalent. When dealing with these conflicts, some actors no longer choose to rely on informal mediation sessions and verbal compromises. Instead, they increasingly relate to a signed agreement, locally known as *"acte d'engagement"*.[11] This has been observed in conflicts between farmers (Babembe and Bafuliiru), pastoralist (Banyamulenge) and customary chiefs in the territories of Uvira and Fizi (Mushagalusa Mudinga & Nyenyezi Bisoka, 2014). Since 1996, customary chiefs, mainly Babembe and Bafuliiru, have accused cattle raisers of not paying their rights of passage (*itulo*), and of allying with armed militia to steal their cattle. In turn, pastoralist accuse the customary chiefs of infringing their freedom of movement and discriminating against them. The *itulo* has always served as a mechanism to regulate relationships between cattle raisers and the customary authorities of the territories they cross and in which they graze with their livestock. Concretely, *itulo* is paid in the form of a gift – traditionally in kind (cassava for farmers, gold for diggers, or cows for cattle raisers) – to the local chiefs in exchange for their kindness, recognition and protection.

In 2011 (Baraka/Fizi) and 2012 (Uvira), thanks to the facilitation of local civil-society organizations, the three conflicting parties met and defined mechanisms to manage and facilitate the cohabitation of agriculturalist and cattle raisers. They developed a text, "agreement for a peaceful transhumance", containing the commitments of each party and how conflicts related to access to livestock, land and water should be managed. These signed agreements introduced some novelties compared to their oral predecessors. They included the organization of a joint prospecting mission to identify and determine the areas of passage and grazing, the establishment of joint committees – including representatives of customary authorities, farmers and cattle raisers – to manage conflicts, and, finally, the maintenance of *itulo*'s non-monetary and symbolic nature. For their part, the customary chiefs committed to invest in the safety of the cattle raisers, in particular by dissociating themselves from armed groups and accepting the possibility of paying the *itulo* collectively. The cattle raisers, on the other hand, committed to disarm, as well as respecting the land and wells of the farmers when grazing and crossing. Today, this document serves as a reference in the management of land disputes related to transhumance in the territories of Fizi and Uvira.

In North Kivu, a similar type of arrangement between local populations, customary leaders and civil society had more far-reaching consequences, since it resulted in the elaboration of a land decree, eventually adopted by the provincial assembly in 2009–10. The initiators of this agreement were not only involved in conducting research on land conflicts in North Kivu, but they also offered suggestions for land reform at the national level. After a careful analysis of the types, causes, actors and consequences of land conflicts, these initiators found that customary authorities had succumbed to the influence of the socio-political context in an opportunistic way. Their analysis criticized the limitations of the local normative framework governing land issues and its role in the perpetuation of land conflicts. In particular, they demonstrated that the unrealistic expectations of the ordinance foreseen in Article 389 of the 1973 land law (see earlier this chapter) led to a continued vagueness with regard to the management of customary land, to the advantage of customary authorities managing these lands. This ambiguity favoured opportunistic customary leaders, who manipulated land rules to facilitate personal access, or the access of their personal network, to the detriment of peasants (Claessens, Mudinga & Ansoms, 2014; Nyenyezi Bisoka, 2016; Utshudi Ona & Ansoms, 2011). To remedy this situation, these organizations undertook consultations with customary leaders, local people and leaders of local organizations, with the aim of making concrete policy proposals. Furthermore, a code of conduct for customary chiefs in land matters was drafted, signed and adopted, in the form of a provincial decree by North Kivu's provincial assembly.

The establishment of these agreements and decrees is linked to a lack of clear regulations regarding transhumance and the role of customary chiefs in land management. This lacuna encouraged several non-state organizations to reflect on land tenure security in line with the new land framework and the newly proposed land law in the DRC. Even if these initiatives are implemented at the micro level, non-state actors sometimes advocate for the integration of positive local practices and concerted local norms into national land reform. The objective is then to arrive at a land reform through a bottom-up process by clarifying the ambiguities, integrating the forgotten elements, and capitalizing on the opportunities not captured by the 1973 law. In this specific case, non-state organizations believed that overarching land regulations at the national level are imperative, while at the same time local specificities must be taken into account, something the 1973 law failed to realize.

Local land arrangements and the state

Three main points arise out of comparison of our three case studies. First, the 1973 land law attributes a clear monopolistic role to the state as the sole deliverer of services in the domain of land management. However, this law was clearly unrealistic in light of the already apparent political struggles over land access and distribution originating from the colonial policies and the postcolonial nationalization policies, and was hence never implemented in practice. This has been recognized by the 2012 land reform process, which states that the 1973 law was never adapted to local realities, and that its de jure implementation led to dysfunctional land governance. Consequently, the state was, and continues to be, incapable of delivering these services, especially in rural areas.

This brings us to the second main point of this chapter, namely that the incapacity of the state to deliver services in the domain of land governance according to the 1973 law does not mean that the state is absent in local land-governance arenas. All three cases clearly show how different non-state actors, such as NGOs, customary leaders and individual actors, take responsibility over roles classically associated with the state, such as land access regulation, tenure security and conflict mediation, and hence are involved in service delivery. Indeed, apparent non-political arenas, such as land governance, then "reveal themselves to be active sites of political negotiations and mediation over the implementation of public goals and the distribution of public authority in which local and regional identities and power relations are shaped and recast" (Lund, 2006a, p. 686). This is a clear example of a twilight institution (Lund, 2006a, 2006b) where non-state actors offer public services in the domain of land governance and thereby exercise public authority.

This offers opportunities for non-state actors. The most obvious example is the plantation of Mukwidja, where the concession holder clearly attempts to control his own land access and to enforce his local power position by actively creating a pool of subjects dependent upon him for their access to land and livelihood. In the two other cases, the political character of the land management arrangements is less ostentatious, but nonetheless present. In these cases, NGOs with the collaboration of customary chiefs participate in the deci-sion-making processes land access rules.

The third main point is that, while these land management prac-tices indeed fill a void in the state's capacity to deliver services, it is fascinating to see that they do so by making references to the state and its instruments.

In the plantation case study, this clearly appears in the form of the receipts containing clear references to ownership documents delivered by the state. Furthermore, the assertion that these docu-ments are recognized by the state, and can be exchanged for official documents at the land registry offices, is a clear reference to state institutions. Also, in the other cases discussed in this chapter, official documents were imitated in order to increase their legitimacy. In addition, the participation of state agents in activities organized by NGOs to convince state institutions to legally recognize documents delivered outside of the state realm clearly link these informal prac-tices to the state. Hence, the state remains an important player, both practically and discursively, in the land governance arena. These arrangements either use elements from the statutory realm to legiti-mize their actions, or seek the explicit involvement of state actors in moving arrangements from the non-statutory realm to arrangements formally recognized by the state.

We provide below examples from our three cases in order to further clarify this point. The different attempts to formalize customary land access and distribution practices in Kalehe and Kabare all took the form of written documents. The mere fact of formalizing social relationships in a written form is a way of mimicking "the sources of legitimacy of property recognized by the state" (Chimhowu & Woodhouse, 2006, p. 257). These actors want these "little papers" to be recognized at the same level as officially registered land titles. Therefore, they contain similar information as official titles, such as the measurement of the plot, the name and signatures of the both parties and their witnesses, and official stamps.

This imitation of the state's practices is always accompanied by the presence of real state actors. In Kalehe, for example, the admin-istrator of the territory was involved as a state representative in the negotiation set up by the NGOs. His presence, however, does not mean that these arrangements will be formally recognized per se. It is rather a deliberate attempt to increase the legitimacy of these prac-tices in order to encourage the local population to adhere.

Also, in Mukdiwja, in establishing his public authority and to boost the legitimacy of the locally negotiated land-access arrangements, the concession holder actively evokes symbols from the statutory realm. This process of legitimation takes two distinct forms. First, it is the use of the state's instruments, in this case the receipts, or locally registered land-property titles which should look as much as possible like formal property titles. Second, in his discourse, he actively instrumentalizes the idea of the state to legitimize local practices. For example, he stresses his alleged collaboration with the land registry office when subdividing the plantation. This is a clear attempt at showing how these arrangements are almost equivalent to formal property titles. The importance of stressing this collaboration with the state is noticeable in the local population's attempts to get hold of the land registry's documents. Furthermore, while stressing his role as a local Big Man, he refers to the role of the state as facilitator of development and security. Through connectedness in official elite circles, he becomes part of the state's image in the eyes of the local population. In this way, Mukwidja's inhabitants attempt to reach the state through the concession holder.

In Baraka, Fizi and Uvira, local NGOs were involved in conflict mediation between cattle raisers and farmers. Again, it would be too simplistic to state that they are simply taking over the state's role to mediate conflicts. They actively sought the compliance of the state in their local arrangements in order to increase their legitimacy. The presence of both customary leaders and state actors is imperative to ensuring the efficiency and the durability of these arrangements. There is thus a certain contradiction in the NGOs involvement. If they need the compliance of the state to be legitimate, why not resort to the state directly? Here, again, it is important to differentiate between the state in its local manifestation through individuals, and the need of the population to see their rights legitimized by the state. The involvement of NGOs points to the dissatisfaction of the local population with state representatives, whereas the *idea* of the state remains important to legitimize local practices. Consequently, while mediating between cattle raisers and agriculturalists, NGOs simultaneously mediate social relationships between the local population and local state elites.

As a final example of how elements from the state arena are used to legitimize local practices, we could refer to dynamics in North Kivu. Here, NGOs were involved in the mediation of land conflicts and drafted a code of conduct for customary chiefs. This code was drafted in statutory language in order to appeal to provincial legislators. Later on, this code was indeed adopted by the provincial assembly as a decree. Local arrangements were thus transformed into state law without the state taking initiative. More than this, non-state actors took ownership of the whole process of drafting new laws. This does not mean that local state actors were not involved. As was said before, their presence was instrumental in assuring local legitimacy and facilitating the code's transformation into an official decree.

In summary, in all three cases active attempts were made to legitimize local arrangements by drawing on elements from the state, which, implicitly, contributes to the legitimation at once of these practices and of the state. In fact, we could speak about a double legitimation process. The state can formally recognize local arrangements, as was the case with the code of conduct eventually adopted as a decree by the provincial assembly in North Kivu. But legitimation might also occur from a bottom-up perspective, whereby clear references to the statutory realm are used to evoke local legitimacy.

Conclusions

The goal of this chapter was to reflect on the different manifestations of the state in Eastern DRC, based on practices of service delivery in the domain of land governance. From the outset, we have analysed the empirical cases through a socio-anthropological perspective on the African state. This perspective suggests thinking of the state beyond its institutions, and rather on the basis of its actions and various manifestations at the local level. These manifestations are always dependent on specific socio-historical processes, to each issue at stake and to each local context. Such a "weblike" description of society shows that the state cannot be understood in isolation from local initiatives that have no a priori link with the state system, and vice versa.

Through different case studies of local land governance, we showed how the imagination and manifestation of the state in this particular field is peculiar. The Congolese are not completely paralysed by the ineffectiveness of the 1973 land law that is supposed to govern the delivery of service in the area of land management. Different non-state actors draw on state symbols to legitimize their actions. On the other hand, the state also "lends" its symbols to individuals and institutions active in the delivery of land services to the population. We called this a double process of legitimization, since the state can formally legitimize (for example, through legal recognition) local land arrangements, whereas legitimation can also be induced from a bottom-up perspective through (discursive and other) references to the state and appropriation of its symbols.

Different non-state actors – such as civil society organizations, individuals and customary authorities – are involved in land governance on three different, but interlinked, levels, with regards to filling a void in the state's capacity to deliver services, as important drivers of processes of social change, and ultimately as part of a process of state-building. First, their involvement might be of pragmatic nature, since locally introduced land arrangements compensate for the 1973 land law's ineffectiveness, which is mainly caused by the inadequacy of the law in relation to specific realities on the ground. This is more widespread in rural areas, where most of the land is not formally registered.

Second, the involvement of non-state actors in the delivery of land management services and distribution is part of a process of social change. In a context where most land is still mainly managed by local and customary practices, the introduction of written documents as instruments to formalize certain access rights is an important element in this process of change. Gradually, the need for written documents to replace oral proof in customary arrangements becomes important and more widespread, since the latter no longer sufficiently secures access rights.

Third, the involvement of non-state actors is part of a process of state-building. The use of written documents introduces new constellations of authority and legitimacy that were irrelevant before. Access rights are no longer only determined by (mostly oral) testimonies of local authorities. It also becomes a matter of questioning the authenticity of the signed papers. What is their legal nature? Who are the witnesses? Which authorities signed them? Who contests them? Our case studies have shown that the formal or informal involvement of state authorities is important in strengthening the legitimacy of these documents, even if they originate outside the state. Moreover, the case of North Kivu showed how non-state actors used the state to legitimize and even legally enforce initially informal arrangements. This important legitimizing role of the state can also be observed in the case of Kalehe's plantation, where an individual transferred property rights to the new occupants of the plantation. To reinforce the legitimacy of these documents, he uses state symbols. Furthermore, he underlines his compliance with the state's requirements in terms of land distribution and registration by insisting that the subdivision of the plantation was recognized by the land registry office.

The question remains as to how the dynamics in the different cases contribute to processes of state-building. Following De Herdt (2011), we distinguish between two different processes of state-building. On the one hand, there is the institutional setting and on the other hand there is the "software" necessary to make the institutional machinery function. Beyond institutional mechanisms, cognitive predispositions are needed before institutional reform can be understood, internalized and applied. Following this logic, the cases we developed in this chapter are examples of how particular local predispositions in the domain of land governance are gradually being built. In the process of state-building, local land management practices are gradually moving towards a specific rationality, similar to that of the state's, that conceives access rights on the basis of (mainly private) land ownership (Nyenyezi Bisoka, 2016).

In short, it is a question of determining the owner of the land before considering its users. The increasing use of written documents and the importance of obtaining state legitimation introduced by non-state actors introduces and internalizes this rationality. This more private rationality can be considered as an element of the "software" in the processes of state-building. This is often done to the detriment of communal notions of ownership, enshrining the inalienability of land – a rationality founded in the customary realm. The successful implementation of land reform is therefore not primarily based on the actors' ability to establish and enforce strong institutions, but rather on people's practices that seemingly reproduce notions of the state, its roles and its different manifestations.

Notes

1 The economic crisis that followed forced Mobutu to revise this policy in 1975 and return 60% of the nationalized enterprises' capital to their original owners.
2 Literally "acquirers".
3 For a historical overview of land reform on the African continent, see Bassett (1993).
4 It should be noted that these reforms were often continuations of policy choices put in place by the colonial administration.
5 In French, these contracts are referred to as "contrat foncier coutumier-type".
6 Interview. Mukwidja concession holder. Mukwidja (14 November 2013).
7 Interview. Mukwidja inhabitant. Mukwidja (14 November 2013).
8 Interview. Mukwidja concession holder. Mukwidja (14 November 2013).
9 The RCD (Rassemblement congolais pour la Démocratie) was a rebel movement that played a major role in the second Congo war (1998–2003). During this conflict, they occupied and managed vast territories in Eastern DRC. Access was (and continues to be) used as a resource to reward allies and to gain proximity to the political centre. The reference in this quote to the alleged relationship between the concession holder and the RCD should be considered in this regard.
10 Interview. Civil society representatives. Mukwidja (15 November 2013).
11 "Act of Engagement".

References

Abrams, P. (1977) Notes on the difficulty of studying the state. *Journal of Historical Sociology* 1 (1): 58–89.

Balandier, G. (1971) *Sens et puissance.* Paris: PUF.

Bassett, T.J. (1993) Introduction: The land question and agricultural transformation in sub-Saharan Africa. In: Bassett, T.J. and Crummey, D. E. (eds) *Land in African Agrarian Systems.* Madison, WI: University of Wisconsin Press, pp. 5–18.

von Benda-Beckmann, F. and von Benda-Beckmann, K. (2006) The dynamics of change and continuity in plural legal orders. *The Journal of Legal Pluralism and Unofficial Law* 38 (53-54): 1–44.

Bourdieu, P. (2012) *Sur l'État: Cours au Collège de France 1989–1992.* Paris: Seuil et Raisons d'agir.

Chimhowu, A. and Woodhouse, P. (2006) Customary vs. private property rights? Dynamics and trajectories of vernacular land markets in sub-Saharan Africa. *Journal of Agrarian Change* 6 (3): 346–71.

Claessens, K. (2013) « Sans plantations, je ne peux pas vivre »: l'accès négocié aux plantations agricoles dans le territoire de Kalehe. In: Reyntjens, F., Vandeginste, S. and Verpoorten, M. (eds) *L'Afrique des Grands Lacs: Annuaire 2012–2013.* Paris: L'Harmattan, pp. 249–67.

Claessens, K. (2017) Land, Access and Power. Case studies from Kalehe, DRC. PhD Dissertation: Institute of Development Policy and Management, University of Antwerp.

Claessens, K., Mudinga, E. and Ansoms, A. (2014) Competition over soil and subsoil: Land grabbing by local elites in South Kivu (DRC). In: Ansoms, A. and Hilhorst, T. (eds) *Losing Your Land: Dispossession in the Great Lakes.*

Woodbridge: James Currey, pp. 82–102.

Clement, P. (2013) The land tenure system in the Congo, 1885–1960: Actors, motivations and consequences. In: Frankema, E. and Buelens, F. (eds) *Colonial Exploitation and Economic Development: The Belgian Congo and the Netherlands Indies Compared.* New York, NY: Routledge, pp. 88–108.

Colin, J.-P., Le Meur P.-Y. and Léonard E. (eds) (2009) *Les politiques d'enregistrement des droits fonciers: Du cadre légal aux pratiques locales.* Paris: Karthala.

De Herdt, T. (ed.) (2011) *A la recherche de l'Etat en R-D Congo.* Paris: L'Harmattan.

Delville, P.-L. (2002) When farmers use "pieces of paper" to record their land transactions in Francophone rural Africa: Insights into the dynamics of institutional reform. *European Journal of Development Research* 14 (2): 89–108.

DRC: MAF (Democratic Republic of Congo: Ministère des Affaires Foncières) (2012) Atelier national sur la réforme foncière: Communiqué final.

DRC: MAF (Democratic Republic of Congo: Ministère des Affaires Foncières) (2013) Réforme foncière: Document de programmation.

Falloux, F. and Rochegude, A. (1988) Land tenure as a tool for rational resource management. In: Falloux, F. and Mukendi, A. (eds) *Desertification Control and Renewable Resource Management in the Sahelian and Sudanian Zones of West Africa.* Washington, DC: World Bank, pp. 10–27.

Griffiths, J. (1986) What is Legal Pluralism? *Journal of Legal Pluralism* 24: 1–56.

Kabila, J. (2011) Speech given during his inauguration. Available from: www.congoplanete.com/download/

DISCOURS%20DE%20
JOSEPH%20KABILA%20
LORS%20DE%20SON%20
INAUGURATION%20LE%20
20%20DECEMBRE%202011.pdf
[Accessed 28 November 2018].
Lund, C. (2000) *African Land Tenure:
Questioning Basic Assumptions.*
London: IIED.
Lund, C. (2006a) Twilight
institutions: Public authority and
local politics in Africa. *Development
and Change* 37 (4): 685–705.
Lund, C. (2006b) Twilight
Institutions: An Introduction.
Development and Change 37 (4):
673–84.
Marenbon, J. (1997) *The Philosophy
of Peter Abelard.* Cambridge:
Cambridge University Press.
Meagher, K. (2012) The strength of
weak states? Non-state security
forces and hybrid governance in
Africa. *Development and Change* 43
(5): 1073–101.
Moore, S. F. (1978) Law and social
change: The semi-autonomous
social field as an appropriate
subject of study. In: Moore, S. F.
*Law as a Process: An Anthropological
Approach.* London: Routledge and
Kegal Paul Books, pp. 719–46.
Mugangu Matabaro, S. (2008) La
crise foncière à l'est de la RDC.
In: Marysse, S., Reyntjens, F. and
Vandeginste, S. (eds) *L'Afrique des
Grands Lacs: Annuaire 2007–2008.*
Paris: L'Harmattan, pp. 385–414.
Mushagalusa Mudinga, E. and
Nyenyezi Bisoka, A. (2014)
Innovations Institutionnelles
des acteurs non-étatiques face
à la Crise foncière en RDC:
Légitimité, efficacité et durabilité
en question. In: Reyntjens, F.,
Vandeginste, S. and Verpoorten,
M. (eds) *L'Afrique des Grands
Lacs: Annuaire 2013–2014.* Paris:
L'Harmattan, pp. 159–79.
Nyenyezi Bisoka, A. (2016) Invention
de la terre et production des
anormaux dans le dispositif
foncier en Afrique: Pouvoir et
résistance à l'accaparement des
terres en Afrique des Grands Lacs.
PhD Dissertation. Université
catholique de Louvain.
Nyenyezi Bisoka, A. and Ansoms,
A. (2015) Accaparement des
terres dans la ville de Bukavu
(RDC): Déconstruire le dogme
de la sécurisation foncière par
l'enregistrement. In: Marysse,
S. and Omasombo, J. (eds)
Conjonctures congolaises 2014. Paris:
L'Harmattan, pp. 217–38.
Nzongola-Ntalaja, G. (2002) *The
Congo from Leopold to Kabila: A
People's History.* London: Zed
Books.
Panaccio, C. (2012) *Textes clés du
nominalisme: Ontologie, langage et
connaissance.* Paris: Vrin.
Peemans, J.-P. (2014) Land grabbing
and development thinking: The
Congolese experience. In: Ansoms,
A. and Hilhorst, T. (eds) *Losing
Your Land: Dispossession in the
Great Lakes.* Woodbridge: James
Currey, pp. 11–35.
Sharma, A. and Gupta, A. (2006)
*The Anthropology of the State: A
Reader.* Malden, MA: Blackwell.
Titeca, K. and De Herdt, T. (2011)
Real governance beyond the 'failed
state': Negotiating education
in the Democratic Republic of
Congo. *African Affairs* 110 (439):
213–31.
Toulmin, C. and Quan, J. (2000)
*Evolving Land Rights, Policy and
Tenure in Africa.* London: IIED/
Natural Resources Institute.
Utshudi Ona, I. and Ansoms, A.
(2011) Reconciling custom,
state and local livelihoods:
Decentralized land management in
South Kivu (DRC). In: Marysse,
S. and Ansoms, A. (eds) *Natural
Resources and Local Livelihoods in
the Great Lakes Region of Africa.*
London: Palgrave Macmillan, pp.
26–48.
Van Acker, F. (2005) Where did all
the land go? Enclosure and social
struggle in Kivu (DRCongo).
Review of African Political Economy
32 (103): 79–98.

Vlassenroot, K. and Huggins, C. (2005) Land, migration and conflict in eastern Congo. In: Huggins, C. and Clover, J. (eds) *From the Ground Up: Land Rights,* *Conflict and Peace in Sub-Saharan Africa.* Nairobi/Pretoria: African Center for Technology Studies/ Institute for Security Studies.

10
Public Services at the Edge of the State: Justice and Conflict-resolution in Haut-Uélé

Kristof Titeca

Introduction[1]

How are public services provided in a marginalized region at the edges of the state? How is it possible to provide services when the presence of the state has dwindled over the years, and the area itself has become affected by violent conflict, further complicating public service provision? These are the questions this chapter is concerned with, and which will be discussed through the case of the Haut-Uélé district, part of Orientale Province, situated in the north-east of the Democratic Republic of Congo.[2] It is literally at the edge of the Congolese state: it borders South Sudan and the Central African Republic in the north, Ituri in the east and south. Both politically and economically, the district is marginalized, and for the last twenty years it has been plagued by series of armed actors.

The chapter aims to address these questions by looking at the functioning of the justice sector, and how conflicts are resolved.[3] Furthermore, it aims to analyse how the justice sector functions in a situation of historical, and increasing, isolation. This isolation not only occurs between the region and the rest of the country, but primarily within the district, where a lack of infrastructure and communication have created a situation of isolation, in which localities are largely disconnected from the rest of the district, and from justice and security structures which go beyond that very locality.

Governance at the edges of the state: Dynamics of expansion and disintegration

The work of Jean-Pierre Olivier de Sardan and Thomas Bierschenk on the anthropology of the state has been important in analysing the functioning of the state, both in areas where there is a relative absence of the state, as well as in areas where the state is very much present. Their much-quoted premise is that "the absence of the state does not mean that a void exists in its place" (Bierschenk & Olivier de Sardan, 1997, p. 441). This means that processes of governance are not limited to state institutions, but instead are characterized by a multiplicity of local power poles and complex political configurations, which are different from one area to another. In other words, their work is useful both in areas with a limited state presence, as well in areas where the state is very much present.

In order to understand governance at the periphery of the state, two (at first sight) contradictory processes are important. First, the disintegration of the state, and, second, the expansion of governance processes – what Bierschenk and Olivier de Sardan call the "stacking up" of layers of governance (see for example Bierschenk, 2010; Olivier de Sardan & Bierschenk, 1993; Olivier de Sardan, 2009). On the one hand, and as shown in the introduction to this book (as well as in the wider literature on the African state), state formation is a long-term and ongoing process, in which "stateness" itself waxes and wanes (Lund, 2006, p. 685). There are, however, particular moments in history during which these processes become particularly intense. One of these periods was the late 1970s and the 1980s, when, as a result of economic crisis, the financial basis of states was profoundly affected, resulting in declining state apparatuses, lower salaries and a reduced number of civil servants (Bierschenk, 2010; Bierschenk & Olivier de Sardan, 1993). This has been extensively shown for the DRC, and is particularly visible in the various strategies adopted by civil servants (De Herdt & Titeca, 2016; Emizet, 1998; Gould, 1980). Administrations were transformed into "parcels of power", in which "each position in the administration provided not only a wage, but also an opportunity for appropriation" (De Herdt, Marivoet & Muhirigwa, 2015, p. 49). Blundo (2006, p. 805) describes this as the "informal privatization" of the state by civil servants. In Bierschenk's words, "the state is clearly unravelling at the edges" (Bierschenk, 2010, p. 9), or "dissolving", as Olivier de Sardan (2010) phrased it. It is these processes – how public services are provided in areas where the state is "unravelling" or "dissolving" – that this chapter is interested in. More particularly, how does the tension between the idea of the state relate to the heterogeneity of practices experienced in places far removed from the centre? In the introduction it has been shown how states should be understood as being embedded in "weblike societies" (Migdal, 1988), and how the state is produced through a variety of processes, described as negotiation (Hagmann & Péclard, 2010), "assemblage" (Li, 2007), real governance (Olivier de Sardan, 2010; Titeca & De Herdt, 2011), and so on. This in itself is the outcome of a historical process – the "stacking up" of different historical layers, in which various modes of governance and political authority are cobbled together, each layer not replacing, but rather adding to, the previous mode (Bierschenk, 2010; Olivier de Sardan & Bierschenk, 1993; Olivier de Sardan, 2009).

As a result, local actors are, within certain limits, able to choose the institutions where they are able to address a problem. The legal pluralism literature refers to this situation as "forum shopping", in which "disputants have a choice between different institutions and they base their choice on what they hope the outcome of the dispute will be" (von Benda-Beckmann, 1981, p. 117). The term also high-lights how the forums themselves are involved in shopping, in which they "usually have interests different from those of the parties, and they use the processing of disputes to pursue these interests" (von Benda-Beckmann, 1981, p. 117). Bierschenk and Olivier de Sardan chose the term "institution shopping" (1998, p. 38) in this context, which is characterized by a high degree of institutional complexity and great fluidity. Politics, and public service provision, does not take place in the context of clear formal rules (which would, in theory, facilitate the role of various actors). Instead, "it is the rules themselves which rather are the object of continuous negotiations" (Bierschenk & Olivier de Sardan, 1998, p. 38), and in which different sets of rules are at play.

Justice and conflict resolution in the DRC

The DR Congo is relying on a hierarchical judicial system of which both "modern" and "customary" courts are part. At the lowest level of modern courts, one finds the Peace Courts (*Tribunaux de Paix*), after which there is the Grand Instance Court (*Tribunal des Grandes Instances*). As described in the introduction and in other chapters, salaries imploded in the 1970s and 1980s, and the Mobutu regime encouraged corruption in the public sector to supplement the meagre income. In addition, courts were largely left to "fend for themselves" (*se débrouiller)*, which meant that salaries had to be raised locally, and that corruption became a widespread practice in the judiciary.[4] Generally, the state justice system is deemed expensive, as the liti-gants themselves have to provide for all costs (Kahombo, Kalombe & Magadju, 2015, p. 109). This situation naturally favours the wealthier and better-connected over the majority of the population,

and particularly the poor, who do not have the resources, connections or knowledge to take cases to court.[5] Moreover, it also means
that the liberation of the accused by police or judiciary often occurs,
not only through corruption, but also through powerful protectors
(Verweijen, 2015, p. 346). The lack of budget for the judicial sector
remains a problem up to the present day (Tekilazaya, Wa Luhindi
& Koso, 2013, p. 56–60). Figures vary between 0.1% of the state
budget in 2008 (Vircoulon, 2009, p. 94, cited in Rubbers & Gallez,
2012, p. 84) and 0.22% of the total state budget in 2009 (Boshoff et
al., 2010, p. 10). Moreover, there is largely insufficient personnel and
qualified staff (Kahombo, Kalombe & Magadju, 2015, p. 105; Tekilazaya, Wa Luhindi & Koso, 2013, p. 63), and overall slowed-down
procedures and high costs. Given insufficient funds and infrastructure, courts are thinly spread over the country, and are only situated
in bigger towns, meaning many people can't afford transportation
to court. Overall, the legitimacy of these modern courts is therefore
limited. Verweijen summarizes this situation in the following way:
"state-led justice and security services in the DR Congo function in
a highly erratic manner. They have insufficient human and financial
resources, suffer from deficient infrastructure and logistics, and are
riddled with complex power structures, often causing them to act
according to patronage logics and to extract resources from citizens"
(2016, p. 2).

As a result, modern courts are largely absent in the resolution
of conflicts, and it is mainly the customary courts which have kept
the judicial system afloat and active. They are perceived to be "less
corrupt", and "fair and amicable" (Carayannis, Bazonzi & Pangburn,
2017, p. 18). Yet the customary system has its range of problems,
in particular the absence of constraints on its decisions – there is
little external control on their judgements and practices. Moreover,
the customary system is seen as time-consuming and expensive
(Verweijen, 2016), and "heavily tilted towards the protection of established interests" (Baaz & Verweijen, 2014, p. 809). The result is that
people will try to mobilize their networks to solve conflicts, which
can involve influential community members or trusted authorities
beyond the modern and customary courts (Meyer, 2014). Baaz and
Verweijen, for example, argue how in the conflict-ridden eastern part
of the country, the "weakening of civilian authority has rendered the
resolution of disputes … a wearying and costly process, with each
party mobilizing wider connections in and outside of the state apparatus to reinforce their position" (2014, p. 804). This mobilization of
social connections is not only because of the retreat of the state, or

low legitimacy, but also because of the lack of knowledge by citizens of the formal rules. As a result of this, a variety of actors are involved in the provision of justice and security provision. For security provision, actors such as "customary chiefs, village elders or business associations work in collaboration with self-defence groups such as hunter associations or youth groups" (Hoffmann, Vlassenroot and Büscher, 2016, p. 1). It also means that soldiers may play an important role in conflict resolution, particularly in the eastern part of the country, where the arrival of soldiers led to the militarization of local governance processes. For example, "it has become common practice to solicit armed actors for dispute processing and score settling, either against payment or in the framework of protection arrangements" (Verweijen, 2015, p. 341; Baaz & Verweijen, 2014, p. 806).

Haut-Uélé: A history of isolation and marginalization.

During pre-colonial and colonial times, Haut-Uélé was rather prosperous. The region considered itself the "breadbasket of Haut Zaire" (Omasombo, 2012, p. 262), with the most important activities being cotton and (particularly) coffee farming. The economic purpose of violent state discipline during colonization was at first bent towards ivory. However, as state institutions bedded in, a new agricultural economy became possible, focussing on cotton and coffee. Across Congo, indigenous households were from 1917 obliged to produce cotton (Likaka, 1997, p. 12). In the Garamba area, heavy labour for cotton production was provided by domesticated elephants, rather than by tractors.[6]

Yet, similar to the rest of the country, Mobutu's "Zairianization" had a strongly negative effect on Haut-Uélé, particularly in the coffee sector, with most of the big coffee plantations being abandoned after their stocks were sold off. In 1972–73, the large cash-crop businesses held by European businessmen in Belgian Congo were passed by government decree into Congolese hands. Those who received these were known as "acquirers" (acquéreurs). In the words of an informant: "Zairinization really disturbed the normal order for the population, and the acquéreurs didn't know how to do their operations."[7] The economic situation further worsened throughout the 1980s, 1990s and 2000s. In this process, Haut-Uélé became increasingly isolated, resulting in regional trade becoming strongly limited, and largely concerned with products of little added value (e.g. bananas, manioc, rice) (Omasombo, 2012, pp. 263–74). Moreover, there was a general degradation of the road infrastructure. In 1934, Haut-Uélé had 3,125 km of roads; at the end of the 1990s, there was 1,942 km left, all of which was in a bad state. Moreover, the outbreak of wars in nearby Uganda and particularly Sudan further affected trading possibilities. According to a trader: "People found difficulties doing commerce. With the war in Sudan the border was blocked and if they were arrested they would lose a lot; so they were also discouraged."[8]

Apart from transport infrastructure (again mirroring developments in the rest of the country), the general infrastructure of the state also detoriated in the 1970s and 1980s. Salaries were no longer paid, and the disconnection with the central state increased.

An important contributing factor to this increasing degradation and isolation is the history of rebellion in the area. From 1996 onwards, the region was attacked by a veritable alphabet soup of rebel groups: the ADFL, RCD, Maï-Maï, RCD-KML, FLC, MLC, RCD-N, the politico-religious movement of Simon Kpologbele.[9] For a time between 1999 and 2005, the SPLA governed part of the area (between Djabir and Faradje). The strongest impact came from the LRA (Lord's Resistance Army) rebellion. Initially peacefully settled in Garamba National Park from late-2005, this changed from late-2008 onwards due to the attack of the Ugandan army ("Operation Lightning Thunder"). The LRA responded to this operation with major attacks in which around 1,500 people were killed in Haut-Uélé and Bas-Uélé, and around 2,300 abducted. The operation largely failed to finish the LRA. Large-scale attacks continued up to mid-2010, after which the LRA entered survival mode, looting for survival, and abducting people for a short period to carry food items, after which they are mostly released. Although few LRA rebels are left in the DRC – most having moved into the Central African Republic (CAR) and Sudan – their presence has had a strong psychological impact, with many people, particularly from hard-to-access villages in the hunting domains of Garamba National Park, preferring not to return home, and instead remaining in Internally Displaced People (IDP) camps (Titeca & Costeur, 2015). Still today, the LRA continues its incursions in the region.

This recent history of conflict has led to the increased geographical isolation of Haut-Uélé. Previously flourishing regional trade, for example with southern Sudan, has come to a standstill over the years. Moreover, communication and transport within the district has become more difficult. In sum, the district has a history of gradual economic, political and physical marginalization and degradation, combined with various cycles of conflict. What, then, does this isolation and degradation mean for the provision of public services, particularly justice and security?

The justice sector in Haut-Uélé

Similar to the rest of the country, courts in Haut-Uélé have little available staff, and courts are mostly (very) far away. The Grand Instance Court (Tribunal des Grandes Instances), based in the district capital Isiro, in theory should have five judges, but in reality only has two out of five judges. For most of the district, Isiro is distant and very difficult to access. While all six territories in Dungu have Peace Courts, they lack personnel and infrastructure. Also, the secondary prosecutor is lacking. Moreover, language seems to be a barrier as judges and magistrates in Haut-Uélé largely come from Kinshasa and speak Lingala, and do not speak Pazande, the language spoken in Dungu. Similar to the rest of the country, actors from all levels of society talk in very negative terms about the judicial sector, reflecting a general belief that the modern justice system only reflects the financial power of the actors involved, with judges easily bribed in order to favour the wealthiest or most influential bidder. Throughout the research, a number of notorious cases were repeatedly mentioned, in which actors bribed their way out of prison and court. Courts are therefore not considered a mechanism readily capable of resolving conflicts, instead being seen as a mechanism which further engenders conflict.[10] Customary courts are perceived to be closer to the population and more accessible, as well as cheaper, since less money is charged than with the state. As a trader summarizes: "they are closer to the population and easier accessible. Also for the most vulnerable: you don't have to always pay for it."[11] As one civilian from Bangadi commented: "it is much easier to see the customary chief, and he doesn't create any problems when people go to see him".[12] The result of this general situation was that in most of the territory, processes of justice have been largely monopolized by customary courts.[13] A final perceived advantage of the customary chief is that he allows things to be solved in a "friendly way",[14] in which there is not too much conflict involved. This mode of functioning also has downsides – the judicial role of the customary court has become severely criticized by human rights and civil society organizations, as customary judicial authorities largely overstep their mandate. For example, people can be kept for a considerable time by customary chiefs, largely overstaying the legally allowed 48 hours; cases were encountered in which people were kept up to a year. Forced labour is often used as a punishment, and as will be explained below, the resolution of conflicts in a "humanitarian way" often leads to conflicts which remain unresolved (e.g. with regards to sexual violence). Many of their practices are therefore in breach of the penal code.

The security sector followed a similar trajectory to the judicial sector. During the Mobutu regime, police (at that time *gendarmes*[15] and civil guards) were in place in every territory, and every administration post (*poste d'administration*) had small jails (*cachots*) in Haut-Uélé. Mirroring the general evolution of the Congolese state, this became more difficult from the 1970s onwards. Many police posts disappeared. The remaining posts are largely concentrated in the large urban centres, which is currently still the case. The police continued functioning during the second Congolese war, but proved powerless in the light of the different invasions. Generally, policemen are insufficient in number to conduct the required work. Their salaries are also insufficient, as a result of which they seek to supplement their salary by extracting revenue from the population. In rural areas these are largely absent. Not only are they not based there, they rarely visit these areas, as they have no funds or means of transport.

The legitimacy of the police is limited. Using the police is seen rather as a retaliatory measure, or something which might further intensify the conflict: "if you really have problems with someone else, and you really want that person to suffer, then you go to the police. But only if you want that person really to suffer!"[16] Abuse of power by the police is common. This is something that is often economically inspired – police agents either try to extort money directly from citizens, or can be bribed by citizens to harass someone else. In this situation, people prefer to solve their problems through customary tribunals.

Isolation and concentration of power

In sum, the above sections describe how the justice and security sectors function in Haut-Uélé. Although historically marginalized, these sectors do not function differently from elsewhere in the country, which face similar problems. Similar to the rest of the country, the state presence is largely concentrated in the few urban areas, with very little state representation – including "modern" courts and police – elsewhere in the territory. In Haut-Uélé, processes of justice are very much localized, as the means to refer cases to a higher level are virtually non-existent. In theory, the most serious cases have to be referred to the Grand Instance Court, in the district capital Isiro. In practice, most of these cases do not reach this level, for the simple reason that the court is very distant and hard to reach. Concretely, villages and towns outside of Isiro (i.e. most of the district) do not have the means or resources to transport the accused to these centres. As described above, the general transport infrastructure in the district is very bad, and the road between the two major towns, Isiro and Dungu, is only accessible by motorbike. Phone communication is difficult too, with the satellite network covering only a limited area of the district.

This, though, does not mean that cases are not treated. In the words of a civil society actor, "there is no politics of empty chairs",[17] as particular functions are taken over by other actors. However, these actors are few, local and geographically variable. In a situation in which "modern" courts are far away or absent, and moreover are seen as largely corrupt, expensive and unfair, they are never the first entry point in the area. Rather, cases always pass through other actors, such as the customary authorities or the police. In other words, the "forum shopping" possibilities are limited, due to the isolation of the area.

The result is that various cases are treated by actors which often do not have the legal authority or expertise to do so. Cases of sexual violence are, for example, not treated by the relevant authority. Instead, they are treated by, for example, customary authorities, kept under the authority of the police, or solved through arrangements between the families involved. This isolation and concentration of power is not only a consequence of geographical isolation and the lack of (transport and communication) infrastructure. It is also a deliberate strategy by actors within the justice and security sector, such as police agents or customary chiefs, to concentrate power and accumulate revenue. In other words, state actors do not only make use of their state power vis-à-vis citizens for survival and enrichment – described in the introduction to this book as the "capacity of legal command" (Englebert, 2009) – they also use this position against other state actors, thereby further concentrating power and authority. While this happens all over the DRC, and at all levels of the state administration, it works particularly well in these circumstances of isolation, fragmentation and a non-transparent legal system. As a civil society actor summarizes: "everyone tries to profit as much as possible on his level".[18] For example, police officers try to keep cases as much as possible under their authority. They do so by convincing the accused that a transfer to a higher authority will land them a significant prison sentence, high judicial expenses, long procedures, and little-to-no satisfactory results. Paying a certain amount of money to them, therefore, is presented as the best option. Although cases of sexual violence are supposed to go to the secondary prosecutor, and the police can only keep the accused for 48 hours, this transfer does not in reality happen. Many of these cases are treated solely by the police. In these cases, payments to the police officers allow charges to be dropped or the accused to "escape".

Also, the public prosecutor tries to keep cases as much as possible under his authority. This means that the accused are kept in prison as long as possible, until they are willing to pay. As a local civil society report summarizes: "there is a total malfunction and lack of collaboration between the prosecutor and the tribunal, which explains why in most cases the prosecutor does not bring cases before the tribunal, which leads to a total dissatisfaction and disappointment among litigants. The proliferation of impunity is a result of this situation" (Dungu Civil Society, 2012).

A factor which contributes to this situation (and similar to other sectors) is the lack of control by the various higher hierarchical levels. This gives the lower-level actors the opportunity to act with relative freedom, particularly in more remote areas, where there are many complaints about the impunity of the actors involved in these situations.

In sum, the retreat of the state has not led to an absence of governance, but instead to a concentration of governance in the hands of a limited number of actors. In this way, processes of governance at the periphery of the state mirror what is happening elsewhere in the country, namely a "weblike" society, in which a variety of actors are involved in the provision of services, and a variety of strategies employed to control these services.

Outcome of this situation: "Sweeping under the carpet" and residual tensions

This concentration of power leads to a number of tensions, as cases remain unresolved, or lead to an outcome which is deemed unsatisfactory. This is particularly so for cases handled by customary authorities. Even if cases are brought before the customary chief, tensions often remain in the community between the family of the victims and the accused, as well as between the family of the victims and the judicial authorities, which are accused of incapacity and bias. As a religious actor summarized in this context: "Conflicts are never fully solved, and uneasy situations remain."[19] This mirrors what Bierschenk and Olivier de Sardan call "sweeping under the carpet", described as the "predominant local strategy for conflict regulation"

(2003, p. 159). Instead of using "exit" or "voice", a common reaction to tensions and conflict is that "of loyalty, e.g. 'bottling up', which leads to conflicts continuing to fester underground" (Bierschenk & Olivier de Sardan, 2003, p. 161). Throughout the field research, several examples were encountered in which the customary chiefs did try to solve serious issues (such as sexual violence) amicably, but which eventually led to strong discontent among one party, eventually leading to conflict and violence.[20]

This concentration of power and geographical isolation also creates other malpractices, for example with regards to arrests and fines – the accused can be imprisoned for extended periods of time without trial, and actors are handling cases for which they often have no authority. It has also created a further monetization of the justice and security sector, thereby extending inequalities: wealthier actors have better access to judicial and security services, unfair judicial practices are created, and so on. For many of the interviewed actors, the judicial system has little legitimacy, something which leads to tensions and conflict. Importantly, many cases remain unresolved, as they are stuck with a particular actor (particularly the police and the customary chief) who is not able to resolve the issue.

In sum, this section has shown the way in which public services are provided in the context of an "unravelled" state. In a manner similar to the rest of the DRC, other actors took over public functions, such as justice and conflict-resolution. At the same time, the strong isolation of geographical areas led to a concentration of power among particular actors, such as customary chiefs. The next section explains how the LRA conflict led to the arrival of a variety of actors engaging themselves in the justice and security sector, further layering the governance processes.

What has been the impact of the LRA conflict?

The LRA conflict had a double effect on processes of justice and security. On the one hand, it led to further isolation, whereas on the other, it led to fragmentation – the "stacking up" of various governance processes – as a range of new actors arrived in the area.

Because of the LRA's extreme violence, many state actors fled to urban centres (particularly Dungu), leaving rural localities with a limited or non-existent state presence. For example, in Duru, a town near the border with South Sudan, all state institutions left the town: the police, border police, immigration services, custom officials, and so on. Moreover, rural areas became even more isolated, due to the insecure roads which were often attacked by the LRA. This made it difficult, even near-impossible, for the judicial system to physically communicate, for example by transporting the accused or victims to higher-level authorities, or for higher-level authorities to visit other places.[21] Because of this, various actors, including customary chiefs, found it more difficult to communicate with their hierarchy.

According to the overall chief, because of the isolation, the *chefs de groupement* "live in a vacuum ... they cannot report messages to us, and we cannot report messages to them". Other actors describe this as a "situation of crisis".[22] In other words, what is meant by a "vacuum" is not a lack of governance processes, but an extreme concentration of power in the hands of the remaining actors. As they are monopolizing processes of justice and security with little or no checks and balances, they are operating in a "vacuum". The LRA conflict, therefore, further exacerbated the isolation (through which people only had limited options for justice and security) and concentration of power in the field of justice and security. In particular, customary chiefs wield much power within their communities.

The "stacking up" of governance actors throughout the LRA conflict

The LRA conflict not only led to an actual reduction of the number of decision-making actors in the field of justice and security – the vacuum described above. It also introduced two new categories of actors to Haut-Uélé, namely the army and international organizations, both of which limited the role of the customary chief.

The army

The army traditionally has a rather weak presence in Haut-Uélé.[23] When the LRA started exactions against the population at the end of 2007, the army slowly increased its presence. By May 2009, it was estimated that between 3,000 and 4,000 Congolese soldiers were in Haut-Uélé and Bas-Uélé districts (HRW, 2010, pp. 52–3). The army was unable to prevent the larger attacks in 2008 and 2009, and the soldiers in themselves were a source of insecurity for the population. Yet, the mere presence of soldiers still acts, to a certain extent, as a deterrent for the LRA threat, as a result of which the population prefers the army's presence to a security vacuum.

The military also play a (limited) role in local processes of dispute resolution. On the one hand, they often are an important factor in abuses of power, in which they prey on the population themselves, or in which they help other actors – such as the customary chief or other local authorities – to do so.[24] In these circumstances, FARDC actors are involved in a variety of cases, which (similar to other areas in the DRC) include "the violent settling of scores (e.g. revenge and rivalries) and accounts (e.g. debts and land disputes) arising from envy and personal or family disputes. Examples are conflicts over heritage, marriage, debts, real estate, love affairs, land, power positions and past wrongdoing" (Verweijen, 2013, p. 74). On the other hand, they can play a role in the resolution of disputes themselves, or by preventing escalation. The case study in Box 10.1 is an example of this.

Box 10.1. Case study 1: How to keep a murder suspect?

In 2012, in one of the localities of research, a man tried to kill someone, but the victim survived the attack. As there is no police presence in the locality, the local chief arrested the suspect and detained him for some time, keeping him in his compound. Transporting the suspect to Dungu, the nearest town with police and relevant judicial authorities, was not possible as the chief only has a bike, and the distance is too far (three hours by car) and dangerous (there are frequent attacks by armed groups on the road). The chief eventually decided to release the suspect, which led to major frustration among the family of the victim, who threatened to kill the suspect. Major tensions remained in the locality for a period. These were only dispelled when the man was re-arrested by the army in order to reduce tensions. Doing so brought back calm to this village, with the army eventually handing the suspect over to the state authorities.

This case study shows the inability of the customary chief to resolve a conflict, and how the army intervened by rescuing a suspect and defusing tensions in a particular village. As a civil society actor argued: "When the soldiers become involved, no one dares to do anything anymore";[25] and the open threats to the accused and his family stopped. As also shown by this example, the involvement of military actors is related with the weakness of the other relevant authorities (customary and other civilian authorities) in providing a solution to particular disputes. Their presence is a double-edged sword for conflict resolution: while the military actors are often the source of problems, they also are able to play constructive roles by preventing those targeted from being killed (Verweijen, 2015, p. 348). Customary chiefs themselves claim that the military do not respect their authority, and that they are powerless in the light of their use of violence.[26]

International humanitarian organizations

A second such category of actors are a range of international humanitarian organizations, which arrived en masse after the outbreak of the LRA conflict. After the Christmas Massacres in December 2008, a wide range of international humanitarian NGOs (MSF, Intersos, Oxfam, Save the Children, and so on) as well as the UN organizations (UNHCR, WFP, Unicef, and so on) arrived in the area.[27] Around 80% of these were based in Dungu, the headquarters of the humanitarian interventions in the area. Active in the field of security and justice are the UN peacekeeping brigade MONUSCO (and more particularly the human rights section).[28] The non-military international actors[29] are organized in the so-called "protection cluster",[30] which is coordinated by UNHCR. The main duty of these international actors is the monitoring and follow-up of security and justice incidents. These organizations helped to tackle the isolation problem, bringing the judicial system closer to the population. This "protection cluster" was doing so through the financing of mobile courts (*chambre foraine*), in which the main tribunal and prosecutor are transported to other places (more particularly Dungu and Faradje).[31]

What did the layering of the justice and security sectors mean in practice?

An important feature of the LRA conflict in Haut-Uélé, which allows us to further look at how justice processes functioned in practice, was the tensions between the displaced and the local population.

The LRA conflict caused major population displacement in Haut-Uélé (in March 2011 around 250,000 people were displaced),[32] which led to many tensions with the local population. These tensions particularly centred around access to land, the use of water and humanitarian aid.[33] Looking at these tensions allows to better understand how various modes of governance coexist and overlap, with various multiplex ties at play.

The case study in Box 10.2 shows the different layers of decision-making structures that are involved in solving conflicts between the displaced and the local population. In contrast to the processes described above, which came before the arrival of the LRA, the breadth of the forum-shopping process has increased. Due to the conflict and displacement, and due to the arrival of new actors, the affected population can involve a range of actors to help resolve conflicts. Yet, notwithstanding their seeming complexity and fragmentation, these conflict-resolution mechanisms still have a large degree of predictability for all actors involved. Generally, the following mechanism is followed to resolve conflicts, both among the local population and the displaced, as well as more generally. In the first instance, it is still primarily the local authorities, and in particular the customary authorities and local civil society, which are involved in the resolution of conflicts. Sometimes the church authorities are also involved,[34] while in certain localities ad hoc solutions are found, such as *comités de suivi* (follow-up committees), which in particular help prevent existing tensions (around land, water or humanitarian aid) erupting into conflict. If conflicts are of a more serious nature, and persist, then a range of higher-level authorities become involved. These are high-level governmental and customary

---

Box 10.2. Case study 2: Stacking up of various forms of power/actors

In one locality of research with a concentration of around 20,000 IDPs, the local customary chief wanted to force the IDPs into labour-intensive communal work as the price to pay for their stay. The IDPs refused to do so, as they refused to accept his authority. The customary chief did not stop there, but involved the military, and through them forced the IDPs to cooperate, i.e. participate in the communal works. This led to the arrest and mistreatment of a number of displaced persons. Two young IDPs, who were severely mistreated by the military, tried to address their situation. They went to their customary chief (outside of Dungu, their locality of displacement), who, however, did not want to implicate himself in this conflict, one reason being that he had family relations with the customary chief in the locality in question. Moreover, he had no power over the locality in which the IDPs were located. The two young men ended up consulting the regional civil society leaders, with whom they went to the highest administrative authority in the territory (Administrateur du Territoire). In addition, representatives from international NGOs were involved, through whom they managed to address the abuses from the military and the customary chief.

authorities, but also international actors, such as MONUSCO civil affairs, or representatives from international NGOs.

This is only a basic scheme, as conflict and displacement continuously create new combinations. The displaced population is, for example, most familiar with the customary chiefs or civil society of their location of origin, who are either also displaced, or remain in the former locality. Particularly in situations where these are tensions or conflicts with the host population, IDPs are distrustful of local authorities, and might be unwilling to accept the customary authority of the locality they reside in. Yet, the power of the displaced (state or civil society) representatives is often contested in these host localities, as they exercise little power over these places.[35] The power of the displaced chiefs is not only contested in this host locality, but also in their home locality, as ruling from a distance is somewhat difficult. This situation has led to further isolation and concentration of power. For example, areas with a higher degree of insecurity can have the majority of existing actors with authority in the field of justice and security displaced, including the customary chief. This does not necessarily lead to a vacuum, as the role of the customary chief is taken over by a representative, but this can lead to problems – in a number of cases, complaints by the home population have arisen about this local representative, who no longer communicates with the chief, is considered to be more corruptible, and so on. This is facilitated by the fact that he is often the only actor present in the field of justice and security.

Conclusions

This chapter discussed processes of justice and conflict resolution in an area where the state is only weakly present, both for geographical reasons, but also because of the (lack of) infrastructure and the presence of conflict.

First, Haut-Uélé has historically been characterized by the state having little presence. Similar to the rest of the country, this was characterized by a strong personalization and privatization of the remaining state institutions and actors, and a concentration of power among certain actors. This means that the available conflict-resolution fora are relatively narrow, with conflicts primarily resolved at a local level by a limited number of actors. The fragmentation and institution-shopping are simply not very elaborated. This was, and is, partly the case because of geographic isolation and limited transport, but also because institutions themselves actively try to monopolize power. It has been shown how the lure of financial profit has further accelerated the concentration of power among particular actors.

Second, the LRA conflict had a mixed impact on this situation. On the one hand, the processes of isolation further increased, as state actors withdrew further from rural areas, and as transport and communication became more difficult. This further increased the power of the customary chief, but did not necessarily increase his legitimacy, as this was further eroded through the conflict. As a religious leader summarized: "part of the void is filled by the customary chief, but the situation remains one of crisis".[36] On the other hand, through the conflict new actors entered the justice and security arena, such as military actors and international NGOs. In this context, the array of forums to "shop" between became wider. However, displacement, and the multiple "shopping" possibilities, further complicated the governance processes at stake. A displaced group may, for example, find their customary chief the most legitimate actor to represent their interests, but his power is contested outside his jurisdiction. Yet, all of this did not mean that there is a lack of governance or predictability. Though there are indeed differences in various localities, and though there are a variety of actors involved, there remains a degree of predictability. The affected actors are aware of who to approach, or who to involve.

Importantly, the processes described are not very different from the rest of the DRC. This chapter shows how, just as in the rest of the country,[37] a messy, and location-specific coalition of actors has taken over public service provision. The provision of justice in Haut-Uélé can be described as a patchwork of relatively isolated locations, in which the application of state law and the provision of justice and security depend on the power configurations at play. What is different "at the edges of the state", however, is that the isolation of the district plays to the advantage of particular local actors, as it closes off opportunities for institution shopping that one may find more often elsewhere.

Notes

1 Part of the field research for this chapter was financed by the Justice and Security Research Program.

2 Haut-Uélé has six territories: Dungu, Faradje, Niangara, Rungu, Wamba and Watsa. It has a surface area of about 91,600 km² (Omasombo, 2012, p. 27).

During the last census in 2008, it was estimated to have 1,652,866 inhabitants (Omasombo, 2012, p.70).

3 The chapter primarily focusses on the justice sector, but given the involvement of a variety of actors in mechanisms of conflict-

resolution, it also pays attention to security actors, such as the military and the police.

4 As Rubbers and Gallez argue with regards to the judicial sector in the 1990s: "if their jobs gave them the opportunity, they might also allow themselves to participate in fraudulent practices for money, e.g. destroying the evidence against someone charged for crime, making a judgment contrary to the law, or moonlighting as legal advizers for private businesses" (2012, p. 83).

5 For example, Carayannis et al. found in Muanda that "justice at the state level has two speeds and two faces, one for the rich and one for the poor, one for the strong and one for the weak" (Carayannis et al., 2017, p. 14).

6 For this reason, the Api domestication centre, established in 1899 (Omasombo, 2011, p. 306), was moved to Gangala na Bodio in 1920 (Schmidt-Soltau, 2007, p. 19).

7 Interview. Civil society actor. Faradje (17 March 2018). Interview conducted by Patrick Edmond.

8 Interview. Displaced senior citizen. Nyalanya camp (15 March 2018). Interview conducted by Patrick Edmond.

9 See Titeca (2016) for more details.

10 In doing so, this finding mirrors research by Rubbers and Gallez in Lubambashi, where they found that the "exchange of complaint after complaint may culminate in the level of the conflict becoming disproportionately high in comparison with the original problem" (Rubbers & Gallez, 2012, p. 99).

11 Interview. Trader. Dungu (10 March 2013).

12 Interview. Civilian from Bangadi. Dungu (7 March 2013).

13 An international judiciary actor summarized this (by referring to the absence of modern courts)

as follows: "there was nothing on the judicial level when we arrived here, it was non-existent … It was only the first time with the *chambre forain* in Faradje, that people saw a tribunal there!" From: Interview. International judicial actor (9 March 2003).

14 Interview. Civilian. Dungu (9 March 2013).

15 With Zairianization in 1975, the police became *gendarmes*, and were installed in several posts on the territory (Ndedu, Bangadi, Doruma, Ngilima, Yakuluku, Gangala Na Bodiyo).

16 Interview. Civil society actor. Dungu (8 March 2013).

17 Interview. Civil society actor. Duru (2 March 2013).

18 Interview. Civil society actor. Dungu (8 March 2013).

19 Interview. Religious actor. Dungu (8 March 2013).

20 A church leader argued how "there only is judicial anarchy here: the police, military and customary chiefs solve everything among themselves à l'amicable". From: Interview. Church leader. Dungu (4 August 2012).

21 In early 2013, for instance, two minors were raped by a teacher in one of the localities of research. Although the *chef de poste* wanted to transfer the cases to Dungu, this was simply not possible, as there is no way to transport the culprit. Due to a lack of other means, this would have to happen by motor-taxi, which would have to travel along highly insecure roads.

22 Interview. Religious actor. Dungu (8 March 2013).

23 During the Mobutu regime, it only established a localized presence in light of specific threats, such as armed poachers in Garamba national park in the late 1980s. The army re-established itself after the Congolese wars: from 2003 onwards, the former rebel groups (MLC and RCD-KML) were integrated in the new Congolese

army, called the Forces Armées de la Républque Démocratique du Congo (FARDC). This also created a weak and undisciplined army presence in Haut-Uélé, and these troops were gradually withdrawn from the area.

24 It is worth noting that this example is nothing new, as there have been previous instances in Haut-Uélé's history in which the military were collaborating with local authorities to act, and prey upon, the displaced/refugees. This was the case in the first half of the 1990s with the Sudanese refugees in Haut-Uélé.

25 Interview. Civil society actor. Dungu (4 August 2012).

26 This is also the case in other areas of the DRC. As Verweijen, for example, highlights regarding the Kivus, the military involvement in dispute resolution is not only a result of civilian demand, it is also the result of the military who "impose themselves in conflicts, sometimes with force" (Baaz & Verweijen, 2013, p. 8; see also Verweijen, 2013).

27 A limited consignment of MONUSCO was present in the area slightly earlier, from 2007 onwards.

28 The Human Rights section of MONUSCO is a collaboration between UNHCHR and MONUSCO. Its main tasks are the sensitization about human rights, and capacity building of state actors (army and police) and civil society. They also have a protection unit, which, for example, protects witnesses.

29 Oxfam, Danish Refugee Council, COOPI, Intersos. Apart from the tasks mentioned, the protection cluster also helps with psychosocial and medical assistance.

30 Working on "protection" issues such as sexual and physical violence, theft, looting, arbitrary arrests, and so on.

31 In which the Danish Refugee Council financed the presence of the court for Faradje (six civilian cases) and Tadu (four civilian cases).

32 Figure for March 2011. Dungu had the most displaced persons – around 120,000 (Omasombo, 2012, p. 73).

33 In the form of the local population contesting that they are not sufficiently benefiting from humanitarian assistance, while also suffering from the LRA conflict.

34 In one case the displaced and the local population tried to solve their conflict in the local church. Since they were praying from the local church, they deemed the priest was the best-placed person to solve this conflict.

35 Further complicating the situation is that new "camp chiefs" were elected as representatives for the displaced in the camps. Local chiefs sometimes formed a committee, but they often lost their power. Also, camp chiefs have very limited power, resulting in disputes with host authorities.

36 Interview. Religious leader. Dungu (8 March 2013).

37 See for example Titeca & De Herdt (2011) for the education sector.

References

Baaz, M. E. and Verweijen, J. (2014) Arbiters with guns: The ambiguity of military involvement in civilian disputes in the DR Congo. *Third World Quarterly* 35 (5): 803–20.

von Benda-Beckmann, K. (1981) Forum shopping and shopping forums: Dispute processing in a Minangkabau village in West Sumatra. *Journal of Legal Pluralism*, 19: 117–60.

Bierschenk, T. (2010) States at work in West Africa: Sedimentation, fragmentation and normative double-binds. University of Mainz, Department of Anthropology and

African Studies. Working Paper
113.
Bierschenk, T. and Olivier De
Sardan, J.-P. (1997) Local powers
and a distant state in rural Central
African Republic. *The Journal
of Modern African Studies* 35 (3):
441–48.
Bierschenk, T. and Olivier de Sardan,
J.-P. (1998) *Les pouvoirs au village:
Le Bénin rural entre démocratisation
et decentralisation.* Paris: Karthala.
Bierschenk, T. and Olivier de
Sardan, J.-P. (2003) Powers
in the village: Rural Benin
between democratization and
decentralization. *Africa* 73 (2):
145–73.
Blundo, G. (2006) Dealing with
the local state: The informal
privatization of street-level
bureaucracies in Senegal.
Development and Change 37 (4):
799–819.
Boshoff, H., Hendrickson, D.,
More, S. and Vircoulon, T. (2010)
Supporting SSR in the DRC:
Between a Rock and a Hard
Place. An Analysis of the Donor
Approach to Supporting Security
Sector Reform in the Democratic
Republic of Congo. The Hague:
Clingendael.
Carayannis, T., Bazonzi, J. and A.
Pangburn (2017) Configurations
of authority in Kongo Central
province: Governance, access
to justice, and security in the
territory of Muanda. Justice and
Security Research Program Paper
35. February 2017.
De Herdt, T., Marivoet, W. and
Muhirigwa, F. (2015) Vers
la réalisation du droit à une
éducation de qualité pour tous.
UNICEF Research Report.
De Herdt, T. and Titeca, K. (2016)
Governance with empty pockets:
The education sector in the
Democratic Republic of Congo.
Development and Change, 47 (3):
472–94.
Dungu Civil Society
(2012) Allocution à l'occasion de
la visite de son excellence madame
le vice-ministre de la justice et
droits humains, Dungu.
Emizet, K. (1998) Confronting
leaders at the apex of the
state. *African Studies Review* 41 (1):
99–137.
Englebert, P. (2009) *Africa: Unity,
Sovereignty, and Sorrow.* Boulder,
CO: Lynne Riener.
Gould, D. J. (1980) *Bureaucratic
Corruption and Underdevelopment in
the Third World: The Case of Zaire.*
New York, NY: Pergamon Press..
Hagmann, T. and Péclard, D. (2010)
Negotiating statehood: Dynamics
of power and domination in post-
colonial Africa. *Development and
Change,* 41 (4): 539–62.
Hoffmann, K., Vlassenroot, K. and
K. Büscher (2016) Governance
as a quick fix? The challenges
of donor-supported, bottom-up
security provision in Ituri (DR
Congo). Justice and Security
Research Program Paper 33. July
2016.
HRW (Human Rights Watch) (2010)
*Trail of Death: LRA Atrocities in
Northeastern Congo.* New York, NY:
Human Rights Watch.
Kahombo, B., Kalombe, J-M.
M. and Magadju, P. M. (2015)
Rapport initial sur la gouvernance
judiciaire et le progress vers
l'instauration de l'Etat de droit
en République Démocratique du
Congo. *Law in Africa* 18: 97–129.
Li, T. (2007) Practices of
assemblage and community forest
management. *Economy and Society*
36 (2): 263–93.
Lund, C. (2006) Twilight
Institutions: Public Authority
and Local Politics in Africa.
Development and Change, 37 (4):
685–705.
Likaka, O. (1997) *Rural Society and
Cotton in Colonial Zaire.* Madison,
WI: University of Wisconsin.
Meyer, A. (ed.) (2014) *Etude
sur l'aide légale en République
démocratique du Congo.* Bruxelles:
Avocats sans Frontières.

Migdal, J. (1988) *Strong Societies and Weak States: State–Society Relations and State Capabilities in the Third World*. Princeton, NJ: Princeton University Press.

Olivier de Sardan, J.-P. (2009) Les huit modes de gouvernance locale en Afrique de l'Ouest. Afrique: Pouvoir et politique. Working Paper 4.

Olivier de Sardan, J.-P. (2010) Développement, modes de gouvernance et normes pratiques (une approche socio-anthropologique) *Canadian Journal of Development Studies/ Revue canadienne d'etudes du developpement* 31: 5–20.

Olivier de Sardan, J.-P. and Bierschenk, T. (1993) Les courtiers locaux du développement. *Bulletin de l'APAD* 5: 71–6.

Omasombo, J. (ed.) (2011) *Haut-Uélé, trésor touristique*. Bruxelles, Le Cri.

Rubbers, B. and Gallez, E. (2012) Why do Congolese people go to court? A qualitative study of litigants' experiences in two justice of the peace courts in Lubumbashi. *Journal of Legal Pluralism* 66: 79–108.

Schmidt-Soltau, K. (2007) ICCN Cadre procédural de Réinstallation du Projet GEF-BM, Rapport Final.

Tekilazaya, K., Wa Luhindi, D. F. and Koso, M. W. (2013) République démocratique du Congo: Le secteur de la justice et l'Etat de droit. AfriMAP and Open Society Initiative for Southern Africa Study. Netherlands Institute

of International Relations Clingendael.

Titeca, K. (2016) Haut-Uélé: Justice and security mechanisms in times of conflict and isolation. JSRP Paper 32.

Titeca, K. and Costeur, T. (2015) An LRA for everyone: How different actors frame their own Lord's Resistance Army. *African Affairs* 114 (454): 92–114.

Titeca, K. and De Herdt, T. (2011) Real governance beyond the "failed state": Negotiating education in the Democratic Republic of Congo. *African Affairs* 110 (439): 213–31.

Verweijen, J. (2013) Military business and the business of the military in the Kivus. *Review of African Political Economy* 40 (35): 67–82.

Verweijen, J. (2015) Armed mobilisation and the nexus of territory, identity, and authority: The contested territorial aspirations of the Banyamulenge in eastern DR Congo. *Journal of Contemporary African Studies* 33 (2): 191–212

Verweijen, J. (2015) The disconcerting popularity of popular in/justice in the Fizi/ Uvira region, Eastern Democratic Republic of the Congo. *International Journal on Minority and Group Rights* 22 (2015): 335–59.

Vircoulon, T. (2009) Réforme de la justice: Réalisations, limites et questionnements. In: Tréfon, T. (ed.) *Réforme au Congo (RDC): Attentes et désillusions*. Paris: L'Harmattan.

Index

subsistence agriculture, viability of, 196

Sudan, 219; southern, 219, 224

Sun City peace agreement, 76

supplementary earnings, quest for, 109, 115

surveillance, 61, 63

survival: ethics of, 107, 115; logic of, 112

Swedish International Development Cooperation Agency (SIDA), 85, 87

sweeping under the carpet, 223-4

Swiss Cooperation, 199

SYGECPAF system, 41, 42

symbols of the state, 59, 206, 208, 209

Système Intégré de Gestion des Ressources Humaines et de la Paie (SIGRH-P), 26-50; implementation of, 40; seen as personal affair, 39

taxation, 17, 80, 129, 179; collection of taxes, 80; decentralization of, 157; informal, 8; municipal, 174, 178; non-registered, 9; of *mamans du marché*, 130; of markets, 131, 175; on Congo river, 124; through schools, 123, 128 see also public lighting tax

taxi buses, 59, 60

teachers, salaries of, administration of, 42

technical control of vehicles, 143, 150-4, 156, 162

technologies of government, 8

ten houses, 171

Tendler, J., 147-8, 163

terres domaniales (state lands), 194

terres indigènes (indigenous lands), 194

Tilly, C., 13

Titeca, K., 12, 17, 75, 78, 120, 123

toilets: digging of, 180, 184; public, need for, 181

trade unions, 27

traditional healers, 78

traffic d'influence (influence peddling), 128

traffic violations, 146

transhumance, 203-4

transport sector, as political support base, 160-1

transportation: difficulties of, 229-30; public, regulation of, 17

trees, planting of, 170

Trefon, T., 30, 125

Tribunal des Grandes Instances (Grand Instance Court), 216, 220, 221

Tribunaux de Paix (Peace Courts), 216, 220

tricycles, 175; public provision of, 170, 173

Trouillot, M.-R., 57

Tull, D., 4, 19, 30

Tungila, I., 150

twilight institutions, 122, 192, 205

Uganda, 10-11, 76, 77, 219

unemployment, 52, 129, 157

United Kingdom (UK), 3

United Nations (UN), 77; peacekeeping operations, 76

UN Children's Fund (Unicef), 227

UN Development Programme/ Harvard Humanitarian Initiative, 81, 84

UN Human Settlement Programme (UN-Habitat), 191, 199

UN Organization Stabilization Mission in the Democratic Republic of the Congo (MONUSCO), 184, 227, 229

UN Refugee Agency (UNHCR), 227

United States of America (USA), 3

unofficial / official, use of terms, 147

Upira, D., 33

user fees, 78, 109, 170, 178, 186; for public toilets, 181-2; in education, 123

users, use of term, 98

Uvira, 207; mediation of land conflicts in, 203-5

vehicles, control of see technical control of vehicles

ventilation system, 78

Verweijen, J., 17, 124

violence, 52, 134, 214; as part of political process, 4-5; in revenue-generating, 126, 130-2, 133; of maintaining state control, 67; of police, 61, 67; of the state, 69; sexual, cases regarding, 222-3, 224

Vlassenroot, K., 195

Politics and Development in Contemporary Africa

Published by one of the world's leading publishers on African issues, 'Politics and Development in Contemporary Africa' seeks to provide accessible but in-depth analysis of key contemporary issues affecting countries within the continent. Featuring a wealth of empirical material and case study detail, and focusing on a diverse range of subject matter – from conflict to gender, development to the environment – the series is a platform for scholars to present original and often provocative arguments. Selected titles in the series are published in association with the International African Institute.

Already published:

About the editors

Tom De Herdt is professor at the Institute of Development Policy, University of Antwerp. He teaches and researches on poverty and inequality, and on local governance of public services, with an empirical focus on sub-Sahara African countries and, more particularly, the Democratic Republic of the Congo.

Kristof Titeca is a lecturer at the Institute of Development Policy, University of Antwerp. He works on governance and conflict in Central and Eastern Africa, specifically the Democratic Republic of Congo and Uganda.